THE TIGHTROPE WALKERS

Studies of Mannerism
in Modern English Literature

by

GIORGIO MELCHIORI

ROUTLEDGE & KEGAN PAUL
London

First published 1956
by Routledge & Kegan Paul Ltd
Broadway House, Carter Lane, E.C.4
Printed in Great Britain
by Butler & Tanner Ltd
Frome and London

Second impression 1957

TO BARBARA

Acknowledgements

I WISH to thank the Editors of the following periodicals in which substantial parts of these essays have appeared, and whose advice and criticism have greatly encouraged me in my work: Mrs. Elena Craveri Croce of *Lo Spettatore Italiano* (Rome); Prof. Mario Praz of *English Miscellany* (Rome); Prof. R. W. Zandvoort of *English Studies* (Amsterdam); and Prof. F. W. Bateson of *Essays in Criticism* (Oxford).

Grateful acknowledgements are due to the following for their generous permission to quote passages from copyrighted works:

Faber & Faber Ltd. and Mr. T. S. Eliot for *Collected Poems 1909–1935, Four Quartets, The Use of Poetry and the Use of Criticism, Poetry and Drama, The Confidential Clerk* and other works by T. S. Eliot.

Eyre & Spottiswoode Ltd. and the owners of the copyright for *The Wings of the Dove* by Henry James.

The Oxford University Press and the copyright owners for *Poems* by Gerard Manley Hopkins and *The Notebooks and Papers of Gerard Manley Hopkins*, edited by Humphrey House; the same publishers and Mr. Christopher Fry for *The Lady's Not for Burning, Venus Observed, A Sleep of Prisoners* and *The Dark is Light Enough* by Christopher Fry.

John Lane the Bodley Head Ltd. and the Trustees of the James Joyce Estate for *Ulysses* by James Joyce; the same

vii

Acknowledgements

Trustees and Jonathan Cape Ltd. for *Stephen Hero* by James Joyce.

William Heinemann Ltd. and Mrs. Frieda Lawrence for the 'Preface to the American Edition of New Poems' by D. H. Lawrence.

The Hogarth Press Ltd. and Mr. Leonard Woolf for *The Common Reader: First Series* and other works by Virginia Woolf; the same publishers and Mr. Henry Green for *Living, Party Going, Concluding* and other works by Henry Green.

J. M. Dent & Sons Ltd. and the owners of the copyright for *Collected Poems* and *Under Milk Wood* by Dylan Thomas, and especially for permission to quote in full Thomas' poem 'The Conversation of Prayers'.

Marguerite Caetani for 'Llareggub' by Dylan Thomas, published in *Botteghe Oscure*, IX, and for a letter by Dylan Thomas published in *Botteghe Oscure*, XIII.

Dates of publication and page references to the passages quoted from these works will be found in the footnotes to the present book.

Contents

Introduction to Funambulism

THE essays here collected deal with several separate aspects of contemporary English literature. They have been written over a period of several years and some of them have appeared in different periodicals. They do not aim at an orderly treatment of the period in question, nor do they try to deal with the greatest or the most influential or the most representative personalities of the period. It will be noticed that such outstanding literary figures as W. B. Yeats, or Edith Sitwell are not even mentioned, while minor ones, like Henry Green or even Christopher Fry, are given full-length studies. The fact is that I was interested not in giving a picture of the literary scene, but in finding out, by subjecting to different critical methods some major and some minor writers, the common characteristics of the style of an age apparently so full of contradiction and uncertainty. I believe, in fact, that there exists a common atmosphere in which works of art are produced and which gives them a common character even if the authors hold opposing political, philosophical or aesthetic views.

A common link among most of the essays may be seen perhaps in the mention, in nearly all of them, of T. S. Eliot. I want to state, though, that, far from sharing his beliefs and principles in the different fields of what he has defined as 'culture', I have taken the position expressed in his poetry and critical writings only as a vantage point from which to look at

I

his times and at the work of other individual authors. But since any critical work needs first of all an understanding of the meaning and value of the words used, I will try in this introduction to give a few schematic definitions of some of the ideas contained in the essays. They will necessarily sound rather dogmatic, but I hope that a fuller justification for them will be found in the different essays where they are applied.

Progress and Decadence. First of all I must disagree with a statement in Eliot's *Notes towards the Definition of Culture*; he says:

We can assert with some confidence that our own period is one of decline; that the standards of culture are lower than they were fifty years ago; and that the evidences of this decline are visible in every department of human activity.[1]

There is no doubt that there have always been periods of confusion and uncertainty, periods when all standards seemed, and were, lost; but that does not mean that the settled standards of ages with well-defined beliefs were higher. And this is particularly true in the field of art and poetry, which certainly Mr. Eliot would include among the human activities. The idea of decline or retrogression is as absurd as that of progress. Confronted with a human nature which is substantially the same in all ages, there can be no progress or decadence. The latter word can be a useful term of definition from the historical point of view of some period in which the political or moral standards in a particular country or field of activity seemed upset; but it does not imply a basic change for the worse in the complex nature of man. There are only changes in position and faith, and in moral outlook, struggles to abolish or reach a faith, or, in art, to abolish or reach a new form of expression. I would therefore substitute for the idea of periods of progress or decline, that of periods when a certain set of beliefs is generally and firmly held and accepted, and periods when uncertainty predominates. The history of thought, and therefore the history of

[1] T. S. Eliot, *Notes towards the Definition of Culture,* London, 1948, p. 19.

literature which is bound up with it, is a sequence, or rather a continuous alternation, of such periods, which we could call periods of certainty and uncertainty, of faith and doubt. And in this alternation of periods, tradition provides the element of permanence and continuity.

Tradition. Tradition, being constituted by the work of the past which is absorbed by individual authors and becomes their common background, allows them to see beyond their immediate predecessors, to establish links with the preceding periods, thus creating a unity in the evolution of a given literature. In this way Eliot's statement on the alteration produced in the existing order of literary monuments (tradition) by the appearance of a new work of art is fully acceptable.[1] An author will exploit freely all that is contained in the repository of tradition and at the same time will be able to make use of the work and of the experience of writers who are at the opposite pole in respect to his sensibility and thought. In fact, in the essays on Joyce and on *Echoes in The Waste Land,* I have tried to illustrate two aspects of the influence of tradition on single authors. We could say then that tradition is a common patrimony permanently increased by the contribution of new works, and from which every author draws freely—but when the series of works of art which form the tradition is looked at in its historical sequence, it shows a continual alternation of antithetical phases. This alternation is determined by the thought and the general conditions of each historical period, by external political factors as well as by philosophical developments brought about by thinkers and mystics. But no author, however steeped he may be in tradition, that is to say aware of the presence of the past, can avoid being influenced by the atmosphere of his own time. On the contrary, his quickened sensitivity will seize upon those elements which are still very vague and indefinite, just beginning to appear; he will give them full expression and in this

[1] *Tradition and the Individual Talent,* now in *Selected Essays,* London, 1932, pp. 13–22.

way he will seem to be ahead of his own time. In the essay on James and Hopkins I have tried to explain this process, showing the similarities between two authors unknown to one another, though contemporaries and in advance of their own period.

Classicism and Romanticism. For one century and a half these two words have been the most elusive and confusing in the field of criticism. I certainly shall not attempt a definition which could only mean adding equivocation to confusion. In the essay on 'Eliot and the Theatre' I have simply tried to trace the meanings that the word 'classicism' has had for the poet, or rather how it changed its meaning for him through the years. But since I have spoken before of art history as an alternation of periods with contrasting characteristics, it may be thought that I tend to identify ages of certainty and ages of doubt with classical and romantic periods respectively. This is not so. I have used at times the word 'neo-classic' or 'classicistic' to denote a precise historical period, an age of certainty in the eighteenth century. But apart from these merely historical acceptations of the words, I consider classic and romantic in a wider sense as two basic attitudes of the spirit present in all ages and frequently, in different proportions, in the same person. In this sense the author who feels a call for a pre-established order and the determination of precise categories is classic, and the one who wants to create a strictly individual order valid only for himself is romantic. Of Eliot it could be said then that he moved from a fundamentally romantic to a fundamentally classic attitude. In view of this conception of the two terms there is clearly no question of advocating the superiority of the one over the other: they are both among the impulses which may, in connection with countless other factors, produce the work of art.[1]

[1] Obviously I don't accept Herbert Read's identification of classicism with abstract art and romanticism with organic art, which implies the superiority of the second (see Sir Herbert Read, *Collected Essays in Literary Criticism*, London,

I cannot however avoid mentioning a further confusion: the current use of the terms 'new classicism' in connection for instance with the poetry of Eliot or Edith Sitwell, and 'new romanticism' in respect of the work of Dylan Thomas, W. S. Graham or W. R. Rodgers. After what has been said of Eliot the use of the term for his poetry is understandable; and if it is accepted, it seems logical to use the definition 'new romantic' for writers who seem to start from an attitude opposed to Eliot's. Indeed, in the essay on Thomas I have suggested that Eliot is approaching a classicistic form of Baroque and Dylan Thomas himself a romantic form of the same style. But I have tried to make clear the provisional character of such a definition by insisting on Thomas' connection with a tradition of visionary poetry which has characteristics of its own and could not be strictly included in either the romantic or the classic current. In conclusion, classicism and romanticism are in my opinion two basic attitudes of the artist towards art, and could therefore be considered also as two permanent streams of poetry present at every stage of the development of literature, irrespective of the predominant style of the period.

Style. Also in respect of the meaning of the word 'style' a clarification is essential, and the more so since in the following essays I have in general limited my demonstration to strictly aesthetic elements—style and technique.[1] The *Pocket Oxford Dictionary* is sufficient for a first working definition: style is the 'distinctive manner of an artist or of a school or period in art'. This is quite clear, but the fact is that while the use of the word in respect to 'the manner of an artist' is current and commonly

1938, especially pp. 19–20). I acknowledge though that, given the necessary explanation, Read's can be a working criterion to assess the vitality of a work of art: all true art will have a form which will be organic to the nature of its inspiration, while the repetition of abstract formal schemes as such will not be vital. But it is better to leave the two dangerous words—classic and romantic—out of the question.

[1] The meaning of technique should be clear from the essay on Joyce, p. 52 of this book.

accepted, when it comes to its application to a period in art, the confusion begins. Dr. Pevsner has put the matter very clearly:

> It is certainly at least one of the legitimate uses of [the word] 'style' to denote the personal mode of expression of an author and an artist, and if you write of Wordsworth's as against Keats's style or Rembrandt's as against Rubens's you are philosophically precise and yet not likely to be misunderstood. . . . But when it comes to introducing such terms as Baroque, nobody can be sure whether it will be taken by the English reading public as a synonym of fantastic or—in the deeper sense —as the final essence distilled out of all the individual qualities of all the leading personalities of one particular age. Hobbes's and Spinoza's philosophy, Bernini's and Rembrandt's art, Richelieu's and Cromwell's statecraft have certain fundamentals in common, and on these we can establish a Baroque style of exact meaning.[1]

Dr. Pevsner makes several important points. There is first of all a definition of style (the final essence, etc. . . . .) which has been adopted throughout this book; and there is the confluence of the philosophy, the politics and the arts of each period into the 'style' of the period itself. A style then is the result of a number of factors; it is indeed the expression, under the guise of art, of the 'climate' of an age. And since, as I said before, periods of stability (political, religious, philosophical, etc.) alternate in human history with ages of change and unrest, in the same way in the history of art there is an alternation of styles: the form and content of a work of art will differ if it is produced in an age of confidence or in one of doubt. According to the sequence of these contrasting features of historical periods, there will be a contrast in the external and inner features of the arts of the same periods. Stability and unrest being the operative words in the definition of historical periods, they will be valid as well in the definition of the successive styles in the arts. The leading features

[1] N. Pevsner, 'The Architecture of Mannerism', in *The Mint*, I, London, 1946, p. 116.

of the style of a stable period (e.g. Renaissance, Baroque, Neo-Classicism, Biedermeier) will be formal balance of the parts, symmetry, solidity (weight), a sense of confidence, a predominance of mass over line; while in the next phase, in a period of uncertainty, the prevailing features in art will be disregard for constructive balance, asymmetry, development line by line (in writing and in the figurative arts) instead of by larger constructive units, a sense of insecurity. Within these two main groups of basic characteristics there is of course ample scope for personal variations—such variations are indeed the individual styles of the single artists which contain the general features of the period, but add to them endless personal characteristics.

I am conscious of the extreme oversimplification of the above statements, and I want therefore to make it clear that period-labels like those I have mentioned before are not meant in any way as limits to the artist's personality, but as basic nuclei from which he develops the expression of his private world of thought, feeling and sensation.

Funambulism. Hardly any period in history has been so acutely conscious of its own unsettledness as the one from the end of the first world war to the present day. This crisis, which is essentially a crisis of beliefs, had of course begun much earlier, before the end of the last century, but it was widely acknowledged and recognized only in the second decade of the twentieth century, when a conflict of unprecedented magnitude made obvious the rift with the past even to the most unprepared man in the street. In the alternation of styles in the history of the arts, the first half of our century will therefore be classed with those dominated by the taste for asymmetry and instability, with Mannerism, or Rococo, or early Romanticism. The connection between the poetry of our time and that of the Mannerist poets, who go under the name of Metaphysicals, is by now such a commonplace of criticism that I shall not try to illustrate it. One could rather question the usefulness of these period-labels: is any work better or worse for being 'Manneristic' or 'Baroque',

'Romantic' or 'Neo-Classic', 'Rococo' or 'Biedermeier'? Of course it does not matter. But the realization of the general stylistic characters of an age helps, I think, to give a background against which the peculiar qualities of a work of art will appear more clearly; and it helps as well to understand some features in such a work which might otherwise discourage certain readers and prevent a full appreciation of the work itself.

The artistic style of our time could be labelled for instance 'new Mannerism' (the recent fashion not only for the early seventeenth-century poetry but also for the *maniera* painters among the art-lovers is a remarkable symptom of the temper of the age); or it could be called 'Metaphysical' (apart from the 'school' of painting which flourished with that name about 1915–20, we could remember that Eliot himself defined Henry James *romancier métaphysique*[1]). But these definitions are dangerous and confusing since they tend to connect too closely the present with one very precise stylistic period of the past. I have preferred to use tentatively in the following essays the word 'Funambulism' to describe the style of our time. I think it is as good a term as any to express the sense of danger—or should we say with Auden, anxiety—and precariousness so vividly reflected both in the form and in the content of the artistic and literary works of the first half of this century. And since a work of art cannot be such if (even expressing uncertainty and doubt) it does not achieve a temporary balance, funambulism seems indeed to convey also that: the achievement of the true artist in our age, who, like the successful acrobat, succeeds in keeping step by step, moment by moment, his balance, while being aware of the void or the turmoil round him. It is of course a balance which has nothing to do with the permanent and pre-established one found in ages of stability and faith. And another purely practical justification for the term could be put forward: any reader of contemporary works of criticism or even book-reviews will find again and again the comparison between

---

[1] T. S. Eliot, 'Note sur Mallarmé et Poe', in *Nouvelle Revue Française*, Nov. 1926.

modern authors and the acrobat, the rope-walker, a comparison used by the critics just as a matter of expediency, as the most apt to convey the distinctive character of the work under discussion when compared with earlier literature.[1]

Towards a New Baroque. In the following essays I have not dealt with Auden, though he might have provided one of the best illustrations of the period and of its evolution; indeed, nobody would question the definition of 'funambulist' in this respect. But I have preferred Christopher Fry as an example of somewhat belated and truly popular Funambulism—of the stage when an artistic movement, developed decades before, becomes acceptable to a very general and unprepared audience. But even

---

[1] I have quoted only one instance of this common comparison: the words of Virginia Woolf about Eliot's early work (see essay on 'Eliot and the Theatre', p. 106). Actually Virginia Woolf—an extremely sensitive critic—used also another image, more particularly for the poets of the generation after Eliot's (the Auden, Spender, Lewis, MacNeice group): that of the leaning tower. She spoke of them as prisoners of an 'ivory tower' (that isolation characteristic of artists in periods of crisis, when they tend to emphasize their individualism); but an ivory tower leaning to the left. She explained the Leaning Tower Influences in the following way: 'If you think of them [the poets of the Auden group] as people trapped in a leaning tower from which they cannot descend, much that is puzzling in their work is easier to understand. It explains the violence of their attack upon bourgeois society and also its half-heartedness; they are profiting by a society which they abuse. . . . It explains the destructiveness of their work; and also its emptiness. . . . How can a writer who has no experience of a towerless, of a classless society create that society?' Apart from the weakness of Virginia Woolf's political argument, there is little doubt, I think, that the image of the leaning tower was suggested to her not only by the content of the poems she attacks, but also by their style. A style which by its very complication and negation of the 'old decorums' of Victorian poetry emphasized the sense of individualism and isolation; and which by its rejection of the principles of symmetry in composition gave the impression of works off their centre, of precarious balance, suggesting indeed a leaning tower. It is exactly this that I mean by 'Funambulism'; and the confusion in political ideas denounced by Virginia Woolf is only one aspect of the more general uncertainty in all fields of human thought and art. (*The Leaning Tower* was written in 1940 and is now collected in *The Moment*, London, 1947, pp. 105 ff.)

in him a process is apparent in the direction of a more balanced form, which we shall be unable to call Funambulism. Indeed the question is now: Whereto is style proceeding? And Auden could help us to find a reply, provisional as it may be. It seems superfluous to insist on the funambulistic character of his early poetry: so much has already been written on his ability as a juggler with words and constructions, as an expert in acrobatics with language and form. But in the books of what could be called Auden's American period there appears a new effort towards not only an established faith but also a stricter form; stricter, that is, not in the sense of the new classicism advocated by Eliot, but in the sense of formal balance and squareness, of symmetry in construction in spite of some fanciful decorative work. Even the *New Year Letter,* as sprawling and uncouth a poem as any, has in the appendix the sonnet sequence *The Quest* which is a remarkable feat of neat and balanced composition. As carefully constructed are *The Sea and the Mirror* and *For the Time Being,* though the first is unbalanced by the rambling speech of Caliban, written in an exasperated Jamesian (and therefore manneristic) style. But more important is *The Age of Anxiety,* which I consider as Auden's most significant and on the whole successful work to date. The title is symptomatic of Auden's awareness of the human condition in the present time,[1] but the subtitle is well worth attention as well. Auden has called his very elaborate composition 'A Baroque Eclogue'; the word Eclogue is an attempt at defining this original form, half dramatic and half lyrical, while the adjective Baroque is meant perhaps as a pointer to the elaborate and flamboyant style and imagery of the long poem, and to its complex structure. The definition is actually most apt: the author has here enclosed in a studiously balanced construction extremely ornate poetic elements, elaborate arabesques of words and ideas,

[1] On this and on the passage from V. Woolf quoted in the preceding note, see Mario Praz, 'The Critical Importance of the Revived Interest in Seventeenth Century Metaphysical Poetry', in *English Studies Today,* Oxford, 1951, pp. 158–66.

exhibitions of technical ability, which are all the same controlled by the general scheme imposed on the whole. It is a structure which could indeed find a parallel in Baroque architecture—an architecture which was, in Prof. Praz's definition,[1] 'a synthesis of dynamically contrasting elements', as compared with the 'unity of converging effects' of Renaissance art, or with the unbalanced serpentine developments of Mannerism. I think that Auden, so quick to seize upon and express the basic climate of his time, has actually detected the tendency in thought, feeling and style towards a stricter balance, a more symmetrical structure, and has tried to express it in the adjective Baroque. A tendency of this kind can be found in other authors with whom I have dealt in the present book: in Dylan Thomas, for instance, though he is being called a 'new Romantic'—and in my essay on his work I have hinted at his development in this direction, towards the 'Romantic' kind of Baroque; and in Eliot who, instead, in his *Quartets* seems to approach the 'classicistic' kind of Baroque.[2] A propos of this, Eliot's by now famous change in favour of Milton appears particularly significant, for Milton in fact is the highest expression of the classicistic kind of Baroque.

The conclusion to be drawn from what I have been saying is, I think, that the middle years of this century, those we are living now, are witnessing one of those fundamental changes of style of which I spoke at the beginning of this introduction: from the Funambulism (the new Mannerism) of the first half of the century—an age of doubt and disillusionment—the artists are groping towards forms expressing a greater stability. For the time being we shall be content to call this new style, which is far from being established yet, which is in the making under our own eyes, new Baroque. It will be objected that our times seem more troubled and unsettled than ever, and it is hard to

[1] In 'Milton and Poussin', in *Seventeenth Century Studies presented to Sir Herbert Grierson,* Oxford, 1938.
[2] See below, pp. 233–4.

believe in the appearance, even in the field of art, of basically stable forms, the normal expressions of faith and certainty. But poets have frequently forerun history and perceived at the very moment of their inception movements of thought which took root only many years later. James and Hopkins, or for that matter Pater, did so over half a century ago, adopting a style which prefigured an age of instability not yet existing in fact. It may be that our contemporary artists are foreshadowing an age of certainty to come while for the present asserting their individual faiths.

Two Mannerists: James and Hopkins

Three or four years ago I re-read *Marius the Epicurean*, expecting to find I cared for it no longer, but it still seemed to me, as I think it seemed to us all, the only great prose in modern English, and yet I began to wonder if it, or the attitude of mind of which it was the noblest expression, had not caused the disaster of my friends. It taught us to walk upon a rope tightly stretched through serene air, and we were left to keep our feet upon a swaying rope in a storm.

w. b. YEATS, *The Trembling of the Veil*

HENRY JAMES' art had a recognizable influence not only on the contemporary novel, but—perhaps less directly —on contemporary poetry as well. This fact has been acknowledged more than once,[1] but it does not seem to have occurred to the critics that there might be an affinity between James and some of the poets living in his own age. I believe that a parallel examination of the most striking characteristics of James and Hopkins will be rewarding and revealing in this respect.

Indeed, except that they were born within a year of each other (respectively in 1843 and 1844) it is hard at first sight to detect any connection between James and Hopkins. It is obvious besides that they completely ignored each other's existence. James' mature novels were written well after Hopkins' death, and Hopkins' poems were only published three years after James' death. And one could easily contrast the Catholic

[1] E.g. M. D. Zabel, 'The Poetics of Henry James', in *Poetry*, Chicago, XLV, 1935, pp. 270–6; and several references in F. O. Matthiessen, *The Achievement of T. S. Eliot,* New York, 1935.

priest relating in his poems his own ecstatic experiences, with the international worldling exploring in his novels the morbid sensitivity of a refined society. But the fact is that each of them has struck readers of later generations by some features so peculiar to himself as to be considered almost personal idiosyncrasies. In view of the utterly different spheres in which they moved it is the more surprising to realize that these very peculiarities, distinguishing each of them from his contemporaries, are common to both. Here is what can be considered as a typical passage from James:

And how much, as it was, for all her bridling brightness—which was merely general and noticed nothing—*would* they work together? . . . Yet, none the less, when, at the end of five minutes, in the cab, Jim Pocock had said nothing either—hadn't said, that is, what Strether wanted, though he had said much else—it all suddenly bounced back to their being either stupid or wilful. It was more probably on the whole the former; so that that would be the drawback of the bridling brightness. Yes, they would bridle and be bright; they would make the best of what was before them, but their observation would fail; it would be beyond them; they simply wouldn't understand.[1]

There is no mistaking the author of this passage: the Jamesian syntax is obvious in each line—the sentences are broken and proceed hesitatingly, feeling their way for the exact word. In this process, grammar is mercilessly twisted, following the involutions of thought; the language too is characteristic and unlike that of the other nineteenth-century novelists: it is on the whole sustained, but it alternates words of the literary usage and colloquialisms; finally, there is a certain concreteness in the imagery (though this is not so apparent in this particular passage): a verb like *bounced back* is vividly descriptive, while *bridling brightness* gives point and flavour to the whole passage.

James is looking for a complexity of effects (expressed in as complex a form) which no other prose writer of his time was pursuing. Even Meredith's prose for all its intellectual subtlety

[1] *The Ambassadors,* Everyman edition, London, 1948, p. 219.

is plainer and less strained. Instead the same type of syntactic elaboration is to be found in the following:

A bugler boy from barrack (it is over the hill there)—boy bugler, born, he tells me, of Irish mother to an English sire (he shares their best gifts surely, fall how things will), this very day came down to us after a boon he on my late being there begged of me, overflowing boon in my bestowing; came, I say, this day to it—to a First Communion.

But this is not prose; it is a transcription, without line divisions, of eight lines of a poem by Hopkins.[1] Here too we find the crowding of secondary clauses in a complex sentence, the breaks and hesitations in the flow of speech, the colloquialisms alternating with the literary words. It is very unlike the work of the poets of the last century, the overflowing sonority of Swinburne, the musical ease of Tennyson, or even the diffused monologizing of Browning. It fits with Hopkins' definition of poetical language, which should be 'current language heightened, to any degree heightened and unlike itself, but not an obsolete one'.[2] This is obvious in all Hopkins' poems: from the current language he gets not only single words and expressions, but also constructions, and those repetitions and interrupting clauses which are characteristic of the spoken language. This can be seen, in the passage already quoted, in the parenthetical sentences, the expressions *he tells me, surely, fall how things will,* and *I say*. And the same interjectional clauses are found in his most complex and elaborate poems, as for instance *The Wreck of the Deutschland*:[3]

1 *The Bugler's First Communion*, in *Poems*, 2nd ed., 1930, pp. 42–3.

2 Passage from a letter quoted in W. H. Gardner, *Gerard Manley Hopkins, A Study of Poetic Idiosyncrasy in Relation to Poetic Tradition*, London, 1948, vol. I, p. 115.

3 *Poems*, ed. quoted, pp. 11–21. Compare with the line of Hopkins' quoted below, 'Finger of a tender of, O of a feathery delicacy', the following from a note of Henry James (*Letters*, ed. P. Lubbock, London, 1920, vol. I, p. xxi): 'Thus just these first little wavings of the oh so tremulously passionate little old wand (now!) make for me, I feel, a sort of promise of richness and beauty and variety.'

> And after it almost unmade, what with dread,
> Thy doing.   (stanza 1)

There are the hesitations, the broken syntax common in normal speech, as in the passage quoted 'came, I say, this day to it—to a First Communion', or again in the *Deutschland*:

> But how shall I . . . make me room there:
> Reach me a . . . Fancy, come faster—
> Strike you the sight of it?   (stanza 28)

And in this same poem we can see other examples of colloquial construction: the exclamation in mid-sentence:

> Finger of a tender of, O of a feathery delicacy.
>   (stanza 31)

or the stammering repetition due to the violence of feeling:

> . . . where, where was a, where was a place?
>   (stanza 3)

Finally there are passages of a deliberately chronicle style:

> On Saturday sailed from Bremen,
> American-outward-bound . . .   (stanza 12)

There is no doubt that these linguistic and syntactic features, that both unite and contrast with the high poetical elaboration, are peculiar to Hopkins, and are among those that most distinguish his style. As for his other characteristics, his striking, compound words, alliteration, assonance, internal rhymes, etc., the difference between himself and his contemporaries is one of degree and intensity rather than original invention;[1] and it was in this preoccupation with the 'current language' that his 'sprung rhythm' also originated, which is, according to his definition, 'the rhythm of common speech and of written prose, when rhythm is perceived in them'.[2]

---

[1] The use of parallel devices by Hopkins' contemporaries has been studied and amply exemplified in W. H. Gardner's two volumes, mentioned above.

[2] 'Author's Preface' to the *Poems*, ed. quoted, p. 5.

The same preoccupation with the 'heightening' of current language and expression seems responsible for the peculiarities of James' style, especially in his later (or 'major') phase. It is significant that James, when revising *The Portrait of a Lady*, as Matthiessen tells us,[1] adopted more colloquial forms—as e.g. *can't, she'd* for *cannot, she would*—and substituted concrete and organic images for abstract descriptions. He reached in this way a sense of greater solidity, but at the same time he complicated the construction of his prose to such an extent as to become the easy target of satire (the early parody by Max Beerbohm is a masterpiece in its kind).

Hopkins' later poems show an identical tendency. His two well-known sonnets, *Tom's Garland* and *Harry Ploughman,* which are considered among his most involved, show a deliberate use of colloquial expressions, to the point of abbreviating *his* to *'s*; and even in subject matter he wants to be as down to earth as possible. But the syntax is utterly broken and the rhythm is extremely loose, so that the structure of the sonnets becomes extremely complicated:

Tom Heart-at-ease, Tom Navvy: he is all for his meal
Sure, 's bed now. Low be it: lustily he his low lot (feel
That ne'er need hunger, Tom; Tom seldom sick,
Seldomer heartsore, that treads through, prickproof, thick
Thousands of thorns, thoughts) swings though.[2]

Like James' prose, these Hopkinsian poems seem unrecitable, but it should be remembered that Hopkins wrote of *Tom's Garland*:[3] 'declaimed, the strange constructions would be dramatic and effective', and of *Harry Ploughman* he said that it was 'altogether for recital, not for perusal'. In the same way

---

[1] F. O. Matthiessen, *Henry James, The Major Phase,* London, 1946. The last chapter contains a thorough study of the changes made in the revision.

[2] *Poems*, p. 63.

[3] This and the next quotation are from letters reproduced in the notes to *Poems*, pp. 114–16.

James, in the preface to *The Golden Bowl*, where his style has reached a maximum of complexity, writes that:

the highest test of any literary form conceived in the light of 'poetry'—to apply that term in its largest literary sense—hangs back unpardonably from its office when it fails to lend itself to *vivâ-voce* treatment.[1]

Both writers then were anxious to produce work which could stand the test of declamation, but were looking at the same time for more complex and penetrating speech forms, such as could render the subtlety, the fineness of their feelings and of their mental processes. This ambition, which distinguishes them among their contemporaries, is at the root of their endless and deliberate stylistic search. It was a search for the utmost precision of expression and immediate communication of feeling and sensation. This effort towards an ever-increasing directness is reflected too in their use of imagery; they tend to avoid abstract descriptions and to use instead concrete images, at times rather precious ones. So Hopkins works out a comparison between a lark and a winch:

> Left hand, off land, I hear the lark ascend,
> His rash-fresh re-winded new-skeinèd score
> In crisps of curl off wild winch whirl, and pour
> And pelt music, till none's to spill nor spend . . .[2]

or describes the action of human muscles in metaphors taken from nature and from military service:

> . . . Each limb's barrowy brawn, his thew . . .
> Though as a beechbole firm, finds his, as at a roll-call, rank
> And features, in flesh, what deed he each must do—
> His sinew-service where do.[3]

James for his part could speak at length of life as

---

[1] H. James, *The Art of the Novel* (critical prefaces, edited with introduction by R. P. Blackmur), New York, 1947, p. 346.

[2] *The Sea and the Skylark, Poems*, p. 28.

[3] *Harry Ploughman, Poems*, p. 64.

a tin mould, either fluted and embossed, with ornamental excrescences, or else smooth and dreadfully plain, into which, a helpless jelly, one's consciousness is poured—so that one 'takes' the form, as the great cook says . . .[1]

or he could change the description of a face of a woman from the earlier abstract terms ('It had an air of intelligent calm—a considering, pondering look that was superior, somehow, to diffidence or anxiety') into a concrete metaphor taken from business life:

It was as calm as a room kept dusted and aired for candid earnest occasions, the meeting of unanimous committees and the discussion of flourishing business.[2]

All these, in James and Hopkins, are images (similes, comparisons, metaphors) bordering on the conceit, unafraid or unaware of the ridiculous which might have sprung from this union of apparently unrelated terms: a lark and a winch, a limb and a military exercise, the form of life and the mould for a jelly, a face and a room. They are at the same time demonstrations of a supreme preciosity, showing how a genuine intellectual power can sustain and make acceptable also extreme exercises in artistry.

We may wonder why two writers unknown to each other should have shared the same peculiarities. But some of them are essentially the products of an exalted artistry, more conscious and more passionately felt than that of most of their contemporaries; and we must remember that these two authors lived through the so-called 'aesthetic period', dominated by the doctrine of 'art for art's sake', when problems of form had assumed an extraordinary importance. Perhaps then the link between the two may be found in a dominant figure of the period: Walter Pater.

Hopkins was, during his formative years, at Oxford, a pupil

---

[1] *The Ambassadors*, ed. cit., p. 129.

[2] The revision of *The Reverberator*, quoted by Matthiessen, *Henry James: The Major Phase*, cit., p. 61.

of Pater, and was certainly influenced by the aesthetic theories that his teacher (only five years older than himself) was then developing. Hopkins' Platonic dialogue *On the Origin of Beauty,* written at this time and, it appears, for Pater, contains theoretical statements that the poet never rejected, and that are the fruit of Pater's teaching.[1] The dialogue insists particularly on the beauty and importance of symmetry and asymmetry both in nature and art, acknowledging the validity of both kinds of pattern, symmetrical and asymmetrical, as the basis of beauty. Transferring the exemplification onto the musical plane, Hopkins says that there are two kinds of beauty, diatonic and chromatic. The first is characterized by parallelism in all its forms, while the second includes, when applied to poetry, 'emphasis, expression (in the sense it has in music), tone, intensity, climax and so on'. Now, this distinction is very important. Hopkins is in this way contrasting the fundamental features of two kinds of artistic expression—the one based on symmetry (parallelism), balance of parts, which had dominated the middle part of his century; the other instead essentially asymmetrical and following a sort of undulating line of development, representing graphically the variations and hesitations of feelings and emotions. What Hopkins calls 'chromatic beauty', then, is that of an art expressing with the utmost intensity and closeness the intellectual reactions to sensations and emotions. The musical terms used by Hopkins in this connection are the more striking when we think that his essay is dated 12 May 1865, and that on the 10th of June of the same year Wagner's *Tristan und Isolde,* the apotheosis of the chromatic scale, had its first performance in Munich. Hopkins' definition of chromatism fits perfectly with the general character of Wagner's opera, in which those features listed by the Welsh poet have an extraordinary prominence. It seems that, with the help of Pater, Hopkins (who was then twenty-two years old) realized that the accepted Victorian standards of formal balance, emotional restraint, and material solidity, were not the only ones by which

[1] See W. H. Gardner, *op. cit.,* vol. I, pp. 6 ff.

a work of art could be created or judged. He put on the same plane the other kind of 'beauty', irregular, unrestrained and at the same time subtler and more elaborate. And though at first he objectively considered the two aspects of beauty as equal, it is apparent from his poems that he adopted the second, the 'chromatic', asymmetric beauty. In other words, Hopkins lived at a time when one style was being succeeded by another contrasting one, and adopted the second.

As for James' debt to Pater, it is a fully acknowledged fact. Stuart Pratt Sherman has amply dealt with the aesthetic ideals shared by Pater and James,[1] throwing light on their passionate love of and search for beauty. This is as well one of the fundamental motives of Hopkins' poetry:

> How to kéep—is there àny any, is there none such,
>   nowhere known some, bow or brooch or braid or
>   brace, làce, latch or catch or key to keep
> Back beauty, keep it, beauty, beauty, beauty, . . . from
>   vanishing away? [2]

And this same anxious quest for beauty (beauty intended as something to be caught in a moment and fixed and kept for endless contemplation) is the mainspring of James' art and the reason for his involved style. The object of his search is so precious that he moves with an extreme caution, feeling his way all the time, trying the different angles of approach. The process is described at length in James' own preface to *The Wings of the Dove*. After fixing the centre of the composition, 'preparatively and, as it were, yearningly—given the whole ground—one began, in the event, with the outer ring, approaching the centre thus by narrowing circumvallations'.[3] He speaks of

establishing one's successive centres—of fixing them so exactly that the portions of the subject commanded by them as by

[1] In an essay reproduced in *The Question of Henry James*, ed. F. W. Dupee, New York, 1947, pp. 86–106, 'The Aesthetic Idealism of Henry James', (written 1917).   [2] *The Leaden Echo and the Golden Echo*, in *Poems*, p. 54.

[3] This and the next two quotations are from *The Art of The Novel*, cit., pp. 294, 296, and 306.

happy points of view, and accordingly treated from them, would constitute, so to speak, sufficiently solid *blocks* of wrought material, squared to the sharp edge, as to have weight and mass and carrying power; to make for construction, that is, to conduce to effect and to provide for beauty.

But we must not be misled by the allusions to *blocks* and in general to a keen architectural sense, and conclude that James saw his novels as balanced classical structures,[1] or that he aimed at the effect of stateliness and serenity given by straight outlines and by the harmonious alternations of symmetrical structural masses. He wanted, it is true, to give depth and roundness to his creations; but in order to do this he always chose the most circuitous line of approach. As his stories deliberately follow these undulating and spiralling lines of development, so do his single sentences. Speaking at the conclusion of the already quoted preface, of Milly Theale, the heroine of the book, James says:

I note how, again and again, I go but a little way with the direct—that is with the straight exhibition of Milly; it resorts for relief, this process, whenever it can, to some kinder, some merciful indirection: all as if to approach her circuitously, deal with her at second hand, . . . All of which proceeds, obviously, from her painter's tenderness of imagination about her, which reduces him to watching her, as it were, through the successive windows of other people's interest in her . . . But my use of windows and balconies is doubtless at best an extravagance by itself, and as to what there may be to note, of this and other supersubtleties, other archrefinements, of tact and taste, of design and instinct, in *The Wings of the Dove*, I become conscious of overstepping my space without having brought the full quantity to light.

[1] Herbert Read, in his introduction to the Eyre and Spottiswoode edition of *The Wings of the Dove,* (London, 1948), has an interesting remark on this subject; 'however baroque, even "mannerist" the *style* of Henry James, his structure must be thought of in terms of Gothic architecture'. The following pages may be considered partly as an indirect discussion of this statement; the definition 'mannerist' should be kept particularly in mind.

James is fully conscious of his supersubtleties and archrefinements; he adopts a form deliberately extravagant, and while trying to communicate deeply human feelings and to penetrate human consciousness, the beauty of expression he pursues becomes identified with preciosity of form. The style of James (and, for that matter, of Hopkins) shows then the characteristics recurring in certain periods in the history of art and poetry—in the periods when the ideals of serenity and formal balance are broken by a spirit of uncertainty and search; the search makes for refinement both in themes and in expression, for a subtler and subtler penetration of meanings and attention to details rather than to the structure as a whole. So that there is a loss of balance and at times of proportion: details are worked out with a goldsmith's care, and this makes for an enormous gain in insight and precision—but the total effect is frequently lost sight of, or is reached through accumulation rather than through a harmonious disposition of the structural parts. Uncertainty too contributes to the lack of total balance or, with reference to graphic representations, lack of symmetry; it induces a preference and a taste for undulating, twining, whorling lines.

These formal features—as I was saying—have characterized the styles of certain artistic periods—the styles that art historians have called (in their chronological succession) Hellenism, Flamboyant Gothic, Mannerism, Rococo. It is what Pater calls, in his *Marius the Epicurean,* Euphuism, widening the terms of reference of a word defining the first phase of Mannerism in the English literature of the Elizabethan age. Euphuism, according to Pater, is based on the passionate love of form, and more specifically of words. It is 'determined at any cost to attain beauty in writing'.[1] But beyond what may seem merely external peculiarities, common to the 'Euphuists of successive ages', like their archaism on the one hand, and their neologies on the other, beyond 'the theory of Euphuism, as manifested in every age in which the literary conscience has been awakened to forgotten

---

[1] *Marius the Epicurean* (1885), 4th ed., London, 1898, vol. I, p. 98.

duties towards language, towards the instrument of expression',[1] there may be deeper motives justifying the departure from the 'simpleness' and 'broadness' of 'the old writers of Greece', the classical art. Cannot this same sense of the 'forgotten duties towards language' be found in Hopkins' ceaseless experiments with words and constructions, in his interest in rhythm and structure, in his extraordinary mixture of neologisms, archaisms and colloquial idioms, his assertion of what Pater calls 'the rights of the *proletariate* of speech'?[2] On the other side, could not this description of the faults and achievements of Flavian (the 'Roman Euphuist' in Pater's book) fit as well Henry James' work? Pater writes:

From the natural defects, from the pettiness, of his euphuism, his assiduous cultivation of manner, he was saved by the consciousness that he had a matter to present, very real, at least to him. That preoccupation of the *dilettante* with what might seem mere details of form, after all, did but serve the purpose of bringing to the surface, sincerely and in their integrity, certain strong personal intuitions, a certain vision or apprehension of things as really being, with important results, thus, rather than thus,—intuitions which the artistic or literary faculty was called upon to follow, with the exactness of wax or clay, clothing the model within. . . . And it was this uncompromising demand for a matter in all art, derived immediately from lively personal intuitions, this constant appeal to individual judgement, which saved his euphuism, even at its weakest, from lapsing into mere artifice.[3]

Indeed, Hopkins and James are both euphuistic writers in this, in Pater's, sense. This means that they adopted a certain attitude to the form of their writing in clear contrast with the rules of the period immediately previous to theirs, or, in other words, shifted the stress from one set of stylistic characters to another. From the clear line of development followed in the narrative of Dickens or Thackeray, or in the poetry of Tennyson or Matthew Arnold, they pass to more tortuous and tormented

---

[1] *Marius the Epicurean* (1885), 4th ed., London, 1898, vol. I, p. 97.
[2] *Ibid.*, vol. I, p. 95.   [3] *Ibid.*, vol. I, pp. 102–3.

forms; to the effects of straightforwardness and harmony they prefer those of nicety in details and preciosity in construction. They represent a different phase of sensibility from that which dominated the middle period of the nineteenth century. They actually usher in a new (or a different) style which will characterize the next half-century. I am using the word style in the sense in which art historians use it—as the complex of formal features and intellectual characteristics common to a certain artistic period. The style of which Hopkins and James are the first major representatives is, as we have seen, of the type that Pater called Euphuism. It is a great merit of Pater to have tried to free the word from that derogatory connotation it had assumed—in fact even now, in the last edition of Roget's *Thesaurus*,[1] we find *euphuism*, together with *mannerism* (historically the style of which Euphuism is just one stage), appearing under the heading *Inelegance*. The fact is that there has always been in England a sort of hostility to precise stylistic definitions,[2] a hostility based on the fear of abstract categories. On the other side there is a still more dangerous conception of 'styles': their division into good and bad styles, the alternation of a vigorous healthy style with a weak decadent style. A very recent and very typical example of this conception, just in connection with 'Mannerism' may be found in a notice of a 'book to come' on Tintoretto, stating that the author of the book 'believes that Tintoretto has suffered by being thrust . . . into the "mannerist" category' and proposes

to rescue Tintoretto from the reckless categorist and to suggest that he at least managed to short-circuit straight from High Renaissance to Baroque: that he was unaffected—or only superficially affected—by that uneasy interlude through which lesser men found it necessary to pass.[3]

[1] Longmans edition, 1936, 579.

[2] Dr. Nikolaus Pevsner in 'The Architecture of Mannerism' (*The Mint*, 1946) deals at length with this subject. See also my 'Introduction', p. 6, and the essay on Christopher Fry, pp. 165–6.

[3] *The Times Literary Supplement*, Nov. 16, 1951, p. 736. The reviewer of the book (*Tintoretto*, by Eric Newton) in the same periodical, in a review which

The statement is obviously based on the conception of Mannerism as a style of transition or decadence, instead of the expression of a certain type of sensibility, the *summa* of the forms that this expression took—as such it cannot be either better or worse than any other expression.

This digression was necessary to dispel possible misunderstandings. The stature of single authors has only an indirect relation to the styles of their respective periods. They will of course adopt them since they speak the language of their age, and they will inevitably modify them, carrying them a stage further through the exceptional powers of their creative personalities. James and Hopkins, as we saw, were both keenly interested in stylistic principles, but their work, as that of all true artists, was not exclusively preoccupied with them. The problems of style and technique were interesting for them only in so much as through them they could construct perfect instruments for the expression of their inner world of meanings. That this world existed and was of paramount importance for them, is obvious. It expresses itself in the powerful visual images of Hopkins—in a poem like *The Windhover* an intellectual image is expressed in extremely vivid visual terms, confirming that predominance of the sense of sight in the nineteenth century which made Emerson remark (as Matthiessen reminds us) 'the age is ocular'.[1] For his own part James stated in the preface to *The Ambassadors* 'Art deals with what we see'.[2] But, as is the case with Hopkins, James' descriptions of places, like those of persons, are from the inside; they not only endow a room or a landscape with personality (a thing Dickens did in a masterly way), but add a wealth of psychological nuances and convey all the subtle interreactions of place, occupant and observer.

appeared after I had written this essay (Feb. 8, 1952, p. 104), speaks too of 'grave misconception' on this point, and argues very much on the same lines as those I have followed here.

[1] Matthiessen, *Henry James*, cit., p. 32.
[2] *The Art of the Novel*, cit., p. 312, quoted also by Matthiessen.

Yet, for all his subtlety, the Victorian faith in progress and scientific discovery was not absent in James. So that he asked the help of a fairly new invention, the camera, to fix finally the vision, the perfect ideal portrait of the settings for his novels. He went round London with a photographer to find suitable subjects for the frontispieces of the New York edition of his works, and describes his experience in these terms:

Nothing in fact could more have amused the author than the opportunity of a hunt for a series of reproducible subjects . . . the reference of which to Novel or Tale should exactly be *not* competitive and obvious, should on the contrary plead its case with some shyness, that of images always confessing themselves mere optical symbols or echoes, expressions of no particular thing in the text, but only of the type or idea of this or that thing. They were to remain at the most small pictures of our 'set' stage with the actors left out; and what was above all interesting, was that they were first to be constituted . . . It was equally obvious that for the second volume of the same fiction (*The Golden Bowl*) nothing would so nobly serve as some generalized vision of Portland Place. Both our limit and the very extent of our occasion, however, lay in the fact that, unlike wanton designers, we had, not to 'create', but simply to recognize—recognize, that is, with the last fineness. The thing was to induce the vision of Portland Place *to* generalize itself. This is precisely, however, the fashion after which the prodigious city . . . does on occasion meet half-way those forms of intelligence of it that *it* recognizes. All of which meant that at a given moment the great featureless Philistine vista would itself perform a miracle, would become interesting, for a splendid atmospheric hour, as only London knows how; and that our business would be then to understand.[1]

It is curious to reflect that, while James was setting out in London streets armed with a camera to catch with it his 'moments of vision', Joyce's *Stephen Hero* was explaining to his friend Cranly, in a Dublin street, that 'the clock of the Ballast Office is capable of an epiphany'. I am referring to Joyce's first

[1] Preface to 'The Golden Bowl', in *The Art of The Novel*, cit., pp. 333, 335.

27

draft of *A Portrait of the Artist as a Young Man,* published only posthumously in 1944, but written at about the same time as James' *The Golden Bowl*; and more particularly to the by now famous passage on the theory of epiphanies, the moments when 'the soul, the whatness [of a thing, e.g. the clock of the Ballast Office] leaps to us from the vestment of its appearance'.[1] But while the younger writer, once he got hold of the principle, held hard to it, writing books which are an endless series of epiphanies, of moments of utter consciousness—the stream of consciousness novels—James aimed instead at seeing, at 'recognizing things with the last fineness', at 'understanding' them, and finally (what Joyce never dreamt of doing) at abstracting 'the type or idea of this or that thing'. In the passage quoted he explicitly speaks of 'intelligence': as Matthiessen rightly remarked, 'James' novels are strictly novels of intelligence rather than of full consciousness'.[2]

But, to return to the other author who is now interesting us, Hopkins too has a conception of photography similar to James'. In a fragment *On the Portrait of Two Beautiful Young People,* he describes the action of a camera:

> . . . The fine, the fingering beams
> Their young delightful hour do feature down
> That fleeted else like day-dissolvèd dreams . . . [3]

He too sees in a photograph one means of fixing the fleeting moment of beauty, or vision. This preoccupation to identify and fix the moment of clarity and beauty has become obsessive during the first half of this century—but we must remember that it has its roots in a hedonistic philosophy, and in the teaching of Walter Pater:

Art comes to you proposing frankly to give nothing but

---

[1] *Stephen Hero*, Star edition, 1944, p. 190. The passage is quoted at length in the essay on 'The Moment as a Time Unit in Fiction', see p. 178.

[2] Matthiessen, *Henry James*, cit., p. 23.

[3] *Poems*, ed. cit., p. 71.

the highest quality to your moments as they pass, and simply for those moments' sake.[1]

It has nothing to do then with the problem of time as it was posed to the modern man after the appearance of the works of Proust, Joyce and Eliot. Hopkins and James were rather concerned with the problems of aesthetic expression, and with the more important one of the interior life (the psychology) of men and things. If for them there is consciousness of moments of vision, there is also that of the effort to penetrate into the depths of the human world of feeling, and the essence of things. James, as he says in the passage quoted above, wanted to attain 'the type or idea of this or that thing'. And how he did it in his writings (both with regard to the feelings of the people and the 'type' of the objects) can be seen from an example from the very first page of *The Wings of the Dove*. Kate Croy, waiting for an interview with her father in the sitting-room of a London boarding house, 'takes in' her surroundings:

She had looked at the sallow prints on the wall and at the lonely magazine, a year old, that combined, with a small lamp in coloured glass and a knitted white centre-piece wanting in freshness, to enhance the effect of the purplish cloth on the principal table: she had above all, from time to time, taken a brief stand on the small balcony to which the pair of long windows gave access. The vulgar little street, in this view, offered scant relief from the vulgar little room; its main office was to suggest to her that the narrow black house-fronts, adjusted to a standard that would have been low even for backs, constituted quite the publicity implied in such privacies. One felt them in the room exactly as one felt the room—the hundred like it, or worse—in the street. Each time she turned in again, each time, in her impatience, she gave him up, it was to sound to a deeper depth, while she tasted the faint, flat

---

[1] *The Renaissance*, 1910 ed., p. 239. In his book *The English Novel* (London, 1954, p. 333) Mr. Walter Allen sees a direct connection between Pater's conception of the moment, and Virginia Woolf's attitude, which is discussed later in the present volume.

emanation of things, the failure of fortune and of honour. . . . To feel the street, to feel the room, to feel the table-cloth and the centre-piece and the lamp, gave her a small, salutary sense, at least, of neither shirking nor lying. This whole vision was the worst thing yet. . . .[1]

Many similar passages could be quoted from James' books: for instance the description of Madame de Vionnet's house in *The Ambassadors* (book VI, chap. I). Here, as well as there, there is a place, an observer and an inhabitant reacting on or against each other. But attention should be called to the last words of the passage quoted, 'this whole vision', where vision is used both in the sense of 'scene' and of 'sudden revelation'. James is conscious of having succeeded in interpreting and representing—through the picture he has drawn of the room, the list of a few articles of furniture—the essential characteristics, the deep nature itself, of a place: this is his vision. He has, in Hopkins' word, *inscaped* that room. And to *inscape* (the word is a coinage of his own) was one of the supreme aims of Hopkins himself. The most satisfactory definition of the word *inscape,* amply used by Hopkins especially in his notes and letters, is that given by W. A. M. Peters: 'inscape is the unified complex of those sensible qualities of an object . . . that strike us as inseparably belonging to and most typical of it'.[2] This obviously is the equivalent of James' *vision,* and Hopkins follows this principle consistently in all his work. The sonnet *Hurrahing in Harvest* may be taken as an example. Here are the last six lines:

And the azurous hung hills are his world-wielding shoulder
  Majestic—as a stallion stalwart, very-violet-sweet!—
These things, these things were here and but the beholder
  Wanting; which two when they once meet,
The heart rears wings bold and bolder
  And hurls for him, O half hurls earth for him off under his
    feet.[3]

---

[1] *The Wings of the Dove,* ed. cit., p. 11.
[2] W. A. M. Peters, *G. M. Hopkins: A Critical Essay towards the Understanding of His Poetry,* London, 1948, p. 1.   [3] *Poems,* ed. cit., p. 31.

The third and fourth lines mark the achievement of the inscape
—the communication between things and the beholder, the
vision, which in Hopkins produces a feeling of exaltation
which he called *instress*. But for Hopkins inscape in itself is not
already poetry. Poetry is inscaping of speech, meaning that after
receiving the inscape of an object (and putting it into ordinary
speech) poetry must inscape this same speech, must make a new
unified complex of the sensible qualities of the words used, so
that they strike us as inseparable from and most typical of the
speech. Poetry is, then, the inscape of objects squared. This is
what Hopkins tried to say in some lecture notes of his:

Poetry is speech framed for contemplation of the mind by the
way of hearing or speech framed to be heard for its own sake
and interest even over and above its interest of meaning. Some
matter and meaning is essential to it, but only as an element
necessary to support and employ the shape which is contem-
plated for its own sake. (Poetry is in fact speech only employed
to carry the inscape of speech for the inscape's sake—and therefore the inscape must be dwelt on. Now if this can be done
without repeating it, *once* of the inscape will be enough for art
and beauty and poetry but then at least the inscape must be
understood as so standing by itself that it could be copied and
repeated. If not repetition, *oftening, over-and-overing, aftering* of
the inscape must take place in order to detach it to the mind
and in this light poetry is speech which afters and oftens its
inscape, speech couched in a repeating figure and verse is
spoken sound having a repeating figure.) [1]

It appears very clearly from this passage that Hopkins was
passionately concerned with the verbal level and the formal
level of poetry. It is, as we saw before, a typical 'euphuistic'
attitude. In this passage one finds the reason for what was called
Hopkins' mannerism, his use of repetition and alliteration, of a
new rhythm and a new syntax, in a word of his bewildering
artistry.

[1] *The Note-Books and Papers of G. M. Hopkins,* ed. H. House, London, 1937,
p. 249.

But let us take now the last passage of James' quoted, from *The Wings of the Dove*. Here are the same characteristics, the alliteration, the repetition, the rhythms, the extra syllables, the breaks:

Each time she turned in again, each time, in her impatience, she gave him up, it was to sound to a deeper depth, while she tasted the faint, flat emanation of things, the failure of fortune and of honour.

We saw that this keen interest in form, style, technique, common to both, was partly due to the influence of the aesthetic movement, but the fact to be emphasised is that James and Hopkins are not akin only for these surface-features: they both used the stylistic and technical achievements which they had developed as instruments to reach and explore deeper levels of consciousness. They actually went so far in this search, and transformed their instruments of expression to such an extent, that James found only very few immediate followers, while Hopkins was ignored by all. They shared the fate of all path-finders: only many years after their disappearance their work was rediscovered and appreciated, and actually became a powerful influence on younger writers. Through their links with the aestheticism at the end of the last century James and Hopkins are firmly rooted in their own time; but by their constant work of deeper and deeper penetration they brought to full maturity already existing tendencies in taste and art. This maturity of a new art became generally apparent and accepted only in the 'twenties of this century, so that the two writers can be considered as transition figures between the age of Biedermeier, of Victorianism, and the *mannerist* age between the two wars. But their work belongs obviously to the second.

One final remark before closing this essay. Hopkins, as we saw, with his sprung rhythm and his use of *current language heightened,* broke the existing formal poetic pattern by including in it technical elements directly derived from prose usage. Conversely James used imagery in a way characteristic of poetry, and introduced, as I had occasion to remark before, alliterative and repetitive patterns taken from the poetic technique. They contributed then to that approach between the techniques of prose and poetry which is more apparent now, when novels assume frequently a lyrical tone while poems have definitely broken the metrical pattern and rejected the 'poetical' language.

James and Hopkins have exercised a parallel action on prose and poetry and on that far reaching exploration of human consciousness which is an achievement of the writers of this century. Hopkins explored in the habit of a priest searching for the secrets of a soul; James in that of a man of the world who inquires into the confused motives behind human action. The ways of approach are different, but the quest is the same.

Joyce and the Tradition of the Novel

IF James' later phase appeared to his contemporaries to be a literary cul-de-sac, it is certain that Joyce's experiments were definitely considered such. On its first appearance *Ulysses* seemed such an extraordinary phenomenon that the disconcerted critics were at a loss, not finding any established tradition to which it could be ascribed. By the time *Finnegans Wake* was laboriously completed, Joyce's previous book had already found so many interpreters, and was safely established so high on the pyramid of their elucidations, as to be quite out of the way of the ordinary novelist, who could now afford to ignore it and proceed safely along the 'traditional' paths.

Even Mr. Eliot, as early as 1923, severed it from the tradition, writing of Joyce's use of the Myth, and the 'continuous parallel between contemporaneity and antiquity':

> It has the importance of a scientific discovery. No one else has built a novel upon such a foundation before. . . I am not begging the question in calling *Ulysses* a 'novel'; and if you call it an epic it will not matter. If it is not a novel, that is simply because that is a form which will no longer serve; it is because the novel, instead of being a form, was simply the expression of an age which had not sufficiently lost all form to feel the need of something stricter. . . . The novel ended with Flaubert and with James.[1]

[1] T. S. Eliot, 'Ulysses, Order and Myth', in *The Dial,* Nov. 1923; reprinted in *James Joyce: Two Decades of Criticism,* ed. Seon Givens, New York, 1949.

The fallacy of this conception lies in the belief that the novel had an established form: that which, grown to maturity in the eighteenth century, had been adopted by the major novelists of the nineteenth century. As a matter of fact, from Jane Austen to Henry James, there had been a shift of stress inside the novel, but no fundamental alteration in its structure. There had been a progressive deepening of the psychological investigation, presented in innumerable styles and from a variety of viewpoints—but always inside the same basic form. And this is the form which Mr. Eliot sees as ending with James and Flaubert. These two writers indeed had stressed the subtle exploration of feeling to such an extent, confining at the same time action and the intrigue to such a secondary role, that there seemed to be no room left for further refinement of the psychological analysis. The fact is that the novel came to be considered as a separate literary form only when its possibilities for the revelation, interpretation and analysis of character were fully realized. These possibilities of the novel having been developed to the full by the end of the nineteenth century, it was logical for those who had adopted this rather one-sided view to consider it exhausted.

But beside this there is another current in the tradition of the English novel: the earlier one derived from the French and Spanish so-called 'picaresque' narratives. To the eighteenth-century writers who did not want to adopt Defoe's naked chronicle style, works like *Don Quixote,* or *Gil Blas* indicated an alternative direction. It is important to realize that up to the eighteenth century, the best vehicle for the narration of incident and the presentation of character had been the theatre. Now it was declining, and the imaginative writers had found that the only other form which could give them similar scope was the prose narrative. They started therefore to acclimatize the new medium, on the basis of the already existing foreign models. The possibilities which it offered were eagerly explored. The adventurousness of the travel novel did not consist only in its story, but also in the technique used by its authors. So, before the psychological novel of plot and character, beginning perhaps with Richardson, established itself, the eighteenth-century writer had time to experiment in a number of directions. That this is normally the case with any new art form, can be observed also in the rapid development of the art of the cinema. By the early nineteen-twenties many exciting experiments in this medium had been made. The film makers had realized the enormous new field opened, and were trying to explore to the limits the territories of which the newborn technique gave them a glimpse. Their daring and thorough exploitation of all kinds of camera tricks was intended for purely aesthetic ends. But since Wiene's *The Cabinet of Dr. Caligari* (1919) and Dreyer's *La Passion de Jeanne d'Arc* (1928), nobody has tried to make an entire film using *only* painted backgrounds or slanting close-ups. Wiene's and Dreyer's films are accomplished works of art, but their peculiar devices are used only incidentally by the makers of more recent good films.

In the same way the English novel developed. Most of the great eighteenth-century novels are thorough explorations of different techniques. There was in them all the excitement of the discovery of a new medium, which made for an extreme eagerness to find where it could lead. Apart from Swift, who worked out the age-old pattern of the satirical Utopia, and Defoe, who exploited on one side the fantastic travel book and on the other the chronicle narrative, Richardson, Fielding, Sterne and Smollett, all determined to sound their chosen medium. Richardson ascertained to what length the epistolary form could be taken, and how it could reveal character and motive; Fielding imposed a definite pattern on the ramblings of the picaresque novel; Sterne decided to loosen the check of consciousness on his imagination; while Smollett exerted, as we shall see later, much verbal ingenuity. But Jane Austen showed what perfectly balanced form could be achieved by straight narrative, excluding whims or extravagant technique, and this method was universally adopted in the nineteenth century.

With James the English novel had reached a maximum of

psychological analysis, and Joyce, to carry it a step further in line with this tradition, saw at first only one means: to plunge into a world of personal introspection, sustained by a constant vein of lyricism. The *Portrait of the Artist as a Young Man* is not so much an autobiographical as a self-searching novel, constantly interlaced with a poetical thread both in sentence-rhythm and in imagery. *Ulysses* moves on from this: the first sections are just an exacerbated development of the novel of introspection, taking several steps further the technique of what is now called the 'stream of consciousness'. But, beside this, the new novel reveals an amazing complexity of structure; so much so that there has been considerable talk about the formlessness of *Ulysses*. It contains indeed much that had never been used before in fiction: a large (but by no means exclusive) use of interior monologue; a continual recourse to myth and symbol; an intentionally wide variety of prose patterns; an unprecedented freedom in word formation and sentence arrangement. All these elements, and dozens more, were very deliberately introduced by Joyce in his attempt to make of *Ulysses* a gigantic all-inclusive record of man's universal failure. The apparent formlessness of the book is of course a reflection of the formlessness of human life, but there is no doubt that Joyce tried, and on the whole succeeded, in imposing on his novel a pattern and a shape. The parallel with the *Odyssey,* the heavy thematic structure of art, colour, symbol, etc., are the obvious unifying devices to hold this flamboyant architecture together. But there is subtler and less external evidence of his unity of inspiration. L. A. G. Strong has pointed out the continuous presence in *Ulysses* of the great shadows of Shakespeare, Swift and Blake.[1] Echoes from these three authors are also detectable in *Finnegans Wake,* and the reasons for their prominence are apparent: Shakespeare as the most complex and universal of English language writers;[2] Blake as the creator of a new gigantic

---

[1] L. A. G. Strong, *The Sacred River,* London, 1950.

[2] D. S. Savage in *The Withered Branch* (London, 1950, pp. 174 ff.) maintains that the character of Stephen Dedalus is closely modelled on that of Hamlet.

mythology representing the conflicts of the modern world; and Swift, Irish born like Joyce, as first revealing frightening regions of the human mind. In his attempt to achieve a superior synthesis of all possible modes of expression, Joyce did not however confine himself to the unifying influence of these three sources (to which one should add Ibsen, apparent in the whole of Joyce's work from *Dubliners* and *Exiles,* to the *Portrait, Ulysses* and *Finnegans Wake*).[1] He also wanted to epitomize all possible techniques in his book, breaking the one that had become established in the nineteenth century. After having outrun the tradition followed by novelists from Jane Austen to Henry James, the only way open to him was to repeat and magnify the experiences of an earlier age. In other words, he resumed and absorbed the individual narrative forms used by the eighteenth-century authors.

Let us see now how the successful experiments in different techniques made by the early novelists re-emerge in Joyce.

As I said, the 'presence' of Swift is plain enough in the grim humour running through *Ulysses,* in the near-morbid interest in physical processes and the action of decay and corruption, and in the meticulous working out of bitterly grotesque ideas. In *Finnegans Wake* Swift keeps turning up with obsessive frequency, and the lisping 'small talk' of the *Journal to Stella* is freely drawn upon.[2] But in any case Swift's influence does not deeply affect the technique of Joyce's two novels, though it is perhaps the main influence on his thought.

Instead I think that the technique, the whole structure of *Ulysses,* has a parallel in Fielding's work. *Joseph Andrews* is taken to be a successful experiment in the picaresque, following closely the models of *Don Quixote* and *Gil Blas.* But there is more to it than that: in his preface Fielding writes that *Joseph*

---

[1] S. Foster Damon, in *The Odyssey in Dublin* (first printed, 1929, included in *James Joyce: Two Decades of Criticism,* quoted, pp. 203 ff.), draws a parallel between *Ulysses* and Dante's *Divine Comedy* which is only partly convincing.

[2] A number of quotations of parallel passages can be found in L. A. G. Strong, *The Sacred River,* cit.

Andrews is 'a comic epic poem in prose'. The model he set himself was not so much *Don Quixote* (to which he acknowledges
his debt in the title-page), but the lost Homeric original, of
which he speaks several times in this preface. Not knowing this
original, the only way open to him was to find a comic
equivalent to Homer's serious epics. That he should follow the
Odyssey rather than the *Iliad* was readily suggested by the books
which directly influenced him: novels of travel. *Joseph Andrews*
is therefore a sort of *Odyssey* in prose, in which the adventures
of an eighteenth-century traveller in England are substituted for
the adventures in fantastic lands and among strange people: the
harbours are roadside inns, the strangers are the odd characters
met on the road. Though Fielding does not, like Joyce, keep a
fairly close parallel with the Homeric poem, there is a resemblance in several themes: the hero resisting the allurements of a
Circe, his friendly or hostile reception at the several inns, and
the burlesque 'battles' told in mock Heroic style. We must
remember that also *Ulysses* is fundamentally mock heroic (see
for instance the *Cyclops* episode). As Mr. E. B. Burgum has
pointed out, 'we have been drenched with full details about the
Ulysses parallel until we have lost sight of the central fact that
it is not simply a parallel but a parallel in reverse'.[1] Joyce chooses
only a few themes of the *Odyssey,* giving them a very personal
interpretation. It is the *Odyssey* of a modern man, or rather *the*
modern man, identified with a lower middle-class Jew. So for
Fielding *Joseph Andrews* was the *Odyssey* of a common man in
contemporary England. In both cases through the Homeric
parallel the authors attempt to show the life of a town (Dublin)
or of a country (England) and of its inhabitants with their
social and cultural background. This is obvious in Joyce, and
said explicitly in Fielding:

I declare here, once for all, I describe not men but manners,
not an individual but a species. Perhaps it will be answered,
Are not the characters then taken from life? To which I answer
in the affirmative; nay, I believe I might aver that I have writ

[1] E. B. Burgum, *The Novel and the World's Dilemma,* New York, 1947, p. 99.

little more than I have seen. The lawyer is not only alive, but hath been so these four thousand years. . . . He hath not indeed confined himself to one profession, one religion, or one country. . . .[1]

The very name of parson Adams suggests his universality, especially remembering that Fielding always gives his characters transparently descriptive names: Joseph, tempted by his master's wife, Mrs. Slipslop, sufficiently defined by those two syllables, Squire Allworthy, or all the minor figures in all his works.

There are also other characteristics common to the two novels. One is the way the narrative of *Joseph Andrews* is frequently broken by discussions of irrelevant topics; then there are the sudden changes of style, a variety by no means comparable with Joyce's, but still noticeable and deliberate in the different short stories inserted in the book and in the imitations of the diction of the Bible, the epic, the law or the sentimental romance. Finally one is struck, in *Joseph Andrews,* by the complexity of aims that the novel is pursuing. We have already pointed out a few: the narrative of travel of the picaresque kind, which makes it also a *recueil* of different tales; the modernization of the *Odyssey,* in a bourgeois setting; the description of manners involving social criticism and moral judgement. To which one should add some more limited satirical purposes; first of all the satire on Richardson's *Pamela,* which seems to have been the original motive of the novel. Besides, the criticism of the shortcomings of the administration of justice recurs again and again in the course of the book, and so does the discussion of theatrical matters. All these themes are interwoven more or less successfully to provide the scaffolding of *Joseph Andrews,* giving it a universal meaning and making of it the reflection of personal interests and idiosyncrasies. There is no need to say that the structure of *Ulysses* and its recurring themes are infinitely more complex, but the fact remains that already as early as 1742 a novel could reveal how the narrative form was able to support

[1] *Joseph Andrews,* book III, chap. I.

40

an elaborate thematic construction and to express a large variety of interests.

Sterne's *Tristram Shandy* records interests of a more esoteric kind, and this is one link with *Ulysses*. In fact, if Fielding's work can be considered in a certain sense a forerunner, Sterne's is a definite influence. His Irish origin has to be taken into account. Joyce, with his enormous knowledge of the languages, cultures and literatures of a number of countries evinced in all his books, and in spite of the universal character he gave them, made a point of constantly keeping Ireland at the centre of his world. It is significant that Blake, one of the presiding spirits in Joyce's work, was thought at the beginning of this century to be of Irish descent.[1] As for Sterne, Joyce must have rated him very highly. There is a significant list of Irish writers in *Finnegans Wake*. Here is the passage, which according to the divisions in Campbell and Robinson's *Skeleton Key* is in the 'Study Period' section:

Force Centres of the Fire Serpentine: heart, throat, navel, spleen, sacral, fon tanella, inter temporal eye.[2]

> Pose the pen, man, way me does. Way ole missa vellatooth fust show me how. Fourth power to her illpogue! Bould strokes for your life! Tip! This is Steal, this is Barke, this is Starn, this is Swhipt, this is Wiles, this is Pshaw, this is Doubbllinnbbayyates.

To each writer Joyce attributes one of the 'force centres' of Yoga. The list gives therefore to Steele heart, Burke throat, Sterne navel, Swift spleen, Wilde sacral, Shaw fontanella, Yeats intertemporal eye. Ingenious and mocking as the whole of *Finnegans Wake*, this passage shows the pre-eminence accorded

---

[1] The hypothesis, in spite of the many substantial proofs to the contrary, is revived by W. P. Witcutt, in his *Blake, a psychological study*, London, 1946.

[2] Faber edition, London, 1939, p. 303.

to Sterne. Of course, given the two lists, of authors and force
centres, and having, so to speak, to couple them, it is fairly
natural that the navel should be attributed to the author of the
book the hero of which is, till the fourth volume, in his
mother's womb, his only connection with the world being the
umbilical cord. The navel had, in Joyce's esoteric doctrines (a
synthesis of widely dispersed notions from the most distant and
improbable sources) an extraordinary importance. Stuart Gilbert tells us that the omphalos 'is at once a symbol of birth . . .
of the strand that links back generation to generation and of a
legendary eastern isle embossed on a smooth shield of sea, a lost
paradise'.[1] Knowing that one of the fundamental purposes of
Ulysses is the linking of the ages, the demonstration of the presence of the past, it is easy to see the enormous importance of the
omphalos theme in Joyce. It is worth while quoting a passage
from the *Proteus* episode in *Ulysses*. Stephen Dedalus, walking
along the strand, meets two midwives; we follow Stephen's
train of thought:

One of her sisterhood lugged me squealing into life. Creation
from nothing. What has she in the bag? A misbirth with a
trailing navelcord, hushed in ruddy wool. The cords of all link
back, strandentwining cable of all flesh. That is why mystic
monks. Will you be as gods? Gaze in your omphalos. Hello.
Kinch here. Put me on to Edenville. Aleph, alpha: nought,
nought, one.
Spouse and helpmate of Adam Kadmon: Heva, naked
Eve. She had no navel. Gaze. Belly without blemish, bulging
big, a buckler of taut vellum, no, whiteheaped corn, orient
and immortal, standing from everlasting to everlasting. Womb
of sin.
Wombed in sin darkness I was too, made not begotten. By
them, the man with my voice and my eyes and a ghostwoman
with ashes on her breath. They clasped and sundered, did the
coupler's will.[2]

[1] S. Gilbert, *James Joyce's Ulysses, A Study,* London, 1930, p. 65.
[2] *Ulysses*, Bodley Head edition, London, 1937. pp. 34–5.

One is reminded of the first chapter of *Tristram Shandy,* the deliberate and casual conception of the hero of the novel. And if we read on in *Ulysses,* some fifteen lines down the same page, we find Stephen suddenly asking himself: 'Am I going to Aunt Sara's or not?' and immediately visualizing the possible visit to his invalid uncle in bed; the scene closes with the bedridden uncle whistling Ferrando's *aria di sortita*:

His tuneful whistle sounds again, finely shaded, with rushes of the air, his fists bigdrumming on his padded knees.

And here one catches a glimpse of Sterne's Uncle Toby:

My uncle Toby instantly withdrew his hand from off my father's knee, reclined his body gently back in his chair, raised his head till it could just see the cornice of the room, and then directing the buccinatory muscles along his cheeks, and the orbicular muscles around his lips to do their duty—he whistled *Lillabullero.*[1]

Uncle Toby's whistling lasts from chapter VI to chapter XI of the third book of *Tristram Shandy.* This happens while Toby, Walter Shandy and Dr. Slop are waiting for the birth of Tristram, and the whistling goes on while the prodigious Latin text of the excommunication is read.

These strange coincidences of character and incident are already evidence of Joyce's debt to Sterne. From what I have said before, other analogies must have appeared. For instance, the Latin excommunication formula, introduced by Sterne on very slight provocation and having a profane and humorously scurrilous tone, cannot fail to remind the reader of the use to which Joyce puts church symbolism, with its Latin ritual, throughout *Ulysses.* The so-called 'black Mass' in the *Walpurgisnacht* or *Circe* episode is the most striking example, but the whole of *Ulysses* from its very first lines (Buck Mulligan's mockery of the Mass ritual) is littered with it. Another Joyce-Sterne link is to be found in the recourse made by Sterne to

[1] *Tristram Shandy,* book III, chap. VI.

little known sources of erudition and knowledge. Burton's *Anatomy of Melancholy* is known to have been one of Sterne's models, and his disquisition on rinology clearly shows the Burtonian inspiration. But *Tristram Shandy* is all interwoven with quotation and erudite information. Past esoteric culture is poured into it as into *Ulysses* to complicate the pattern of the present with that of the past, and to give a dimension of depth to the whole. Indeed, the excursions into out-of-the-way provinces of knowledge, common to both books, are the external manifestations of their authors' eagerness to explore undiscovered regions of man's consciousness. Joyce, coming after Freud and Jung, found a more or less scientific basis for his exploration. Sterne was content with giving his narrative the erratic quality of semi-automatic writing. The techniques of the two authors present, for this reason obvious similarities. A random example from *Tristram Shandy*, will serve to illustrate this point:

—Bonjour!—good morrow!—so you have got your cloak on betimes!—but 'tis a cold morning, and you judge the matter rightly—'tis better to be well mounted, than go o' foot—and obstructions in the glands are dangerous—And how goes it with thy concubine—thy wife,—and thy little ones o' both sides? and when did you hear from the old gentleman and lady —your sister, aunt, uncle, and cousins—I hope they have got better of their colds, coughs, claps, toothaches, fevers, stranguries, sciaticas, swellings, and sore eyes.

—What a devil of an apothecary! to take so much blood— give such a vile purge—puke—poultice—plaister—night-draught—clyster—blister?—And why so many grains of calomel? santa Maria! and such a dose of opium! periclitating, pardi! the whole family of ye, from head to tail—By my great-aunt *Dinah's* old black velvet mask! I think there was no occasion for it.

Now this being a little bald about the chin, by frequently putting off and on, *before* she was got with child by the coach-man—not one of our family would wear it after. To cover the MASK afresh, was more than the mask was worth—and to

44

wear a mask which was bald, or which could be half seen through, was as bad as having no mask at all—

This is the reason, may it please your reverences, that in all our numerous family, for these four generations, we count no more than one archbishop, a *Welch* judge, some three or four aldermen, and a single mountebank—

In the sixteenth century, we boast of no less than a dozen alchymists.

'It is with Love as with Cuckoldom'—the suffering party is at least the *third*, but generally the last in the house who knows anything about the matter: this comes, as all the world knows, from having half a dozen words for one thing; and so long, as what in this vessel of the human frame, is *Love*—may be *Hatred*, in that—*Sentiment* half a yard higher—and *Nonsense* —no, Madam,—not there—I mean at the part I am now pointing to with my forefinger—how can we help ourselves? [1]

Sterne is obviously registering a private train of thought, and giving free rein to word-sounds and word-associations. Joyce in practically all the first part of *Ulysses* objectifies the same process, following the mental ramblings of his characters. The verbal juggling, the typographical devices, the brusque transitions are so many points of contact between *Tristram* and *Ulysses*. And finally they both achieve that infinite expansion of the moment which abolishes all time sequence. Sterne effects this by giving what he calls a 'rhapsodical' structure to his work;[2] Joyce instead by pouring all the physical and mental experiences of the past into the present fleeting moment. Motives and methods differ, but the resulting total impression of the two works is nearly the same: the sense of a prodigious accumulation of all knowledge, of the growth of a monstrous architecture, which is nevertheless governed by a hidden logic of proportion, rhythm and historic development. A sort of fascination with birth and the parent-son relationship dominates both works, and Sterne and Joyce are both irresistibly attracted and at the same time revolted by the lowest physical human reactions—the animal processes. From all this it appears that the

---

[1] Book VIII, chap. III and IV.   [2] Book I, chap. XIII.

part played by *Tristram Shandy* in the conception of *Ulysses* has been underrated, and is well worth pointing out.

J. W. Beach [1] speaking of the infinite expansion of the moment to be observed in *Ulysses*, remarks that this method is exactly the opposite of that used in Smollett's novels, *Peregrine Pickle* and *Roderick Random,* where all the attraction lies in the rapid shift from episode to episode. As a matter of fact, if the heritage of Swift, Fielding and Sterne is present in Joyce's work, Smollett seems at first sight to be alien to it. His 'picaresqueness' is too complete and exclusive: he proceeds by accumulation of incident, with no thought for pattern or significance. V. S. Pritchett, though, has pointed out a peculiar connection, not with *Ulysses,* but with the composite language of *Finnegans Wake,* a hardly explorable language where each word carries two and more contradictory meanings. [2] Now in Smollett's last and perhaps most shapely novel, *Humphry Clinker,* there is a superb example of the art of misspelling in the letters of the Welsh maid Winifred Jenkins. They are only ten letters, some sixteen pages scattered among the 330-odd of the novel. The complications and involutions of Winifred's style had begun with the simple intention of introducing misspelling as a diversion and a pretext for equivocation. In the first letter the mistakes are those of a Mrs. Malaprop: 'importunity' for 'opportunity', 'mare' for 'mayor', 'asterisks' for 'hysterics', and so on. But by the time we reach the eighth letter, the implications of her misspellings are much subtler—the author had discovered that he could take advantage of them to form new composite words with a higher concentration of meaning, and tell a story on different levels, implying in it two separate trains of thought. Here is a fair example:

. . . Who would have thought that mistriss, after all the pains taken for the good of her prusias sole, would go for to

[1] In his essay on Joyce in *The Twentieth Century Novel—Studies in Technique,* New York, 1932.

[2] V. S. Pritchett, 'The Shocking Surgeon', in *The Living Novel,* London, 1946.

throw away her poor body? that she would cast the heys of infection upon such a carrying-crow as Lashmihago! as old as Matthewsullin, as dry as a red herring, and as pore as a starved veezel— . . . The young 'squire called him Dunquickset; but he looked for all the world like Cradoc-ap-Morgan, the ould tinker that suffered at Aberdeen for steeling of kettle. Then he's a profane scuffle, and, as Mr. Clinker says, no better than an imp-fiddle, continually playing upon the Pyebill, and the new burth. . . . O! that ever a gentlewoman of years and discretion should tare her air, and cry, and disporridge herself for such a nubjack! [1]

The transformation of personal names is typical. It is one of the most striking characteristics of *Finnegans Wake*: the list of Irish writers quoted before is sufficient evidence of this method. In the passage from Smollett Dunquickset and Matthewsullin are on the same plane. And it is interesting to see the metamorphosis of Lismahago, who in the sixth letter is Kismycago (with an indecent innuendo from the Italian in the last two syllables), in the eighth Lashmihago, and finally settles in the tenth to Lashmiheygo. It should be noted then how the 'tinker' suggests the substitution of 'cattle' with 'kettle', and the 'infidel mocking the Bible', has an elaborate musical overtone in the 'imp-fiddle playing on the pyebill and the new burth'(burthen). 'Disporridge' and 'nubjack' are among Smollett's happier creations. The letter proceeds:

But, as I was saying, I think for sartain this match will go forewood; for things are come to a creesus. . . . I believes as how, Miss Liddy would have no reversion if her swan would appear; and you would be surprised, Molly, to receive a bride's fever from your humble sarvant. But this is all suppository, dear girl; and I have sullenly promised to Mr. Clinker, that neither man, woman, nor child, shall no that arrow said a civil thing to me in the way of infection.

Here the associations are still more surprising: apart from the 'arrow' which is most appropriately 'infected', we find Miss

[1] *Humphry Clinker,* Everyman edition, London, 1943, pp. 291–2.

Lydia Melford and her modest lover projected into the mythological past, re-enacting the fable of Leda and the swan. Joyce
himself could not have improved on it. Even Joyce's trick of
availing himself of foreign words to complicate the poly-
significance of his new vocabulary is found in Smollett. For
instance 'mentioned' becomes 'minchioned'[1]—now *minchione* in
Italian means 'fool, gullible person', and has too a less decent
undertone (Smollett shows elsewhere that he knows Italian).
It is significant too that, as *Finnegans Wake* echoes throughout
with nursery rhymes and popular songs, so the maid's letters
maintain the loose rhythm of popular verse:

. . . we bathed in our birth-day soot . . . and behold, whilst
we dabbled in the loff, Sir George Coon started up with a
gun.[2]

Profanity, in Smollett as in Joyce, is never far away: 'church' is
constantly spelt 'crutch', and here is the beginning of the last
letter:

Providinch hath bin pleased to make great halteration in the
pasture of our affairs. We were yesterday three kiple chined by
the grease of God, in the holy bands of mattermoney . . .[3]

Towards the end of this letter, the last in the book, there is one
sentence which is a masterpiece of grim humour: that courting
of decay which, beyond Joyce, has been popularized by the
easy surrealism of a Salvator Dali:

. . . Now, Mrs. Mary, our satiety is to suppurate. . . .

(our society is to separate). I wonder if Mr. Savage would
transfer to *Humphry Clinker* what he said of *Finnegans Wake*: 'it
expresses a malady of the spirit through a corruption of the
language'.[4] The fact is that Smollett, like Swift and Sterne, felt
the fascination of the repulsive. Pritchett sees one link with
Joyce in 'the physical realism of Smollett and his chamber-pot

---

[1] *Op. cit.,* p. 249.   [2] *Op. cit.,* p. 249.   [3] *Op. cit.,* p. 336.
[4] D. S. Savage, *The Withered Branch,* p. 194.

humour',[1] and remarks: 'his coarseness, like that of Joyce, is the coarseness of one whose senses were unprotected and whose nerves were exposed'.[2]

This coarseness and chamber-pot humour, present even in Fielding, disappeared with Jane Austen and are not to be found in the novels of the last century; but they well up afresh in Joyce. They are partly due to a frankness which Victorian convention had obliterated, and partly to that effort of the explorers of the new medium of the novel, to confront and express life in its totality. They were inventing a new means of expression and enthusiastically availed themselves of it to reveal those sides of eighteenth-century life (and life in general) which could no longer be expressed by the pre-existing literary forms, developed already to the point of formulas. Moreover Swift, Fielding, Sterne and Smollett set out deliberately as humorous writers, since the novel was taken to be mainly a vehicle for light entertainment. One element which is too frequently over-looked by Joyce's critics and interpreters is the constant under-current of humour throughout his later writings. The difference between Joyce and the eighteenth-century writers from the point of view of humour, is this: in the early novelists humour was deliberate and open, emphasized to hide (to a certain extent) more serious concerns; in Joyce, who wrote when the novel had already become the conscious expression of serious thought and psychological analysis, humour is a hidden undercurrent, springing from the past tradition. When in the nineteenth century the novel assumed an objective attitude, increasingly stressing its function as expositor of the inner motives of the characters, the highly personal, subjective, position of a Sterne or a Swift was thought to suit better the poetic form, where the author, availing himself of an elliptical diction, could express the zones of dimmed consciousness, the simultaneity of perception, the strange and seemingly absurd transitions of thought and even the mysterious word-associations and deformations which develop in some dark corner of the mind. Browning provides

[1] V. S. Pritchett, *The Living Novel*, p. 22.   [2] *Ibid.*, p. 20.

examples of it in his *Dramatis Personae* and *The Ring and the Book*. Sterne's conversational style, proceeding by leaps, bounds and rebounds, is clearly echoed in passages like this, the beginning of part VIII of *The Ring and the Book, Dominus Hyacinthus De Archangelis, Pauperum Procurator*:

> Ah, my Giacinto, he's no ruddy rogue,
> Is not Cinone? What, to-day we're eight?
> Seven and one's eight, I hope, old curly-pate!
> —Branches me out his verb-tree on the slate,
> *Amo -as -avi -atum -are -ans,*
> Up to *-aturus*, person, tense, and mood,
> *Quies me cum subjunctivo* (I could cry)
> And chews Corderius with his morning crust!
> Look eight years onward, and he's perched, he's perched
> Dapper and deft on stool beside this chair,
> Cinozzo, Cinoncello, who but he?
> —Trying his milk teeth on some crusty case
> Like this, papa shall triturate full soon
> To smooth Papinianian pulp!
>   It trots
> Already through my head, though noon be now,
> Does supper-time and what belongs to eve.

Note how a Latin pronoun receives the ending of an English verb (*Quies me cum subjunctivo*) and the relish with which the Italian exuberance in diminutives is drawn upon—Giacinto becomes Cinone, Cinozzo, Cinoncello, and later on in this passage Cinuolo, Cinicello, Cinino, Ciniccino, Cinuciattolo, and at least a dozen others. A complicated law-case and the celebration of the birthday of his son are the two thoughts running parallel in the lawyer's mind, and inextricably interwoven. Sterne's wandering narrative is developed by Browning into a series of interior monologues, the basis of so much post-Joycean fiction. The whole plan of the book presents interesting analogies with Joyce's writing. A murder and murder-trial in Rome in 1679 are analysed and developed to such formidable lengths as to be comparable only with a book like *Ulysses*. The story is repeated over and over again (about a dozen times) by all the persons concerned, each one providing his own version from a different angle. Something very similar happens in *Finnegans Wake,* where one of the main themes, recurring every few pages, is the 'crime' and trial of H. C. Earwicker. With obsessive (one might say maniacal) deliberation, Joyce leads us back to it again and again, giving us an incredible number of versions of the elusive happenings in Phoenix Park between Earwicker, the two maids and the three soldiers. Indeed the only result of the enormous accumulation of evidence and of its symbolical interpretation is that at the end of the book we still do not know what has happened. The same could be said of several other contemporary works; the most obvious examples are Kafka's *Trial* (1925) and Pirandello's *Così è (se vi pare)* (1917).

Joyce, in an age that questions everything, has used Browning's pattern not to search for, but to abolish truth. It should be noted besides that actually it was Smollett himself who first used this method of presenting the same fact through different eyes leaving the reader in doubt. The first few letters of *Humphry Clinker* relate the episode of the challenge between Melford and Wilson from the points of view of different correspondents, and it takes some time before the reader can discover what has actually happened. Smollet of course had no higher object than the mystification of the reader to awaken his interest, and later in the book the different views of the correspondents are used only for satirical contrasts. But the fact remains that Smollett has the priority also in this field.

From what I have been saying it appears that Joyce is by no means to be regarded only as the destroyer of the English narrative tradition. In diction *Ulysses* is the sublimation of the nineteenth-century aesthetic movement, carrying to incredible lengths the precious formalism of Pater and Wilde, together with the exhibition of an equally precious culture. But as for his structural technique, or rather techniques, he links back, beyond the nineteenth century, with the experiments in novel-writing of the eighteenth century. He does not break but resumes a tradition. I am speaking of course of a technical tradition, and not of a stylistic one; between the two terms technique and style there is, I believe, a difference like the one existing between the work of the builder and of the architect. The first is interested in the proper use and arrangement of the building materials, so that the house should not collapse; the second, over and above this, aims at an aesthetic result. From the stylistic point of view elements deriving from Fielding, Sterne or Smollett run through the whole of the nineteenth-century narrative; only their technical devices had largely disappeared, and are reassembled only in Joyce's work.

A final remark may be appropriate here: the fact that the technique of some eighteenth-century novelists has passed through the poetry of Browning before reaching Joyce witnesses to that progressive approach of prose to poetry and vice versa which I mentioned in the preceding essay. There is no doubt that the whole of Joyce's work has in it a vein of lyricism, and even its rhythms are deliberately close to verse-rhythms. We must remember that even in Dickens and Trollope there are passages of real blank verse partly unconsciously used. Giving to prose the quality of poetry was one of the aims of the aesthetic movement, and it is natural that Joyce should have adopted it. But the fact that the connection should have occurred not only in style, but also (*via* Browning) in technique, is a proof that the fusion of the various literary forms of expression reached in Joyce one of its highest degrees.

Echoes in 'The Waste Land'

JOYCE is *the* revolutionary in the English novel. Probably the same cannot be said of Eliot in poetry since Ezra Pound's experiments before his seem even more daring. But Eliot's greater popularity as compared with Pound's makes him more important for the development of the style of our age. We saw, in respect of Joyce, how his revolution did not exclude the presence of a strong and well-established tradition. The same could be said of Eliot. But while with Joyce I have tried to show one way in the working of tradition (the return to earlier experiments), with Eliot I shall endeavour to demonstrate the other way in which tradition operates in the new artists: the memory of words and images and past experiences which constitute that tradition; a memory different for each single artist and contributing therefore to his individuality while linking him with the past.

The Waste Land has been annotated by T. S. Eliot himself, and he has taken care to identify most of his direct references to other authors. His habit of introducing into his poems references which amount very nearly to quotations from other literary works has been frequently commented upon. The transference of a passage, already well known and compact with an emotional and intellectual weight of its own, into a different context, is not just a show of erudition, or cashing in on pre-fabricated emotions, but serves a very definite creative purpose. On one hand it shows definite emotional patterns in a new light, modifying them by contrast and association with the 'modern' way of feeling; on the other it conveys a sense of the modern poets' consciousness of the past as history and as poetry.

But alongside these conscious though not artificial associations there is in *The Waste Land,* as in any other poem practically since the beginning of poetry, that stream of more or less unconscious echoes and recollections which reassemble and rearrange themselves to form the unit of a new poem. The realization of this process of creation is one of the reasons for Eliot's use of quotation, and this is a major difference between Eliot and Pound. Pound tended to use quotations as evocative tags, whereas for Eliot they are the outcrops of the deep strata of past culture.

To identify the materials which went into the making of a poem is always a fascinating task, giving, as it does, an insight into the workings of the imagination. And *The Waste Land,* no less than *Kubla Khan* or the *Ancient Mariner,* will prove a most rewarding hunting ground for those who are interested in the associative process which takes place in the mind of the artist. In the poems of Coleridge's which Prof. Lowes has so thoroughly examined as to leave nothing to be discovered, the most amazing associations took place, always below the level of consciousness. *The Road to Xanadu* is a feat of mental detection which can hardly be equalled; and in any case it would be impossible to cast afresh the magic spell which holds the reader of Prof. Lowes' book from the moment he realizes that he is actually meandering through the mind of a poet. On the other hand, in Eliot's case the interest will centre on the constant interplay between the two levels: the fully conscious one, and that which (to avoid a dangerous trespass into the field of psychology) I will call simply 'not conscious'.

I propose only to point out some of the materials which went into the building of a short section of *The Waste Land*: the first thirty-odd lines of the second movement, *A Game of Chess*. The reason for this choice is fairly obvious; this being a mainly descriptive passage, it contains a number of recollections of similar descriptions which are not difficult to retrace.

Eliot sets out, in *A Game of Chess,* to represent a scene of richness and splendour to be contrasted with the sordidness of the following pub. scene, but he also implies a more immediate contrast. As we realize that this extreme refinement belongs to another age, the sumptuous room becomes a modern boudoir. The poem begins with a deliberate reference to the barge scene in *Antony and Cleopatra.* The evocative power of Shakespeare's voluptuous description of Eastern splendour cannot fail to excite an immediate response in the reader. This is perhaps the most evident example of the use of quotations as a stage set: but a host of similar scenes immediately press on the mind. The Cupidon in the fourth line may well come from the same passage of *Antony and Cleopatra:*

> . . . on each side her
> Stood pretty dimpled boys like smiling Cupids . . .[1]

But how many sculptured Cupids have we met! Later I shall consider yet another Cupid in a passage which may have deeply influenced this.

Laura Riding and Robert Graves have already pointed out one poem which has largely contributed to the imagery of *A Game of Chess:* Keats' *Lamia.*[2] Here is a ghost-woman, serpent-born, appearing at a rich nuptial feast. So Eliot's lady, unsubstantial as a ghost in her rich dressing-room, is linked with Cleopatra, the 'serpent of old Nile'. And even an early poem by Eliot shows the impression *Lamia* had made on him. It is one of the poems published in the *Harvard Advocate* during Eliot's University years:

> Among a crowd of tenuous dreams, unknown
> To us of restless brain and weary feet,
> Forever hurrying, up and down the street,
> She stands at evening in the room alone.

---

[1] *Antony and Cleopatra,* II, ii, ll. 200–1.
[2] L. Riding and R. Graves, *A Survey of Modernist Poetry,* London, 1927, pp. 170–1.

Not like a tranquil goddess carved of stone
But evanescent, as if one should meet
A pensive lamia in some wood retreat,
An immaterial fancy of one's own.[1]

The description of the banquet-room in *Lamia* is one of the purple patches of the poem:

Of wealthy lustre was the banquet-room,
Fill'd with pervading brilliance and perfume:
Before each lucid pannel fuming stood
A censer fed with myrrh and spiced wood,
Each by a sacred tripod held aloft,
Whose slender feet wide-swerv'd upon the soft
Wool-woofèd carpets: fifty wreaths of smoke
From fifty censers their light voyage took
To the high roof, still mimick'd as they rose
Along the mirror'd walls by twin-clouds odorous.
Twelve sphered tables, by silk seats insphered,
High as the level of a man's breast rear'd
On libbard's paws, upheld the heavy gold
Of cups and goblets, and the store thrice told
Of Ceres' horn, and, in huge vessels, wine
Came from the gloomy tun with merry shine.
Thus loaded with a feast the tables stood,
Each shrining in the midst the image of a God.

When in an antichamber every guest
Had felt the cold full sponge to pleasure press'd,
By minist'ring slaves, upon his hands and feet,
And fragrant oils with ceremony meet
Pour'd on his hair, they all mov'd to the feast
In white robes, and themselves in order placed
Around the silken couches, wondering
Whence all this mighty cost and blaze of wealth could spring.[2]

Here are the perfumes which, as in Eliot, and Shakespeare's

[1] Now in *The Harvard Advocate Anthology*, ed. D. Hall, New York, 1950, p. 107.

[2] *Lamia*, part II, ll. 173-98.

barge scene, play such an important part in the heightening of
the sensuous atmosphere; here are the mirrors, reflecting the
smoke of the censers ('The glass . . . Doubled the flames of
sevenbranched candelabra'.[1]) Gold, fragrant oils, exquisite
words, the idea of pouring giving a sense of affluence: all these
are used by Eliot and Keats in exactly the same way, conveying
a sense of untold magnificence with a shadow lurking somewhere amidst the profuse beauty of the scene. And not only the
tone, but the full rhythm of Eliot's lines is very close to Keats'.

But the dressing-room at a certain stage acquires a sordid
undertone which eventually becomes sinister. The beauty is
ostentatious: it is cruel. From the real charm of taste and art, we
pass on to the showy profusion of a shop window, with its
aquarium lights, and its lifeless figures. It is, in fact, the profusion Mr. Bloom saw in a Dublin shop-window, while
wandering in the heat of the day, looking for somewhere to eat:

He passed, dallying, the windows of Brown Thomas, silk-
mercers. Cascades of ribbons. Flimsy China silks. A tilted
urn poured from its mouth a flood of bloodhued poplin:
lustrous blood.[2]

Ulysses was published in its final form in the same year as *The
Waste Land* was written; besides, the *Lestrygonians* episode, from
which this passage is taken, is among those published two or
three years before in *The Little Review,* a periodical to which
Eliot himself contributed. There can be little doubt that the
poet had read it before writing *The Waste Land,* and, reviewing
it in 1923, he acknowledges that it had made a deep impression
on him: 'It is a book to which we are all indebted and from
which none of us can escape.'[3] It would not be surprising
that the scene from the *Lestrygonians,* where the suggestion

[1] T. S. Eliot, *The Waste Land*—II: *A Game of Chess* (in *Collected Poems 1909–
1935,* London, 1936, pp. 64–5), ll. 78, 82.

[2] J. Joyce, *Ulysses,* Bodley Head edition, London, 1937, p. 156.

[3] I have already quoted from this review in the previous essay (see p. 34) and
other passages can be found in the second part of the present essay (p. 71), and
on p. 131.

of sumptuousness in the window-display rouses voluptuous thoughts (together with a hint of sexual disgust) leading to the merely physical and sordid stimulus of food, should have wandered into the poet's imagination while he was dealing with a not very different subject. (The parallel is completed in the pub. scene in the later part of this section:

> Well, if Albert won't leave you alone, there it is, I said,
> What you get married for if you don't want children?
> HURRY UP PLEASE ITS TIME
> Well, that Sunday Albert was home, they had a hot gammon,
> And they asked me in to dinner, to get the beauty of it hot.)[1]

The fragrant oils poured on Lamia's guests, and the flood of rich stuffs poured from a tilted urn in the silk-mercer's window (in *Ulysses*) reappear in the vision of the lady's jewels 'from satin cases poured in rich profusion'.[2] There is in both Eliot and Joyce the same arrested motion in the act of pouring (whereas 'pour' normally implies movement): a still life with drapery. The China silks and the tilted urn seem to have coalesced in Eliot's satin cases. As in *A Game of Chess* the fleeting evocation of Cleopatra at the beginning conveys a feeling of Eastern sensuality, which is maintained in the following lines, so in Joyce's *Lestrygonians* passage there is a strong exotic flavour (and exoticism is always connected with sensuality). There are 'China silks', 'cascades', and a few lines later:

> Sunwarm silk. . . . All for a woman, home and houses, silk webs, silver, rich fruits, spicy from Jaffa. . . . Wealth of the world.

It may be useful to read on in *Ulysses*:

> Wealth of the world. A warm human plumpness settled down on his brain. His brain yielded. Perfume of embraces all him assailed. With hungered flesh obscurely, he mutely craved to adore.[3]

---

[1] *The Waste Land*, cit., ll. 163-7.   [2] *The Waste Land*, cit., l. 85.
[3] *Ulysses*, cit., p. 157.

Here are the perfumes and their sensuous appeal (in Eliot: 'her strange synthetic perfumes . . . troubled, confused and drowned the sense in odours'.[1]) And so we come to a line of blank verse and some more prose:

> He turned Combridge's corner, still pursued. Jingling hoof-thuds. Perfumed bodies, warm, full. All kissed, yielded: in deep summer fields, tangled pressed grass, in trickling hall-ways of tenements, along sofas, creaking beds.[2]

The last sentences seem to foreshadow the sordid loves of the third part of *The Waste Land*:

> And I Tiresias have foresuffered all
> Enacted on this same divan or bed.[3]

The hoofthuds have the same disturbing effect as 'Footsteps shuffled on the stairs', in this section of Eliot's poem; but what seems most striking is the echo of Joyce's line 'He turned Combridge's corner, still pursued', in Eliot's

> And still she cried, and still the world pursues.[4]

Joyce's hero pursues his way to a restaurant and is pursued by physical hunger and sensual visions; are not these animal impulses those of the 'world' which is pursuing inviolable Philomel in *A Game of Chess*? The presence of Joyce's novel can also be detected in other parts of *The Waste Land*, but which are not immediately relevant to the passage that I am examining.

The next entry is one noted by Eliot himself; *laquearia*, in line 92—V. *Aeneid*, I, 726. The process of mental associations which I have tried to follow tentatively and intermittently up to this point seems to be thrown into new light by this note. A barge on the Nile and Lamia's ghostly banquet-room have contributed to the dressing-room of Eliot's lady. Now we find a

---

[1] *The Waste Land*, cit., ll. 87–9.   [2] *Ulysses*, cit., p. 157.
[3] *The Waste Land*, cit., ll. 243–4.
[4] *The Waste Land*, cit., ll. 107 and 102.

confirmation of the interplay of classical reminiscence and modern refinement. The Corinthian banquet-room in *Lamia,* lurking in the back of Eliot's mind from the beginning, recalls, this time consciously, another banquet-room in a classic poem, where Dido provides a feast for Aeneas. *Lamia* is the hidden link between Cleopatra's barge and Dido's Carthaginian banquet. The two tragic African queens (whose frequent appearances together in literature include the Fifth Canto of Dante's *Inferno*) have much in common with the medieval ghost-woman seen by Keats in all the glamour of a decadent Greek setting. The former have become, through their literary developments, the prototypes of the 'aesthetic' conception of love, of which Lamia is a further example.

And indeed a decadent poet like Swinburne had already made the connection between Cleopatra and Lamia in what is the fullest description of his conception of the fatal woman. In spite of its length the passage in worth reproducing:

But in one separate head there is more tragic attraction than in these: a woman's, three times studied, with divine and subtle care; sketched and re-sketched in youth and age, beautiful always beyond desire and cruel beyond words; fairer than heaven and more terrible than hell; pale with pride and weary with wrong-doing; a silent anger against God and man burns, white and repressed, through her clean features. . . . Her eyes are full of proud and passionless lust after gold and blood; her hair, close and curled, seems ready to shudder in sunder and divide into snakes . . . her mouth crueller than a tiger's, colder than a snake's, and beautiful beyond a woman's. She is the deadlier Venus incarnate . . . upon earth also many names could be found for her; Lamia re-transformed, invested now with a fuller beauty, but divested of all feminine attributes not native to the snake—a Lamia loveless and unassailable by the sophist, readier to drain life out of her lover than to fade for his sake at his side; or the Persian Amestris, watching the only breasts on earth more beautiful than her own cut off from her rival's living bosom; or Cleopatra, not dying but turning serpent under the serpent's bite; . . . There is a drawing in the furthest room at the Buonarroti Palace which recalls and almost reproduces the design of these three. Here also the electric hair, which looks as though it would hiss and glitter with sparks if once touched, is wound up to a tuft with serpentine plaits and involutions; all that remains of it unbound falls in one curl, shaping itself into a snake's likeness as it unwinds, right against a living snake held to the breast and throat. This is rightly registered as a study for Cleopatra; but notice has not yet been accorded to the subtle and sublime idea which transforms her death by the aspic's bite into a meeting of serpents which recognize and embrace, an encounter between the woman and the worm of the Nile, almost as though this match for death were a monstrous love-match, or such a mystic marriage as that painted in the loveliest passage of 'Salammbô', between the maiden body and the scaly coils of the serpent and the priestess alike made sacred to the moon; so closely do the snake and the queen of snakes caress and cling. Of this idea Shakespeare also had a vague and great glimpse when he made Antony murmur, 'Where's my serpent of old Nile?' mixing a foretaste of her death with the full sweet savour of her supple and amorous 'pride of life'. For what indeed is lovelier or more luxuriously loving than a strong and graceful snake of the nobler kind? [1]

Now, Eliot's early interest in Swinburne is testified by the two essays collected in *The Sacred Wood* (1920): 'Swinburne as Critic' and 'Swinburne as Poet'. It may well be that he had read this passage, in Swinburne's *Essays and Studies*. Eliot's intention was to represent, in Miss Bradbrook's words,[2] 'a neurotic fine lady of the present day', the heiress, in a 'Waste Land' world, of the Romantic and Decadent fatal woman. Probably he recalled the Swinburnian prototype, as suitable material for his telescoping of past though morbid splendour and present squalor. His recollection of Swinburne would

[1] C. A. Swinburne, 'Notes on Designs of the Old Masters at Florence', collected in *Essays and Studies* (1875). The passage is quoted in full by Mario Praz, *The Romantic Agony*, Oxford, 1933, pp. 240–1.
[2] M. C. Bradbrook, *T. S. Eliot*, London, 1950, p. 16.

naturally include its associations, Cleopatra and Lamia, which worked independently on the mind of the poet, taking him back directly to Shakespeare and Keats.

We can say, then, that the projection of the modern into the ancient is an essential element in Eliot's poetry. The examples just noted are a clear demonstration of this method. And it is interesting to note how the method itself is only partly consciously employed. This proves that the presence of past culture and history in the modern artist is not just an abstract theory but responds to an instinctive need in the contemporary man. This section of *The Waste Land* is particularly compact with classical allusions: as Eliot points out in another note, Ovid is made to contribute to the Philomel theme (lines 99 ff.).

Eliot proceeds with his review of the lady's room, and we focus now on the fire-place:

> Huge sea-wood fed with copper
> Burned green and orange, framed by the coloured stone,
> In which sad light a carved dolphin swam.[1]

A dead aquarium. But, granting the relevance of the water-theme to the whole of the poem, one may trace the tributaries of this new stream. *Lamia's* already quoted 'a censer fed with myrrh and spiced wood' is echoed in the first of these lines; but the 'copper' is already a departure, and the association of the sea-images with those of burning recalls to the memory one of the best-loved poems in English literature:

> The water, like a witch's oils,
> Burnt green, and blue, and white . . .[2]

and a few stanzas before, also in the *Ancient Mariner,* we see the 'hot and copper sky'.[3] Surely if Prof. Lowes had written a *Road from Xanadu,* recording the Romantic and post-Romantic works on which the *Ancient Mariner* left its mark, it would have been as revealing and exciting as his first great exploration itself. But

---

[1] *The Waste Land,* cit., ll. 94–6.
[2] *The Rime of the Ancient Mariner,* ll. 129–30.　　　　[3] *Ibid.,* l. 111.

here I must be content to point out this stray recollection of Coleridge's poem.

The description of the mantelpiece leads us on to the Philomel episode, one of the basic symbols of *The Waste Land*. The importance of Philomel for the whole structure of the poem is fundamental. The motif of violation and inviolability symbolized in it sounds through *The Waste Land* to the end, and contributes to its unity. But why Philomel? Of course, if you care to beat in the bush of English (or any other) literature, you can rouse whole swarms of Philomels. Yet in this case Philomel is not the threadbare synonym of nightingale or swallow (she can be either): here the stress is on the rape. The search for the source of this passage could therefore be restricted to a poetic context where Philomel appears connected with the idea of rape, and with an interior (instead of the usual nightingale thicket) or possibly a bedroom scene.

We do not need to consult rare texts to find something in this line: it is sufficient to look up Shakespeare: *Cymbeline*, Act II, Scene ii; Imogen's bed-chamber:

> She hath been reading late
> The tale of Tereus; here the leaf's turned down
> Where Philomel gave up.[1]

The speaker is Iachimo, who has secretly entered the chamber where Imogen is asleep, to collect the evidence which will prove her pretended infidelity to Posthumus. It is definitely a rape, though a mental one. Iachimo himself, advancing into the room, recalls the rape of Lucrece:

> Our Tarquin thus
> Did softly press the rushes ere he waken'd
> The chastity he wounded.[2]

The choice of the story of Philomel as the book Imogen was reading when she fell asleep, may be merely accidental. But if we turn to Shakespeare's *Rape of Lucrece* we shall find the

---

[1] *Cymbeline*, II, ii, ll. 44-6.   [2] *Cymbeline*, II, ii, ll. 14-16.

heroine, left alone after having suffered violence, invoking
'Philomel, that sing'st of ravishment'.[1] (It is worth noticing that
this passage of *Lucrece* contains the description of a waste land:

> And for, poor bird, thou sing'st not in the day,
> As shaming any eye should thee behold,
> Some dark deep desert, seated from the way,
> That knows nor parching heat nor freezing cold,
> We will find out; and there we will unfold
> > To creatures stern sad tunes, to change their kinds:
> > Since men prove beasts, let beasts bear gentle minds.

One is reminded of the whole purport of Eliot's poem.)

The allusions to Tarquin at the beginning and to Philomel
at the close of the scene in *Cymbeline* emphasize the idea of the
rape which Iachimo is consummating in his mind. In this
atmosphere Iachimo takes stock of the room, like the poet in *A
Game of Chess*. Perfume and candlelight have the same suggest-
iveness in both passages:

> 'Tis her breathing that
> Perfumes the chamber thus: the flame o' the taper
> Bows toward her . . .[2]

Shakespeare can create a three-dimensional room with these
scanty hints, but the claim I am putting forward for the fundamental importance of *Cymbeline* in the creation of *A Game of
Chess* cannot rest simply on a reference to Philomel, and one or
two corresponding items in an inventory of bedroom furnishings. Actually the description of Imogen's bed-chamber does
not end with this scene. It becomes much more detailed when
Iachimo repeats it to Posthumus, as evidence of her guilt, in the
fourth scene of the same act. I will quote his lines, leaving out
Posthumus' interruptions:

> It was hang'd
> With tapestry of silk and silver; the story
> Proud Cleopatra, when she met her Roman,

---

[1] *The Rape of Lucrece*, ll. 1142–8.   [2] *Cymbeline*, ii, ii, ll. 18–20.

And Cydnus swell'd above the banks, or for
The press of boats or pride: a piece of work
So bravely done, so rich, that it did strive
In workmanship and value; which I wonder'd
Could be so rarely and exactly wrought,
Since the true life in't was.—
    . . . The chimney
Is south the chamber; and the chimney-piece
Chaste Dian bathing: never saw I figures
So likely to report themselves: the cutter
Was as another nature, dumb; outwent her,
Motion and breath left out.
    . . . The roof o' the chamber
With golden cherubins is fretted: her andirons,—
I had forgot them,—were two winking Cupids
Of silver, each on one foot standing, nicely
Depending on their brands.[1]

Here we find the other furnishings of the room in Eliot's poem,
and we have a glimpse into the creative process. It is only a
brief glimpse, but sufficient to give us an insight into the constant shifting and re-arranging of known images and words in
the artist's mind. Since there is no note by Eliot referring to
Cymbeline, I am inferring that he was not conscious of this
secret play of the imagination. He began with a deliberate
reference to Shakespeare's Cleopatra, and proceeded with the
description of a room. Dido's banquet-room presented itself to
his mind, and Lamia's feast added touches of sensuous splendour to the whole. But, somewhere in what James called 'the
deep well of unconscious cerebration', the memories deposited
by the reading of another Shakespearian play must have begun
to move. Cleopatra established the link. She was the secret hook
which drew to the surface—not in their original order and
structure, but already transformed—the descriptive elements
which build the lady's room in Eliot. (There is little doubt that
Shakespeare himself was remembering the barge scene of his

[1] *Cymbeline,* II, iv, ll. 66–76, 80–5, 87–91.

previous play when writing *Cymbeline*.) So the 'golden cherubins' in the roof of Imogen's chamber became assimilated with
her andirons: 'two winking Cupids Of silver', and with the
boys in Cleopatra's barge, 'like smiling Cupids', producing
Eliot's peeping Cupids:

> a golden Cupidon peeped out
> (Another hid his eyes behind his wing).[1]

Dian bathing may perhaps have prompted the sea imagery connected with the chimney-piece, where the 'carvèd dolphin' may
be a cross between another Keatsian context (*Eve of St. Agnes,*
stanza IV) and the irresistible Shakespearian line referring to
Antony; 'his pleasures, Were dolphin-like'[2]—but I grant that
this connection is rather far-fetched, even admitting the united
presence in the poet's mind of Keats' poems and *Antony and
Cleopatra.*

Instead, what is really revealing is the Cleopatra-Philomel
exchange. The story in the book Imogen was reading here
takes the place of the picture decorating the room, a picture
which in *Cymbeline* represented Cleopatra's story. But Cleopatra had already been evoked in *A Game of Chess,* so the blank
space left on the wall by her picture was filled by the rape of
Philomel, which had obviously been lurking in some corner
of the poet's mind, from the other *Cymbeline* context. Through
associative processes of this kind the work of the poet is done:
the new pattern is a different arrangement of the elements of the
old one, and the crossing of this with a number of other recol-
lected patterns which can be called poetic even if they come
from a prose work like *Ulysses.*

Joyce and Keats, Shakespeare and Swinburne, lead this
dance of images. But the authors mentioned are only a minority
in comparison with the wealth of not conscious references to
past literature of which each new work is compact. In the
Philomel passage Eliot refers in his notes to Ovid and Milton
(the *Waste Land* is after all a *Paradise Lost*). And the next few

---

[1] *The Waste Land,* cit., ll. 80-1.   [2] *Antony and Cleopatra,* v, ii.

lines, the last which I am dealing with, yield more wealth of recollection. The 'staring forms' which

Leaned out, leaning, hushing the room enclosed,[1]

send us back once again to Keats: in the stanza of *The Eve of St. Agnes* where there are the 'carved angels', the whole passage reads:

The carved angels, ever eager-eyed,
Star'd, where upon their heads the cornice rests,
With hair blown back, and wings put cross-wise on their
breasts.[2]

That Eliot had Lamia's banquet-room in his mind has already been demonstrated; only a few lines before its description (quoted at the beginning of this essay) Keats shows us Lamia who, after having surveyed the host of her 'viewless servants' setting out the banquet, 'fades'

And shut(s) the chamber up, close, hush'd, and still.[3]

In Eliot's imagination the staring angels of *The Eve of St. Agnes* become part of Lamia's banquet room at this point.

In *A Game of Chess* even the electrical phenomenon of the lady's hair sparking under the brush has an uncanny quality, culminating with its glowing into words. But we need only recall Cleopatra's 'electric hair, which look as though it would hiss and glitter with sparks if once touched', in the Swinburne passage already quoted, to realize whence the image comes. Another reference is added to it, though: the words out of the flame are a clear recollection of Dante, in the two Cantos (*Inferno*, XXVI and XXVII) on the false counsellors. Dante gives a most vivid description of how the tips of the flames enclosing the spirits of the damned would move and 'glow into words'. Eliot was obviously familiar with this part of the poem, and must have been deeply moved by it, since two tercets from

---

[1] *The Waste Land*, cit., l. 106.   [2] *The Eve of St. Agnes*, stanza IV.
[3] *Lamia*, II, l. 143.

Canto XXVII form the motto of *The Love Song of J. Alfred Prufrock.*

> S'io credessi che mia risposta fosse
> A persona che mai tornasse al mondo
> Questa fiamma starìa senza più scosse.
>
> Ma perciocché giammai di questo fondo
> Non tornò vivo alcun, s'i'odo il vero,
> Senza tema d'infamia ti rispondo.

This image of hell closes the passage I have chosen to illustrate. Certainly a more searching and competent analysis would be sure to unearth many more treasures of hidden association. This was only an attempt to uncover the first layer, and I hope that some provisional conclusions may be reached at this stage.

First of all, it is most important to make a clear distinction between deliberate echoes—old materials that the poet includes in his work for the overtones they have acquired (examples are Cleopatra's barge, Virgil's *laquearia,* Milton's 'sylvan scene') on the one hand, and, on the other, the hidden associations of which the whole poem is woven. It is mainly with the latter that the present discussion is concerned. Eliot had based 'the plan and a good deal of the incidental symbolism' of his poem on Miss Weston's *From Ritual to Romance* and Frazer's *The Golden Bough*: it will be noticed that I have not had occasion to mention either book. The reason is obvious: I am not looking here for the symbolic meaning, the contents of thought and ideas in the poem; in other words, I am not considering the whole impression of the structure before me, but am looking at the building materials. There is a limitation in this kind of analysis; but the risk of not seeing the wood for the trees is compensated by the excitement of getting an insight, restricted as it is, into the creative process.

In this particular case we are able to see how a sensuous atmosphere of splendour and vague mystery (a sense of foreboding, as Eliot called it apropos of another of his poems) evoked Keats; this very connection helps us to realize the power of the modern poet, who succeeds in giving, in a single word, a completely new twist to a Keatsian scene, transferring it to our own industrial time: 'her strange *synthetic* perfumes'—the adjective seems to us to be obviously connected with perfumes, but at the same time it introduces a startlingly modern note into the classic description.[1] The echoes from Joyce's *Ulysses* are due to a demonstrable closeness of aim and conception in the poet and in the novelist. Actually in this particular passage they are less apparent than in other sections of *The Waste Land,* or, for that matter, than in the poem as a whole.

Cymbeline seems to me the most surprising and the most significant thread in the whole pattern of associations. *Cymbeline* must have been very much in Eliot's mind at the time of the composition of *The Waste Land.* Further evidence of this may be found in the sequence to the scene I have quoted, where Iachimo gives Posthumus proof of Imogen's pretended infidelity. Posthumus, left alone, imagines the scene:

> This yellow Iachimo in an hour,—was't not?
> Or less,—at first?—Perchance he spoke not, but,
> Like a full-acorn'd boar, a German one,
> Cried O! and mounted; found no opposition
> But what he look'd for should oppose, and she
> Should from encounter guard. Could I find out
> The woman's part in me! For there's no motion
> That tends to vice in man, but I affirm
> It is the woman's part . . .[2]

Turning now to *The Waste Land,* section III (*The Fire Sermon*):

> I Tiresias, old man with wrinkled dugs
> Perceived the scene, and foretold the rest—
> I too awaited the expected guest.

---

[1] Since writing this I found the following remark in Elizabeth Drew, *T. S. Eliot: The Design of His Poetry,* London, 1949, p. 102: 'It is the startling intrusion of the word synthetic, in the description of the perfumes, . . . that prepares us for the atmosphere of the artificial and unnatural which is to colour the following scene.'

[2] *Cymbeline,* II, v, ll. 14–22.

He, the young man carbuncular, arrives,
A small house agent's clerk, with one bold stare . . .
The time is now propitious, as he guesses,
The meal is ended, she is bored and tired,
Endeavours to engage her in caresses
Which still are unreproved, if undesired.
Flushed and decided, he assaults at once;
Exploring hands encounter no defence;
His vanity requires no response,
And makes a welcome of indifference.
(And I Tiresias have foresuffered all
Enacted on this same divan or bed; . . .[1]

The two scenes of lust, both reconstructed in the mind of the speakers, who figure as blind witnesses emotively engaged in what is happening, show obvious even rhythmic analogies. But a further significant link is represented by Posthumus' outburst: 'The woman's part in me!' The idea of man being bisexual is not only Shakespeare's. As Eliot points out in a note, 'the two sexes meet in Tiresias', who is the narrator of the sordid romance of the typist and the clerk. Shakespeare uses the idea simply as a pretext for an attack on women, while Eliot gives it a much more complex meaning. But the connection remains in both authors between this dubious figure and the animal lust of the scene described.

There may have been merely contingent reasons (a recent reading, a performance, and in general Ezra Pound's insistence on the value of Shakespeare's last plays) for the recollections of *Cymbeline* at the time of the writing of *The Waste Land*. But the form such recollections have taken is typical: an imaginary rape has substantiated the idea of pollution arising from the rites described in Miss Weston's book and from the state of modern civilization. This is not surprising when we consider the new interpretation of Shakespeare's 'romances' as fully mature works, in which more than one level of reality is revealed at one and the same time. *Cymbeline* shares therefore some of the features of

[1] *The Waste Land,* cit., ll. 228–32, 235–44.

that Metaphysical poetry to which our contemporaries and Eliot in particular are deeply indebted. And the debt is due to the similarity in the historical and in the stylistic climate between the two periods in question: the Jacobean and our own age. I shall not go into more details for the time being since I have dealt with this point in some of the following essays.

I shall be content to point out that these not conscious echoes demonstrate that all real poetry is born in the same way, absorbing and transforming the work of the past. Even such a conscious artist as Eliot, who realized this mental assimilation and actually laid it bare by quoting his own sources, reveals, in a close analysis, how secretly this intricate process works.

We have seen the mass of conscious and unconscious reminiscence from the most various sources going into the making of a few lines of *The Waste Land*. I suggest that we should now give at least a cursory look at the influence on the same poem as a whole of a single contemporary author. I have already quoted a sentence from Eliot's tribute of admiration to Joyce's *Ulysses*; and in the same review of what he considered as 'the most important expression which the present age has found', Eliot goes on to say that Joyce's parallel use of the *Odyssey*

has the importance of a scientific discovery. . . . In using the Myth, in manipulating a continuous parallel between contemporaneity and antiquity, Mr. Joyce is pursuing a method which others must pursue after him. . . . Psychology (such as it is, and whether our reaction to it be comic or serious), ethnology, and *The Golden Bough* have concurred to make possible what was impossible even a few years ago. Instead of the narrative method, we may now use the mythical method.[1]

While writing this Eliot was obviously thinking as much of his own work as of Joyce's. Hardly any critic has failed to point out

[1] T. S. Eliot, *Ulysses, Order and Myth*, cit., see pp. 34 and 57.

the connection between Joyce and Eliot, and the points of contact between the two authors have been very clearly illustrated
by Claude-Edmonde Magny,[1] who reaches the conclusion that
this contact was closest at the time of the writing of *Ulysses* and
The Waste Land, while after that period they took separate and
diverging roads. My purpose in this essay is to point out the
debt of *The Waste Land* to *Ulysses* not only from the point of
view of the general method followed by Eliot and so neatly
enunciated in his review of Joyce's book, but also on the level
of imagery, symbolism and vocabulary.

I speak of 'debt' because, as I have said in the first part of this
essay, there is hardly any doubt that Eliot had read at least the
first episodes of *Ulysses* in *The Little Review* before writing his
major poem. My analysis will centre therefore mainly on the
third section of Joyce's novel, (now known under the name of
the *Proteus* episode) for the obvious reason that it appears as the
most 'poetical' of the book and therefore the most likely to be
absorbed into the work of a contemporary poet. As Mr. Philip
Toynbee has rightly remarked, 'the first two sections [of
Ulysses] are narrative interspersed with interior comment. This
section [*Proteus*] is a continuous interior monologue, interspersed with short passages of description'. And he has contrasted the 'high' language of Stephen, 'rich, supple and
poetical', with the 'low' language of Bloom, 'earthly, colloquial
and disjointed', in the later sections of the book, where Joyce is
following a strict plan, ruling out poetry.[2]

Assuming then that the *Proteus* episode is the most likely to
have influenced the diction of *The Waste Land,* we can attempt
to proceed by parallel quotations from the two works. In the
Ulysses episode Stephen Dedalus walks along the Dublin
strand. As in *The Waste Land,* the fundamental themes of the

[1] C.-E. Magny, 'A Double Note on T. S. Eliot and James Joyce', in *T. S.
Eliot, A Symposium,* compiled by R. March and Tambimuttu, London, 1948,
pp. 208–17.

[2] P. Toynbee, 'A Study of Ulysses', in *James Joyce: Two Decades of Criticism,*
ed. Sean Givens, New York, 1949, pp. 243–84.

Water (the sea) and the Dry Land are immediately established. Stephen thinks:

Signatures of all things I am here to read, seaspawn and sea-wrack, the nearing tide, that rusty boot.[1]

We may think of the 'heap of broken images' in line 22 of *The Waste Land* which will become one of the leading motifs of the poem, as the flotsam and jetsam is a basic symbol in *Proteus*. This is made clear later on in the same section:

These heavy sands are language tide and wind have silted here. And there, the stoneheaps of dead builders, a warren of weasel rats. . . . Sands and stones. Heavy of the past.[2]

We could turn to the conclusion of *The Waste Land* and find there how this theme has been transformed. Monologizing like Stephen Eliot says:

> I sat upon the shore
> Fishing, with the arid plain behind me . . .[3]

and he quotes fragments of lines in different languages, which are indeed 'heavy of the past', commenting:

These fragments I have shored against my ruins.

The analogy of the two passages and of their significance seems very clear, especially if we keep in mind another context in *The Waste Land* where the lonely fisher (the Fisher King, the human sinner) appears:

> A rat crept softly through the vegetation
> Dragging its slimy belly on the bank
> While I was fishing in the dull canal . . .
> White bodies naked on the low damp ground
> And bones cast in a little low dry garret,
> Rattled by the rat's foot only, year to year.[4]

---

[1] *Ulysses*, cit., p. 33.   [2] *Ibid.*, p. 41.

[3] *The Waste Land*, cit., ll. 423–4.   [4] *Ibid.*, ll. 187–9, 193–5.

Here then is the warren of weasel rats; and the dead landscape represented in Eliot's lines (a landscape which we have seen so many times reproduced with utter complacency in recent years by a whole generation of fashionable surrealist painters) is very similar to the one drawn by Joyce only two lines before the passage quoted:

He climbed over the sedge and eely oarweeds and sat on a stool of rock, resting his ashplant in a grike. A bloated carcass of a dog lay lolled on bladderwrack. Before him the gunwale of a boat, sunk in sand.[1]

And another passage which may have stuck in Eliot's mind is found in the same page of *Ulysses*, a few lines before: Stephen thinks of the martello tower which he has rented with Buck Mulligan, and the key to its door, which he has given to Mulligan two hours earlier: 'He has the key', he remarks to himself, and goes on with his endless stream of literary associations:

I will not sleep there when this night comes. A shut door of a silent tower entombing their blind bodies . . .[2]

Joyce was not thinking of Dante in this passage, but Eliot was half-remembering probably also Joyce's passage when he introduced in the last movement of *The Waste Land* the reference to the Count Ugolino episode in the *Inferno*:

> *Dayadhvam:* I have heard the key
> Turn in the door once and turn once only
> We think of the key, each in his prison
> Thinking of the key, each confirms a prison
> Only at nightfall, aethereal rumours
> Revive for a moment a broken Coriolanus.[3]

It is just after thinking of the 'sands and stones heavy of the past' that Stephen sees the dog: 'A point, live dog, grew into sight running across the sweep of sand.' His first reaction is of

---

[1] *Ulysses*, cit., p. 41.   [2] *Ibid.*, p. 41.
[3] *The Waste Land*, cit. ll. 411–16.

fear: 'Lord, is he going to attack me? Respect his liberty . . . I
have my stick'.[1] Since the apparition of the dog seems relevant
both to Joyce and Eliot, I will follow it in the next few pages
of the book. Here it comes, half a page later: 'The dog's bark
ran towards him, stopped, ran back. Dog of my enemy.' And
after another half-page:

Their dog ambled about a bank of dwindling sand, trot-
ting, sniffing on all sides. *Looking for something lost in a past life.*
Suddenly he made off like a bounding hare, ears flung back,
chasing the shadow of a lowskimming gull. The man's
shrieked whistle struck his limp ears. He turned, bounded
back, came nearer, trotted on twinkling shanks. On a field
tenney a buck, trippant, proper, unattired. At the lacefringe of
the tide he halted with stiff forehoofs, seawardpointed ears. His
snout lifted barked at the wavenoise, herds of *seamorse*. . . .
Unheeded he kept by them as they came towards the drier
sand, *a rag of wolf's tongue redpanting from his jaws.* His speckled
body ambled ahead of them and then loped off at a calf's
gallop. The carcass lay on his path. He stopped, sniffed,
stalked round it, brother, nosing closer, went round it, sniffing
rapidly like a dog all over the dead dog's bedraggled fell . . .
His hindpaws then scattered sand: *then his forepaws dabbled and
delved. Something he buried there,* his grandmother. He rooted in
the sand, dabbling, delving and stopped to listen to the air,
scraped up the sand again with a fury of his claws, soon ceasing, a
pard, a panther, got in spousebreach, *vulturing the dead.*[2]

It is not a loving picture of a dog, as Joyce himself pointed out
when Frank Budgen told him: 'I don't know a better word-
picture of a dog. . . . English and Irish, we are all dog-lovers.'
To which Joyce reportedly replied: 'This certainly was not done
by a dog-lover. . . . I don't like them. I am afraid of them.'[3]
   Now, one of the most discussed passages in *The Waste Land*
is in the first section of the poem, *The Burial of the Dead.* After
the speaker has greeted 'Stetson, You who were with me in the

[1] *Ulysses,* cit., p. 42.   [2] *Ulysses,* cit., p. 43 (italics mine).
[3] F. Budgen, *James Joyce and the Making of Ulysses,* London, 1934, p. 54.

ships at Mylae!' establishing in a startling and masterly way the connection between present and past (Joyce was doing exactly the same thing in *Ulysses*; e.g. 'Francis was reminding Stephen of years before when they had been at school together in Conmee's time. He asked about Glaucon, Alcibiades, Pisistratus. Where were they now?'[1]), he goes on asking:

> That corpse you planted last year in your garden,
> Has it begun to sprout? Will it bloom this year?
> Or has the sudden frost disturbed its bed?
> Oh keep the Dog far hence, that's friend to men,
> Or with his nails he'll dig it up again! [2]

Why, it has been asked, 'The wolf . . . that's foe to men' in the Dirge of Webster's *The White Devil* (so suggestive a passage as it stands) has been changed by Eliot into 'the Dog . . . that's friend to men'? And why has the word Dog been spelt with a capital? Matthiessen (and Leavis before him) saw in the passage 'the sense of the agonizing, since futile, effort to escape those memories (of war), to bury those dead for good.'[3] But that would hardly have required the change from wolf to Dog. A similar point of view has recently been maintained by Mr. John Peter in his original new interpretation of *The Waste Land*. Mr. Peter though speaks of 'guilty memories' and of the reluctance to expose oneself 'to the probes of others, even of those whose motives are sympathy and compassion'; the Dog therefore typifies 'this class of inquirer'.[4] Even this does not account for the use of the capital in 'Dog'. Cleanth Brooks seems to have given more attention to this point:

I am inclined to take the Dog as Humanitarianism and the related philosophies which, in their concern for man, extirpate

---

[1] *Ulysses*, cit. p. 396.

[2] *The Waste Land*, cit., ll. 71–5.

[3] F. O. Matthiessen, *The Achievement of T. S. Eliot*, 2nd ed., New York, 1947, p. 22.

[4] J. Peter, 'A New Interpretation of The Waste Land', in *Essays in Criticism*, II, n. 3, July 1952, p. 249.

the supernatural—dig up the corpse of the buried god and thus prevent the rebirth of life.[1]

Though the allusion to Humanitarianism seems somewhat vague, Mr. Brooks appears nearer the mark in connecting the Dog to the fertility rites described in Miss Weston's book, and in noticing that for Eliot the Dog is not necessarily a friendly force; the poet seems rather to fear its intervention. Helen Gardner went still further in this connection, by quoting the Biblical Dog, the power of Evil: 'Deliver my soul from the sword, my darling from the power of the dog.'[2] And actually this identification of the Dog with evil is supported by at least two later contexts in which the word appears in Eliot's work. In *Marina* we find in fact:

> Those who sharpen the tooth of the dog, meaning
> Death

among the beings which are 'become unsubstantial' thanks to a saving grace, alongside

> Those who sit in the stye of contentment, meaning
> Death
> Those who suffer the ecstasy of the animals, meaning
> Death [3]

The dog is actually here a symbol of evil. And the other context, from the fifth Chorus of *The Rock* makes the point even clearer; speaking of the House of God, the Church, Eliot writes:

O Lord, deliver me from the man of excellent intention and impure heart . . .
Preserve me from the enemy who has something to gain: and from the friend who has something to lose . . .
Those who sit in a house of which the use is forgotten: are like snakes that lie on mouldering stairs, content in the sunlight.

[1] C. Brooks, *Modern Poetry and the Tradition*, London, 1948, pp. 145–6.
[2] H. Gardner, *The Art of T. S. Eliot*, London, 1949, p. 92.
[3] *Collected Poems*, cit., p. 113.

And the others run about like dogs, full of enterprise, sniffing
    and barking: they say, 'This house is a nest of serpents, let
    us destroy it,
And have done with these abominations, the turpitudes of the
    Christians.' And these are not justified, nor the others . . .
. . . we are encompassed with snakes and dogs: therefore some
    must labour, and others must hold the spears.[1]

And the image in *Marina* comes back again in the sixth
Chorus, where Eliot deals with the superficiality of modern
civilization, for those who do not realise that civilization in its
deepest meaning is due, as he thinks, to Christianity. He
exclaims:

Men! polish your teeth on rising and retiring;
Women! polish your fingernails:
You polish the tooth of the dog and the talon of the cat.[2]

The dog is therefore the busy inquirer who founds his search on
areligious, or rather on purely animal bases. And this, I think,
Eliot meant also when introducing the dog in *The Burial of the
Dead* (the title of this section of *The Waste Land* is significant).
Stetson had buried his and the world's past—he had done like
the Robin-red-breast and the wren in Webster's Dirge, which

with leaves and flowres doe cover
The friendlesse bodies of unburied men.

The corpse may be that of the 'drowned Phoenician sailor' of
line 47, who becomes one of the most permanent and recurring
symbols in Eliot's poem. Like the drowned sailor who would
be transformed into something rich and strange, so the corpse
will sprout and bear fruit, unless disturbed by an evil power of
inquiry which is not even satisfied with letting dead bodies lie.
This could not be expressed with a better image than that of
Webster's wolf, and Eliot indeed nearly quoted the lines of the
Dirge.

[1] *Collected Poems*, cit., p. 169.   [2] *Ibid.*, p. 170.

It is at this point, I think, that the reminiscence of the extremely vivid word-picture of the dog digging and delving in *Ulysses* came into play, bringing about the change from Webster's wolf to Eliot's dog, especially since the latter could afford an even wider range of symbolic references. We saw that in Stephen's mind the dog, which at a certain moment resembles a wolf, was 'looking for something lost in a past life . . . vulturing the dead'. And the relevance of the *Ulysses* passage which might have prompted the substitution will appear even more clearly when we shall see that in it there are also several references to the drowned sailor and to the sea-change in Ariel's song. But for the time being I shall try to conclude on the subject of the Dog, passing to the second question: Why is the word spelt with a capital? I think that Eliot, in his search for the polivalence of his symbols, took advantage of it to introduce a further meaning in his lines. The explanation has already been given by Miss Elizabeth Drew [1] and, more concisely, by Mr. Maxwell, who refers to Eliot's previous use of the word Dog (with a capital) in *Sweeney among the Nightingales*:

> Gloomy Orion and the Dog
> Are veiled; and hushed the shrunken seas;

'In this context—Mr. Maxwell says—the Dog is obviously Sirius, the Dog star, which for the Egyptians foretold the coming of the fertilizing floods of the Nile'.[2] And here is the relevant passage from the section of *The Golden Bough* on the Ritual of Osiris, mentioned by Eliot himself as one of the sources of *The Waste Land*:

> . . . in the early days of Egyptian history, some three or four thousand years before the beginning of our era, the splendid star of Sirius, the brightest of all the fixed stars, appeared at dawn in the east just before sunrise about the time of the summer solstice, when the Nile begins to rise . . . [To the

[1] E. Drew, *T. S. Eliot, the Design of His Poetry*, cit., pp. 100–1.
[2] D. E. S. Maxwell, *The Poetry of T. S. Eliot*, London, 1952, p. 83.

Egyptians] apparently the brilliant luminary in the morning sky seemed the goddess of life and love come to mourn her departed lover or spouse and to wake him from the dead.[1]

(We might note that, peculiarly enough, the dog in *Ulysses* belonged to a couple of gypsies whom Joyce—whose fondness for associations and plurality of meaning was at least as great as Eliot's, calls Egyptians.) Now, in the first sections of *The Waste Land* the rebirth of life is dreaded (*April is the cruellest month*) by the lost inhabitants of Eliot's arid landscapes who, like *Geron-tion*, are 'old men in a dry month' and 'have lost their passion'. Only years later the poet will consider them as 'snakes that lie on mouldering stairs'; but at the time of writing *The Waste Land* they are still the true essence of modern man, passive and unwilling to act, wanting to forget his own past, and consider-ing as evil any agency which will try to revive it. The Dog is a symbol of these disturbing agencies—it is the star Sirius of the Egyptians and it is the exact equivalent of that 'April' in the first line of the poem 'stirring dull roots with spring rain', while 'Winter kept us warm, covering Earth in forgetful snow'. In these very lines (as Miss Drew has observed) there is the first allusion to Webster, winter has the same function as 'the ant, the field-mouse and the mole' in the Dirge, which, will 'rear him hillocks, that shall keep him warm'. And we have seen already why, when Eliot went back to the Webster passage in the closing lines of the section to mention the opposing force, he turned the wolf into a dog: Frazer's book and Joyce's treat-ment of the dog in *Ulysses* must have been the two main elements which suggested the change.

---

[1] J. G. Frazer, *The Golden Bough,* abridged edition, p. 370. The words 'her departed lover' occur also in *The Waste Land* (l. 250):

> She turns and looks a moment in the glass,
> Hardly aware of her departed lover . . .

It is typical of Eliot's 'Mythical method' to transform the meeting of the Egyptian gods into the barren loves of the typist and the 'small house agent's clerk'.

But the echoes of Joyce's novel on *The Waste Land* do not end here. In the *Proteus* episode Stephen, after his first movement of fear at the sight of the dog, reproaches himself: 'He saved men from drowning and you shake at a cur's yelping,' and that reminds him of a recent accident: 'The man that was drowned nine days ago off Maiden's rock. They are waiting for him now.'[1] This is not the first time that the drowned man is mentioned in *Ulysses*. In the first section of the novel Stephen had overheard the conversation between a business man and a boatman:

—There's five fathoms out there, he said. It'll be swept up that way when the tide comes in about one. It's nine days today. The man that was drowned.[2]

And Stephen is again reminded of him in the second section while, during his lesson at Mr. Deasy's school, one of his pupils recites *Lycidas*: 'Sunk though he be beneath the watery floor.'[3] But in the *Proteus* episode the drowned man becomes still more important. Its relevance to *The Waste Land* is obvious and has been noticed long ago by Stuart Gilbert and Prof. Ernst Robert Curtius:

'The sea', Prof. Curtius has remarked, 'that primordial element, giver and taker of life, beats about the Ulyssean world of life-experience. As in Mr. T. S. Eliot's *Waste Land*, so through the work of Joyce runs the motif of the Drowned Man.' It is interesting to note that Mr. Eliot's drowned man was, like the prototype of Odysseus himself, a Phoenician trader . . . The drowning man is said to have a flash of insight into 'the vast repository where the records of every man's life as well as every pulsation of the visible cosmos are stored up for all eternity', that is to say the 'Akasic records' alluded to by Stephen in the Aeolus episode. Mr. Bloom observes: 'Drowning they say is the pleasantest. See your whole life in a flash.'[4]

[1] *Ulysses*, cit., p. 42.   [2] *Ibid.*, p. 19.   [3] *Ibid.*, p. 23.
[4] S. Gilbert, *James Joyce's Ulysses*, cit., pp. 122-4.

This needs no comment. I should only like to draw attention to section IV of *The Waste Land, Death by Water*:

As he rose and fell
He passed the stages of his age and youth . . .[1]

And the similarity is still more striking when we compare a later passage of Stephen's interior monologue in the *Proteus* section with other parts of *The Waste Land*:

Five fathoms out there. Full fathom five thy father lies. At one he said. Found drowned. High water at Dublin bar. Driving before it a loose drift of rubble, fanshoals of fishes, silly shells. A corpse rising saltwhite from the undertow, bobbing landward, a pace a pace a porpose. There he is. Hook it quick. Sunk though he be beneath the watery floor. . . . A seachange this, brown eyes saltblue. Seadeath, mildest of all deaths known to man.[2]

This passage, which crystallizes Stephen's experiences (the overheard conversation, the line from *Lycidas*) seems to contain many of the basic images of *The Waste Land*. The quotations from Ariel's song are also a recurrent theme in *The Waste Land*. They appear for the first time after the mention of the Phoenician sailor in line 47 (*Those are pearls that were his eyes. Look!*). The same line from the *Tempest* is repeated in the second section of the poem (line 125), and in *The Fire Sermon* there are at least two references (lines 192 and 257) to Shakespeare's play, pointed out by Eliot himself in his notes. Still more interesting is another reference to it in the very brief fourth section, *Death by Water*, dealing with the drowned Phoenician sailor, 'a fortnight dead'. There the lines occur:

A current under sea
Picked his bones in whispers. As he rose and fell . . .[3]

This seems to me another reminiscence from Ariel's song: not

[1] *The Waste Land*, cit., ll. 316–17.   [2] *Ulysses*, cit., pp. 46–7.
[3] *The Waste Land*, cit., ll. 315–16.

only 'of his bones are coral made', but also the line in the previous part of the song:

> The wild waves whist.

It is known that *Death by Water* is a nearly literal translation from Eliot's earlier poem in French *Dans le Restaurant*. But at this point the French original had only:

> Un courant de sous-mer l'emporta très loin,
> Le repassant aux étapes de sa vie antérieure.[1]

'Picked his bones in whispers', then, and the undulating movement in the second half of the line, are new additions in the version written for *The Waste Land*. I wonder if they can have been suggested by Joyce's description of the movement of the weeds only a few lines before the last *Proteus* passage quoted:

> Under the upswelling tide he saw the writhing weeds lift languidly and sway reluctant arms, hising up their petticoats, in whispering water swaying . . .[2]

There is, I think, a strict parallelism in the use of the Drowned Man symbol in Joyce and Eliot, and in my opinion the poet must have more or less consciously absorbed Joyce's lyrical prose, interweaving the images evoked by the novelist with his own in *The Waste Land*. It is well to remember that the drowned man fused in Stephen's mind with the image of his dying mother—a bitter death because he had crossed her dying will. This appears in the *Proteus* episode:

> A drowning man. His human eyes scream to me out of horror of his death. I . . . With him together down . . . I could not save her. Waters: bitter death: lost.[3]

and is made clearer later in *Ulysses*:

> She is drowning. Agenbite. Save her. Agenbite. All against

[1] *Collected Poems*, cit., p. 52.   [2] *Ulysses*, cit., p. 46.
[3] *Ibid.*, p. 42.

us. She will drown me with her, eyes and hair. Lank coils of
seaweed hair around me, my heart, my soul. Salt green death.
   We.
   Agenbite of inwit. Inwit's agenbite.
   Misery! Misery! [1]

The drowned man becomes therefore a symbol of remorse and
is identified with what the dog was trying to dig up—we saw
the word 'seamorse' occurring in the dog passage quoted. It
seems to me therefore that both for Eliot and Joyce the drowned
man and the dog were objective correlatives of the same feelings.

A further proof of the presence of at least the *Proteus* episode
in Eliot's mind is provided by the imagery in the following
passage in Joyce:

Come. I thirst. Clouding over. No black clouds anywhere,
are there? Thunderstorm Allbright he falls, proud lightning
of the intellect, *Lucifer, dico, qui nescit occasum.* No. My cockle hat
and staff and his my sandal shoon. Where? To evening lands. [2]

'My cockle hat', etc. comes of course from Ophelia's song in the
madness scene. Here again another scene of death by drowning,
remembered by Eliot himself at the end of the second section of
The Waste Land, where he quoted Ophelia's last words in this
very scene of *Hamlet*: 'Good night ladies, good night, sweet
ladies, good night, good night'. As for the other references in
the passage from *Ulysses,* we can compare them with those in
the last section of *The Waste Land, What the Thunder Said.* This
section, as is known, begins with an evocation of Christ's
passion (lines 322–8); and in Joyce there is a definite allusion
to the Crucifixion: 'I thirst'. Eliot introduces us to a barren
thirsty landscape of

      no water but only rock
   Rock and no water and the sandy road
   . . . mountains of rock without water
   If there were water we should stop and drink. . . [3]

---

[1] *Ulysses* cit., p. 230.   [2] *Ibid.,* p. 47.
[3] *The Waste Land,* cit., ll. 331–5.

In this fragment of the poem there are more elements which may have been inspired by *Proteus*. A line like

> Sweat is dry and feet are in the sand [1]

reminds us of the opening paragraphs of *Proteus,* where Stephen Dedalus describes in extreme detail his sensations in treading on the 'grainy sand', at one stage with his eyes shut ('Am I walking into eternity along Sandymount strand? Crush, crash, crick, crick'). Eliot's metaphor:

> Dead mountain mouth of carious teeth that cannot spit [2]

may have been suggested by Stephen's

> My teeth are very bad. Why, I wonder? Feel. That one is going too. Shells [3]

which occurs just after the passage beginning with 'Come. I thirst' quoted above. And returning to this we find mention of clouding over and a thunder-storm. Eliot follows the same sequence in *What the Thunder Said,* where there is an allusion to the 'dry sterile thunder without rain' (line 342). At the close of the movement there finally comes the voice of thunder but, as in Joyce, it does not bring rain. There is indeed a presentiment of it:

> In a flash of lightning. Then a damp gust
> Bringing rain [4]

but the sentence is left unfinished and we go back to a thirsty landscape:

> Ganga was sunken, and the limp leaves
> Waited for rain, while the black clouds
> Gathered far distant . . .
> Then spoke the thunder [5]

---

[1] *Ibid.,* l. 337. [2] *Ibid.,* l. 339.
[3] *Ulysses,* cit., p. 47. [4] *The Waste Land,* ll. 393–4.
[5] *Ibid.,* ll. 395–9.

and at the very end of the poem the land is still dry:

> I sat upon the shore
> Fishing, with the arid plain behind me
> Shall I at least set my lands in order?
> London Bridge is falling down falling down falling down.[1]

At this point Eliot gives the fragments of quotations from past literatures and different languages, 'shoring them against his ruins'. In this way he tries to represent the broken state of our civilization in which the past and time itself seem to be 'falling down' (like London Bridge in the popular song) in a universal cataclysm. This feeling is expressed earlier in the same section of the poem:

> What is the city over the mountains
> Cracks and reforms and bursts in the violet air
> Falling towers
> Jerusalem Athens Alexandria
> Vienna London
> Unreal[2]

which in turn sends us back to the first section of *The Waste Land* where the condition of the modern city life is presented:

> Unreal City,
> Under the brown fog of a winter dawn,
> A crowd flowed over London Bridge, so many,
> I had not thought death had undone so many.[3]

But this conception is in Joyce very concisely expressed in one sentence:

> I hear the ruin of all space, shattered glass and toppling masonry, and time one livid final flame.[4]

We realize the importance of this theme for Joyce if we remember that the 'fall' is a basic motif of *Finnegans Wake*, where H. C. Earwicker is identified with Humpty Dumpty.

---

[1] *The Waste Land*, ll., 423–6.   [2] *Ibid.*, ll., 371–6.
[3] *Ibid.*, ll. 60–3.   [4] *Ulysses*, cit., p. 21.

After this I think we can say that the two authors, as Eliot himself clearly saw, were trying to express the same ideas, and it is therefore not completely unjustified to maintain that the central nucleus of *The Waste Land* is to be found in *Ulysses,* and especially in the most lyrical episode of the book, the *Proteus* section.

In this essay I have deliberately avoided pointing out the similarities and the differences in method and principles between Eliot and Joyce (e.g. their use of the symbol of the city, their quotations from different languages) because other critics, and particularly F. O. Matthiessen and Miss Gardner, have already covered this ground. My purpose has been instead to suggest that *Ulysses* has actually been an active agent in the making of *The Waste Land* not only on the conceptual plane, but also on the verbal level. And this influence of the very sound of Joyce's words on Eliot, the echoes they left in his mind, may be proved by a comparison of the first line of the *Sirens* episode in *Ulysses,*

Bronze by gold heard the hoofirons, steelyringing[1]

with the opening lines of Eliot's *Triumphal March*:

Stone, bronze, stone, steel, stone, oakleaves, horses' heels
Over the paving.[2]

Here, except for the fact that the progress of the viceroyal carriage in Joyce's Dublin and the parade of the leader in Eliot are both representative of pomp and authority, there seems to be no ideal connection between the two passages (incidentally, with his 'bronze' and 'gold' Joyce was not referring to the emblems of pomp, but to the colour of the hair of two barmaids). And besides, by 1930, when *Triumphal March* was presumably written, Joyce's and Eliot's ways had widely diverged both in the literary and in the philosophical fields. It is unlikely therefore that Eliot meant his lines as a precise reference to the *Sirens* passage. We are faced more probably with an unconscious

[1] *Ulysses*, cit., p. 242.   [2] *Collected Poems*, cit., p. 135.

reminiscence. Matthiessen spoke of Eliot's 'auditory imagination'; we could speak in the present case of 'auditory memory', since the reminiscence seems merely verbal, and come to the conclusion that a large part of the artist's creative activity and indeed of his imagination *is* memory.

This conclusion applies, I think, not only to the second but also the first part of this essay, and involves as well the problem of tradition—tradition in fact is a memory so deeply linked with the growth of the creative artist that it seems inborn or inherited from previous generations. But its real essence is instead in the power of absorption, in the power of memory of the artist's mind.

The Lotus and the Rose

━━━

ELIOT'S opinion of D. H. Lawrence is well known. He made it clear in the Page-Barbour lectures of 1933, published a year later under the title of *After Strange Gods*. There, in discussing orthodoxy, he spoke of Lawrence as 'an almost perfect example of the heretic', and contrasted him with James Joyce, 'the most ethically orthodox of the more eminent writers of our time' (p. 38). Though recognizing Lawrence's spirituality, Eliot believes that 'the daemonic powers found an instrument of far greater range, delicacy and power in Lawrence than in the author of *A Group of Noble Dames*' (p. 60.) Matthiessen tells us that in another unpublished lecture Eliot returned to this point criticizing the inadequacy of Lawrence's interpretation of life and saying that in Joyce one has 'a sense of history', while in Lawrence there is only 'a sense of the moment'. Eliot's strictures—Matthiessen adds—'did not blind him to the extraordinary sensibility that enabled Lawrence to describe, in a way that Joyce could not, the pain and ecstasy of individual relationships, and to communicate, in visionary flashes, the sensuous fullness of "the moment"'.[1]

The political, religious or philosophical beliefs of different artists may be widely divergent; but when it comes to the act of creation, an artist may well make use, consciously or unconsciously, of materials or intuitions belonging to one who is,

[1] F. O. Matthiessen, *The Achievement of T. S. Eliot,* cit., pp. 147–8.

ideologically, opposed to him. Such is the case, I think, with Eliot and Lawrence. A minor borrowing from Lawrence's *The Rainbow* in the third movement of *The Waste Land* was pointed out many years ago.[1] More relevant still is the echo of Lawrence's short story *The Shadow in the Rose Garden* noticed by Louis Martz,[2] in *Burnt Norton,* the first of the *Quartets.* Eliot had dealt at some length with this story in *After Strange Gods,* and the context in which the images drawn from Lawrence appear is a fundamental one in the *Quartets.* The Rose Garden is the most significant objective correlative of Eliot's moment of revelation, the deep instantaneous intuition of all time concentrated in one single luminous point. It is the basis of a new conception of time and its relation to eternity.[3] It is the real theme of the *Four Quartets.* The clearest statement of what Eliot was trying to communicate in these poems, a statement actually of what the *Quartets* are about, is to be found in the third of them, *The Dry Salvages*:

> to apprehend
> The point of intersection of the timeless
> With time, is an occupation for the saint . . .
> For most of us, there is only the unattended
> Moment, the moment in and out of time,
> The distraction fit, lost in a shaft of sunlight,
> The wild thyme unseen, or the winter lightning,
> Or the waterfall, or music heard so deeply
> That it is not heard at all, but you are the music
> While the music lasts. These are only hints and guesses,
> Hints followed by guesses; and the rest
> Is prayer, observance, discipline, thought and action.
> The hint half guessed, the gift half understood, is Incarnation.

This moment of Incarnation, which in the lines quoted is expressed through a series of natural images (sunlight, the wild

[1] F. Fergusson, 'D. H. Lawrence's Sensibility', in *The Hound and Horn,* 1933.

[2] L. L. Martz, 'The Wheel and the Point: Aspects of Imagery and Theme in Eliot's Later Poetry', in *The Sewanee Review,* Winter 1947. Reprinted in *T. S. Eliot: A Selected Critique,* ed. L. Unger, New York, 1948.

[3] For this new conception of time, see pp. 175 ff. below.

thyme unseen, the lightning, etc.), was most forcibly suggested
right at the beginning of the first of the *Quartets,* by the complex and inclusive image of the Rose Garden:

> Footfalls echo in the memory
> Down the passage which we did not take
> Towards the door we never opened
> Into the rose-garden. My words echo
> Thus, in your mind.
> > > But to what purpose
> Disturbing the dust on a bowl of rose-leaves
> I do not know.
> > > Other echoes
> Inhabit the garden. Shall we follow?
> Quick, said the bird, find them, find them,
> Round the corner. Through the first gate,
> Into our first world, shall we follow
> The deception of the thrush? Into our first world.
> There they were, dignified, invisible,
> Moving without pressure, over the dead leaves,
> In the autumn heat, through the vibrant air,
> And the bird called, in response to
> The unheard music hidden in the shrubbery,
> And the unseen eyebeam crossed, for the roses
> Had the look of flowers that are looked at.
> There they were as our guests, accepted and accepting.
> So we moved, and they, in a formal pattern,
> Along the empty alley, into the box circle,
> To look down into the drained pool.
> Dry the pool, dry concrete, brown edged,
> And the pool was filled with water out of sunlight,
> And the lotos rose, quietly, quietly,
> The surface glittered out of heart of light,
> And they were behind us, reflected in the pool.
> Then a cloud passed, and the pool was empty.
> Go, said the bird, for the leaves were full of children,
> Hidden excitedly, containing laughter.
> Go, go, go, said the bird: human kind
> Cannot bear very much reality.

Time past and time future
What might have been and what has been
Point to one end, which is always present.

(Burnt Norton, I)

As many commentators have already pointed out, the significance of the vision in the Rose Garden is made even clearer in *The Family Reunion,* and can be traced back to some of Eliot's early poems, as well as to *The Waste Land,* to *Ash Wednesday,* and to *Coriolan.*[1] It is the exact equivalent of 'the still point of the turning world', and 'the moment in and out of time', which recur so frequently in Eliot's poetry and are the objects of his meditations.

What has not been noticed, however, is the relevance to this conception of Eliot's comment on Lawrence quoted by Matthiessen. How else could Eliot communicate his sense of this moment to his readers, except through sensual images? His statement on the art of the Metaphysical poets has been very frequently quoted: they 'feel their thoughts as immediately as the odour of a rose'. It is well known that his aim was to reach again that unification of sensibility, that 'direct sensuous apprehension of thought', which he had found in early seventeenth-century poetry. In the *Four Quartets* the thought he wanted to express was his conception of the moment of revelation. But had he not said that Lawrence was able 'to communicate, in visionary flashes, the sensuous fullness of the moment'? It seems natural therefore that Eliot, in spite of the difference in beliefs, should turn instinctively to Lawrence when he wanted to express in sensual terms his spiritual experience.

This, I think, he did, not only by recalling Lawrence's Rose Garden in *Burnt Norton,* but by deriving most of his symbols and the very image-structure of the first *Quartet* from another, and much more relevant, Lawrence context. I mean Lawrence's preface to the American edition of his *New Poems* (1920). It is

[1] See, e.g. H. Gardner, *The Art of T. S. Eliot,* cit.; L. Unger, 'T. S. Eliot's Rose Garden', in *The Southern Review,* 1942, reprinted in *T. S. Eliot: A Selected Critique,* cit.; and the essay by L. L. Martz already mentioned.

an essay which passed unnoticed at first, and was reprinted in the posthumous collection *Phoenix* in 1936. I find it strange that none of the numerous commentators on Eliot's works (as far as I know) have noticed the similarity in conception between *Burnt Norton* (first printed in 1936, the same year as *Phoenix*) and Lawrence's essay, since both deal with an identical theme, the 'moment'. Lawrence, in fact, launching into a defence of *vers libre* (the *right sort* of free verse) maintains that it is the only metric form able to express the 'immediate present', the 'incandescence of the immediate moment'. Let us now make a close comparison between the splendid poetic imagery used by Lawrence to illustrate this conception in his essay, and that to be found in the *Four Quartets*. The relevance of Lawrence's prose to Eliot's poems will, I believe, appear very clearly.

We can start from the long passage from the opening section of *Burnt Norton* which I have quoted above. Several complex images contribute to the creation of the magic atmosphere of the Rose Garden, dreamy and sensual, in and out of time, a momentary apparition or vision. It is introduced and closed by the bird, a messenger of the unknown: but the two main symbols are those of the rose and of the lotus: ambiguous, as all those used by Eliot (Mr. Empson would probably class them in his fourth type of ambiguity, where 'the alternative meanings combine to make clear a complicated state of mind in the author'). The rose is a metaphysical symbol—Dante's mystic rose—which maintains all the same the appeal of its sensuous beauty, the sensual associations it had in the *Roman de la Rose*. The lotus, the flower of forgetfulness, implies a languid ecstasy, rapture and sensuality; in Eliot, the lotus rising out of the imaginary waters of an empty pool is the clearest pointer to the atmosphere of unreality created by the moment of absolute ecstasy; but its sexual implications must not be forgotten: the lotus is a phallic symbol.[1] We have only to turn to Joyce's

[1] All these meanings, and a deeper mystical and philosophical significance, were implied in the lotus symbol in Oriental lore. See W. E. Ward, 'The Lotus

Ulysses, a book that Eliot knew well: there at the end of the fifth section, the so-called *Lotus-Eaters* episode, the scene of Mr. Bloom in his bath makes the allusion clear, and the whole episode is permeated by an atmosphere of lazy sensuality, mental more than physical. With the lotus symbol, as with the rose, Eliot realizes once again that fusion of the physical with the metaphysical which is his main objective.

Let us see now how the same symbols, the same images, are prefigured in Lawrence's essay:

> The perfect rose is only a running flame, emerging and flowing off, and never in any sense at rest, static, finished. Herein lies its transcendent liveliness. The whole tide of all life and all time suddenly heaves, and appears before us as an apparition, a revelation. We look at the very white quick of nascent creation. A water-lily heaves herself from the flood, looks around, gleams, and is gone. We have seen the incarnation, the quick of the ever-whirling flood. We have seen the invisible. We have seen, we have touched, we have partaken of the very substance of creative change, creative mutation. If you tell me about the lotus, tell me of nothing changeless or eternal. Tell me of the mystery of the inexhaustible, forever-unfolding creative spark. Tell me of the incarnate disclosure of the flux, mutation in blossom, laughter and decay perfectly open in their transit, nude in their movement before us.

Here the first connection with the *Burnt Norton* passage quoted above is made by the appearance of the rose (and we shall see later how in the very last line of the last *Quartet* Eliot tells us that 'the fire and the rose are one'). Then Lawrence states what Eliot implies: 'an apparition, a revelation, of all life and all time'. And what is Lawrence's 'white quick of nascent creation' but Eliot's 'heart of light', the core of vision? The very words used by Eliot to describe the phantomatic apparition of the water in the empty pool ('the surface glittered out of heart of light') send us back to the scene in the 'Hyacinth garden', in the

Symbol: Its Meaning in Buddhist Art and Philosophy', in *Journal of Aesthetics and Art Criticism,* XI, n. 2, Dec. 1952.

first movement of *The Waste Land,* where the poet was trying to
convey the same feeling of the moment:

> and my eyes failed, I was neither
> Living nor dead, and I knew nothing
> Looking into the heart of light, the silence.
>
> (*The Waste Land,* 39–41)

A moment of rapture beyond life and death, beyond the normal
temporal dimensions—the very incarnation of the moment. Or,
as Lawrence puts it, 'we have seen the incarnation . . . we
have seen the invisible'. It is here that he introduces the image
of the water-lily (which is called, a few lines below, the lotus):
'A water-lily heaves herself from the flood, looks around,
gleams, and is gone.' We remember Eliot's lines:

> And the pool was filled with water out of sunlight,
> And the lotos rose, quietly, quietly,
> The surface glittered out of heart of light . . .
> Then a cloud passed, and the pool was empty.

Here is the invisible (Eliot's pool is a mirage—the pool is dry,
'dry concrete', all the time). Here is incarnation, a word that for
Lawrence has an authentic physical carnal meaning, while in
Eliot, capitalized as we have seen, it acquires a religious
significance. Both authors have used the images of the lotus
and the rose in the same way: as symbols of the fullness of
life in a momentary phase of extreme physical and spiritual
intensity.

But also later the similarities continue. Lawrence, defining
'the incarnate disclosure of the flux', speaks of 'laughter and
decay perfectly open in their transit'. In *Burnt Norton* decay is
represented by the cloud that sweeps away the vision—the pool
is empty; and the laughter is that of the children excitedly
hidden among the foliage (a recurring image in Eliot, already
studied by other critics). As for the bird ('Quick, said the bird
. . . The bird called . . . Go, go, go, said the bird') that opens
and closes the instantaneous vision, I think that it can be

connected with the wild birds of which Lawrence speaks at the beginning of his preface:

Our birds sing on the horizons. They sing out of the blue, beyond us, or out of the quenched night. They sing at dawn and sunset . . . The wild birds begin before we are awake, or as we drop into dimness, out of waking . . . As we arrive and as we go out our hearts surge with response. But whilst we are in the midst of life, we do not hear them.

Also Eliot's bird sings at the awakening and at the fading of consciousness.

After having spoken of the revelation, symbolized by the lotus, Lawrence proceeds:

Let me feel the mud and the heavens in my lotus. Let me feel the heavy, silting, sucking mud, the spinning of sky winds.

If we read on in *Burnt Norton,* we find, right at the beginning of the second movement:

> Garlic and sapphires in the mud
> Clot the bedded axle-tree . . .
> The dance along the artery
> The circulation of the lymph
> Are figured in the drift of stars . . .

All the rest of this lyrical section is relevant, but the few lines quoted are sufficient for an essential comparison. Lawrence wants to *feel physically* in the moment both 'the mud and the heavens'. So does Eliot. His 'drift of stars', the image of heaven, corresponds to Lawrence's 'spinning of sky winds'. As for the axle-tree, bedded in the mud, its symbolic significance (the image recurs in earlier poems, *Burbank with a Baedeker,* and *Gerontion*) has been fully explored by a classical scholar, Robert Goheen,[1] who has convincingly identified it, in the last analysis, with the axis of the world. He further demonstrated how this cosmic symbol is the same as 'the still point of the

---

[1] R. F. Goheen, 'Burbank with a Baedeker: The Third Stanza (Thematic Intension through Classical Allusion)', in *The Sewanee Review,* Winter 1953.

turning world', that very moment of revelation which was expressed also by the physical image of the lotus. Mud, heaven, the moment of revelation: the same highly significant image-cluster is present in both authors, deepening and clarifying the meaning of Eliot's poem and Lawrence's essay: the presence in an instant of the totality of the cosmos, the earthly and the spiritual indivisibly fused.

Burnt Norton underlines this immediately after:

At the *still point of the turning world.* Neither flesh nor fleshless;
Neither from nor towards; at the still point, there the dance is,
But neither arrest nor movement. And *do not call it fixity,*
Where past and future are gathered. Neither movement from
      nor towards,
Neither ascent nor decline. Except for the point, *the still point,*
There would be no dance, and there is only the dance . . .
The release from action and suffering, release from the inner
And the outer compulsion, yet surrounded
By a grace of sense, *a white light still and moving* . . .

And now the next few sentences in Lawrence's preface:

Give me nothing fixed, set, static. Don't give me the infinite or the eternal: nothing of infinity, nothing of eternity. Give me the *still, white seething, the incandescence and the coldness of the incarnate moment*: the moment, the quick of all change and haste and opposition: the moment, the immediate present, the Now.

This time the correspondence is so clear that there is no need for comment. I have only italicized the most obvious *verbal* echoes. Actually Lawrence's words could stand as an explanatory note to Eliot's lines.

After this, however, the two conceptions seem to diverge, though the formal echoes of Lawrence in Eliot are still apparent. For instance, in both the wind obviously stands for transience, but Lawrence gives it a positive connotation:

This is the unrestful, ungraspable poetry of the sheer present, poetry whose very permanency lies in its wand-like transit. Whitman's is the best poetry of this kind. Without beginning

97

and without end, without any base and pediment, it sweeps past for ever, like a wind that is for ever in passage and unchainable. Whitman truly looked before and after. But he did not sigh for what is not. The clue to all his utterance lies in the sheer appreciation of the instant moment, life surging itself into utterance at its very well-head.

In Eliot instead the symbol is wholly negative:

> Men and bits of paper, whirled by the cold wind
> That blows before and after time,
> Wind in and out of unwholesome lungs
> Time before and time after.
>
> (*Burnt Norton,* III)

In the same way the conclusions on the literary plane are at least in partial contrast. Lawrence, defending free verse of the type Whitman produced, writes:

From the foregoing it is obvious that the poetry of the instant present cannot have the same body or the same motion as the poetry of the before and after. It can never submit to the same conditions. It is never finished. There is no rhythm which returns upon itself, no serpent of eternity with its tail in its own mouth. There is no static perfection, none of that finality which we find so satisfying because we are so frightened.

Eliot instead insists on a pattern, though a moving one:

> Only by the form, the pattern,
> Can words or music reach
> The stillness, as a Chinese jar still
> Moves perpetually in its stillness . . .
> The detail of the pattern is movement . . .
>
> (*Burnt Norton,* V)

Lawrence advocated a freedom in verse which amounted to formlessness, and the result can be seen in his own poems. Eliot, though not adopting an absolutely rigid and symmetrical form, a 'serpent of eternity with its tail in its own mouth', wants the Chinese dragon, not a closed form but a serpentine one, which maintains a precise though moving pattern.

The conclusions of Lawrence, the heretic, and Eliot, the orthodox, on the spiritual plane are necessarily different. The first stresses the physical side of the momentary experience, connecting it with his sex-mysticism:

It is the instant; the quick; the very jetting source of all will-be and has-been. The utterance is like a spasm, naked contact with all influences at once. It does not want to get anywhere. It just takes place.

Eliot transfers the experience of the instant onto the plane or religious mysticism. But in the beautiful last lines of *Burnt Norton* he summarizes and concentrates several images used in the course of the poem, some of which are directly drawn from Lawrence: *81597*

> Sudden in a shaft of sunlight
> Even while the dust moves
> There rises the hidden laughter
> Of children in the foliage
> Quick now, here, now, always—
> Ridiculous the waste sad time
> Stretching before and after.

The last line but two is an obvious evocation of the bird in the first movement of the poem ('Quick, said the bird . . .'). How much clearer this image becomes when seen in the light of these lines from Lawrence, near the end of his preface:

The bird is on the wing in the winds, flexible to every breath, a living spark in the storm, its very flickering depending upon its supreme mutability and power of change. Whence such a bird came: whither it goes: from what solid earth it rose up, and upon what solid earth it will close its wings and settle, this is not the question. This is a question of before and after. Now, *now*, the bird is on the wing in the winds.

The close unity of the *Four Quartets,* the consistency of their image-structure, is well-known. It would be easy, therefore, to point out the recurrence in all of them of the symbol originally used also by Lawrence. I shall be content with a few examples. In the fourth movement of *East Coker* we find the 'purgatorial fires of which the flame is roses'. Reconsidering now Lawrence's statement 'the perfect rose is only a running flame', we realize the deep religious significance that Eliot gave his poems, as compared with the novelist's sensuality. From *The Dry Salvages* I have already quoted (at the beginning of this essay) the most relevant passage on the significance of the 'moment', and I have remarked on the different connotation that the word 'Incarnation' has for the two authors. In the last Quartet, *Little Gidding,* the final stanza is particularly important since it summarizes the content of the four poems:

> We shall not cease from exploration
> And the end of an our exploring
> Will be to arrive where we started
> And know the place for the first time.
> Through the unknown, remembered gate
> When the last of earth left to discover
> Is that which was the beginning;
> At the source of the longest river
> The voice of the hidden waterfall
> And the children in the apple-tree
> Not known, because not looked for
> But heard, half-heard, in the stillness
> Between two waves of the sea.
> Quick now, here, now, always—
> A condition of complete simplicity
> (Costing not less than everything)
> And all shall be well and
> All manner of thing shall be well
> When the tongues of flame are in-folded
> Into the crowned knot of fire
> And the fire and the rose are one.

The exploration of which Eliot speaks is of course the exploration of the moment, the moment which is the pivot on which all the *Quartets* turn. This is the 'earth left to discover'.

But also for Lawrence the instant was *terra incognita* to be conquered:

One realm we have never conquered: the pure present. One great mystery of time is *terra incognita* to us: the instant. The most superb mystery we have hardly recognized: the immediate, instant self. The quick of all time is the instant.

But the whole passage in Eliot is compact with references to those images which we trace back to Lawrence, though here they are rather alluded to than fully expressed: here are the children (the laughter), the bird, and finally in the very last line there is repeated on a purely mystical level that identification of the fire and the rose which for Lawrence was another way of expressing the fullness of life in the fleeting moment.

The rose closes the *Quartets* like the emblem on a seal. It contains, in an extremely concentrated form, all the meaning, or all the meanings, of the poems. It certainly is infinitely more complex than Lawrence's rose. At the same time we may notice that the other symbol, the lotus, which for Lawrence was practically an equivalent of the rose, has appeared only at the beginning of the *Quartets,* while it was dropped later. I think we can see the reason for this. The strongly sensual connotation of the lotus image was useful to convey the nearly physical impact of the first intuition of the 'moment'. But in transferring this experience onto a truly metaphysical plane, as he intended to do in the later parts of the *Quartets,* this image would no longer serve: the rose was much more comprehensive. The lotus was instead the aptest to create immediately in the reader as well as the author the readiness to accept a suspension in the time sequence. It suggested the atmosphere of reverie, of timelessness which Tennyson had evoked in a masterly way in his *Lotus-Eaters* (and Joyce in his). Of course, neither Tennyson nor Joyce had connected the image of the lotus with the moment of revelation. Lawrence did. But it seems to me very significant that another writer made the same connection in a book which was published in 1919, the year when Lawrence was presumably writing his preface.

The writer is Marcel Proust and the book is *Du côté de chez Swann*,[1] the first volume of his great exploration of time, *A la recherche du temps perdu*. And the experience that sent Proust on his quest for his own past was the experience of an instant; the passage where he describes this momentary experience is perhaps the most famous of the whole *Recherche*:

. . . je portai à mes lèvres une cuillerée de thé où j'avais laissé s'amollir un morceau de madeleine. Mais à l'instant même où la gorgée mêlée des miettes du gâteau toucha mon palais, je tressaillis . . .

Proust started because, in a moment of extreme intensity and penetration, he saw the whole of his past. It is the real beginning of his long saga of memory:

Et comme dans ce jeu où les Japonais s'amusent à tremper dans un bol de porcelaine rempli d'eau de petits morceaux de papier jusque-là indistincts qui, à peine y sont-ils plongés, s'étirent, se contournent, se colorent, se différencient, deviennent des fleurs, des maisons, des personnages consistants et reconnaissables, de même maintenant toutes les fleurs de notre jardin et celles du parc de M. Swann, et les nymphéas de la Vivonne, et les bonnes gens du village et leurs petits logis, et l'église et tout Combray et ses environs, tout cela qui prend forme et solidité, est sorti, ville et jardins, de ma tasse de thé.

The sudden unfolding of memory in the instant of supreme revelation finds expression in the comparison with the Japanese 'flowers', which open and fill out like magical lotuses (and the image is made concrete a few lines below, with the mention of the *nymphéas*, the water-lilies).

In the three writers, first in Proust, then in Lawrence and finally in Eliot, the instant of absolute clarity, of rapture and plenitude, is expressed through the same symbol: that of the lotus. The flower of forgetfulness becomes for them the flower of memory; it creates that sense of physical and spiritual ecstasy,

[1] Proust had had the novel printed at his own expense in 1913, but it attracted attention only when Gallimard took it over and republished it in 1919.

of languid and luminous beauty that they wanted to communicate. And it makes time stand still.

I hope that from this analysis we gain an insight into the significance of a fundamental image of the *Four Quartets*. The lotus, thanks to the significance it had acquired in the pages of Proust and Lawrence, set the mood in which the basic theme of the *Four Quartets* (the moment of Incarnation) could be expressed. It introduced timelessness. Having performed this essential function, the lotus disappeared, and the much more complex and inclusive image of the rose took its place. The *Quartets* move from the sensual apprehension of timelessness to its mystical interpretation, from the lotus to the rose.[1]

[1] On the symbol of the rose and its connection with the moment of revelation, the timeless moment, see the letter by W. B. Yeats to Mrs. Shakespear, written in Nov. 1931 and quoted by R. Ellmann, *The Identity of Yeats* (London, 1954, p. 269): 'The night before [your] letter came I went for a walk after dark and there among some great trees became absorbed in the most lofty philosophical conception I have found while writing "A Vision". I suddenly seemed to understand at last and then I smelt roses. I had realized the nature of the timeless spirit. Then I began to walk and into my excitement came—how shall I say— that old glory so beautiful with its autumnal tint. The longing to touch it was almost unendurable. The next night I was walking on the same path and now the two excitements came together. The autumnal image remote, incredibly spiritual, erect, delicate featured, and mixed with it the violent physical image. . . .' Compare Eliot's already quoted remark in 'The Metaphysical Poets' (1921, in *Selected Essays*, p. 287) on 'feeling thought as immediately as the odour of a rose'. And with Yeats' sentence, 'The longing to touch it was almost unendurable' compare Virginia Woolf's description of a similar experience in her *Diary* for Aug. 15, 1924 (p. 65): 'Coming back the other evening from Charleston, again all my nerves stood upright, flushed, electrified (what's the word) with the sheer beauty—beauty astounding and superabounding. So that one almost resents it, not being capable of catching it all and holding it all at the moment.'

Eliot and the Theatre

THERE seems to be hardly anything left to be said of Eliot and of poetic drama. So much has been written recently on the two subjects that any addition will be largely repetitive. In spite of this I think it worthwhile to follow Eliot's attempts in the theatrical field, for the light they may throw not only on the rest of his work, but also on the development of his critical ideas. I believe that Eliot has dedicated more critical thought to drama than to any other subject, and in his essays he seems permanently to revert to the theatre even when he is dealing with other artistic forms. This constant interest may well provide a vantage point from which to survey the phases of development of his poetical and critical work. I intend therefore to look from this angle at what I would call his 'poetics', that is to say his aesthetic and critical principles not as mere theories, but as a working complex of ideas actuated in his poetic practice.

From the first a dramatic element has been at work in Eliot. He stated that his starting points were Laforgue, Corbière and the Elizabethan dramatists; and to them we can add Browning's *Dramatis Personae* since, as Mr. J. Isaacs remarks, 'as far back as 1911 Eliot had combined the dramatic monologue of Browning and of Laforgue in *The Love Song of J. Alfred Prufrock*',[1] and by 1920 he could produce blank verse

[1] J. Isaacs, *An Assessment of Twentieth-Century Literature*, London, 1951, p. 139. For the influence of Browning on modern poetry, see Carlo Izzo's preface to his *Poesia inglese contemporanea*, Parma, 1951.

modelled on the Elizabethans and of a quality comparable to them. The first group of Eliot's poems seems indeed a gallery of dramatic portraits, sketched very lightly but represented in action; it is well to remember, though, that the title of the collection is *Prufrock and Other Observations*. While partly identifying himself with Prufrock, and in spite of the fact that many poems use the first person singular, Eliot prefers the role of observer—his characters then, the lady of *Portrait of a Lady*, Aunt Helen, Cousin Nancy, Mr. Apollinax, are seen from the outside, without that direct participation in the life of each single character which is, I think, essential to a dramatist. The second group of poems, the *Poems 1920,* where the figure of Sweeney is substituted for Prufrock, is even more concerned with the 'I', even more subjective—but on the other hand it reaches a sort of intellectual detachment which can best be seen in *Gerontion*, the last and the most complex and mature of this group of poems. Here again, in the very title, is a character, which goes much deeper than the earlier light sketches. Besides Eliot has here at last reached an absolutely personal style, absorbing and fusing completely the French symbolist and the Elizabethan element. From the French poets he has derived the capacity for producing realistic visual portraits, which are dramatic even in their brevity:

> by Mr. Silvero
> With caressing hands, at Limoges
> Who walked all night in the next room;
> By Hakagawa, bowing among the Titians;
> By Madame de Tornquist, in the dark room
> Shifting the candles; Fraülein van Kulp
> Who turned in the hall, one hand on the door . . .[1]

From the late Elizabethans he has derived and made his own the technique of dramatic speech, here emphasized by the fact that the poem is written in the first person:

> I have lost my passion: why should I need to keep it
> Since what is kept must be adulterated?

---

[1] *Collected Poems,* cit., pp. 37–8.

I have lost my sight, smell, hearing, taste and touch:
How should I use them for your closer contact? [1]

This is great dramatic poetry—but reading the whole poem
one realizes that it is further removed from the theatre than most
of the previous shorter pieces. Why? A comparison with
Prufrock or with its distant models, Browning's *Dramatis Personae*, will clarify this point. In Browning, in *Prufrock* or for
that matter in *Portrait of a Lady* there is a certain conversational
quality, a fluency and discursiveness which bridges over the
sudden transitions, the shocks given by unexpected juxta-
positions or unexplained gaps in the logical texture of the poem.
In *Gerontion* instead, aiming at a greater intensity, the poet has
concentrated his images omitting completely the logical links,
so that the resulting impression is that of an accumulation of
fragments ('fractured atoms. . . . Thoughts of a dry brain in a
dry season') subtly connected but still such as to render to the
reader 'the immense panorama of futility and anarchy which is
contemporary history'.[2] This fragmentariness—though only
apparent because it hides a close structure of thought—is essentially antidramatic, since drama requires a clear and open communication between author and audience, drama is meant to
help the intellectual effort of the public towards understanding,
while a poem like *Gerontion* stimulates the intellectual powers
not by its immediacy of communication, but by its very
'obscurity'. Speaking of the poems of this period, of *Gerontion*
as well as *The Waste Land,* which has the same fragmentary
appearance ('these fragments I have shored against my ruins')
though its construction is more complex and solid, Virginia
Woolf said:

. . . Again with the obscurity of Mr. Eliot. I think that Mr.
Eliot has written some of the loveliest single lines in modern
poetry. But how intolerant he is of the old usages and politeness
of society—respect for the weak, consideration for the dull! As
I sun myself upon the intense and ravishing beauty of one of

[1] *Collected Poems,* cit., p. 39.   [2] Eliot, *Ulysses, Order and Myth,* cit.

his lines, and reflect that I must make a dizzy and dangerous
leap to the next, and so on from line to line, like an acrobat
flying precariously from bar to bar, I cry out, I confess, for the
old decorums. . . .[1]

Eliot was indeed at this stage an acrobat, in the same sense
in which Donne can be called one; his poems were dramatic in
the same way as the act of the acrobat or the funambulist is
dramatic. As Mr. Cecil Day Lewis has pointed out,[2] the
dramatic effect was reached by his 'use of concentrated images
and paradoxically juxtaposed ideas', by 'a perpetual interplay
between the surface images and an underlying dramatic situation or series of situations'. Eliot, he remarked, 'was the first
person in England to exploit the dramatic-situation kind of
poetry through the medium of "modern" imagery'. One could
add, of course, that the imagery was 'modern' as Donne's
imagery, dealing with the new scientific discoveries, was
modern in *his* time. Eliot was then at his point of closest contact with the Metaphysicals. His favourite late Elizabethan
dramatists—Webster, Tourneur, Chapman, Middleton—who
had more than one point in common with Donne, had led
him to understand and appreciate (the first perhaps in his
generation) Metaphysical poetry. He had already in 1918 put
side by side, in his *Whispers of Immortality*, Webster and Donne,
and it was natural that, since he was writing poems instead of
plays, he should adopt Donne's method rather than Webster's
or even the late Shakespeare's, which is of necessity looser
though pursuing the same ends. The affinity between Eliot's
poetry and the Metaphysicals' has been illustrated so many
times—best of all indirectly by Eliot himself in his critical
essays—that I shall not insist on it, since it is only incidental to
the subject of this essay. I need only mention that the 'dramatic-
situation kind of poetry' of which Lewis speaks and which
could be applied as well to Donne's works, has very little to do

[1] V. Woolf, *Mr. Bennett and Mrs. Brown* (1924), now in *The Captain's Death
Bed*, London, 1950, p. 109.
[2] C. Day Lewis, *A Hope for Poetry*, Oxford, 1934, pp. 64-5.

with drama as theatre. Dramatic situations of this kind are to be found plentifully in *The Waste Land,* a work which nobody could dream of associating with the theatre. Actually we can see in it the disappearance of the 'character' in the theatrical sense of the word. Prufrock, Sweeney, Gerontion could in different degrees be associated with living beings on the stage of life, but the elusive hero of *The Waste Land* is Tiresias, of whom Eliot himself says in his much quoted note:

Tiresias, although a mere spectator and not indeed a 'character', is yet the most important personage in the poem, uniting all the rest. Just as the one-eyed merchant, seller of currants, melts into the Phoenician Sailor, and the latter is not wholly distinct from Ferdinand Prince of Naples, so all the women are one woman, and the two sexes meet in Tiresias. What Tiresias *sees,* in fact, is the substance of the poem.[1]

This shows, if anything, that Eliot, who at first under the influence of the Elizabethans had written poems with a technique approaching to a certain extent that of the stage, was now conscious of the difference between what could be called lyrical or even intellectual poetry, and poetic drama. It is true that in his essay on *The Metaphysical Poets* (1921) he insists on the close connection between Donne and the Jacobean dramatists, noticing in all of them that 'telescoping of images and multiplied associations' which is 'one of the sources of the vitality of their language'; [2] and it is true too that he says that poetic drama 'must take genuine and substantial human emotions, such emotions as observation can confirm, typical emotions, and give them artistic form; the degree of abstraction is a question for the method of each author'.[3] This could have been said not only of poetic drama, but also of poetry in general. But at the same time Eliot had realized a substantial difference: 'the stage appeals to too many demands besides the

---

[1] *Collected Poems,* cit., p. 80.
[2] *Selected Essays,* 2nd ed., London, 1934, pp. 281 ff.
[3] *'Rhetoric' and Poetic Drama* (1919); now in *Selected Essays,* cit., p. 41.

demand for art'. So that he could write in a very early essay on
The Possibility of Poetic Drama:

Possibly the majority of attempts to confect a poetic drama
have begun at the wrong end; they have aimed at the small
public which wants 'poetry'. . . . The Elizabethan drama was
aimed at a public which wanted *entertainment* of a crude sort,
but would *stand* a good deal of poetry; our problem should be
to take a form of entertainment, and subject it to the process
which would leave it a form of art. Perhaps the music-hall
comedian is the best material. I am aware that this is a dangerous suggestion to make. For every person who is likely to consider it seriously there are a dozen toymakers who would leap to
tickle aesthetic society into one more quiver and giggle of art
debauch.[1]

Taking into account these principles and those contained in
a review of 1923 [2] where rhythm is recognized as the fundamental element of drama ('what makes of Massine and Chaplin
the great actors they are'), it is clear that the first attempt by
Eliot in the theatre should have been *Sweeney Agonistes*, which
he defined 'Fragments of an Aristophanic Melodrama'. The
Aristophanic element is in the bitter humour, charged with
sinister overtones, of the two scenes. Eliot was probably
thinking of what he called 'farce' in his essays on Marlowe,
Jonson and Massinger, all written between 1920 and 1921: 'I
say farce, but with the enfeebled humour of our times the word
is a misnomer', he writes about Marlowe's *Jew of Malta*; 'it is
the farce of the old English humour, the terribly serious, even
savage comic humour. . . .' [3] Indeed this kind of humour
begins in the very title of *Sweeney Agonistes*: the modern
Samson is the shady hero of Eliot's earlier poems, the ape-like
man oppressed by a sense of guilt, so very different from that of
the Biblical hero, but in some way his equivalent, since the

[1] *The Sacred Wood,* 4th ed., London, 1934, p. 70.
[2] Quoted by Matthiessen, *The Achievement of T. S. Eliot,* cit., p. 156.
[3] *Christopher Marlowe;* now in *Selected Essays,* cit., p. 123.

motive of action in our present age is no longer the feeling of having a mission, of leading the people on the path of God; now instead

> That's all the facts when you come to brass tacks:
> Birth, and copulation, and death,[1]

and guilt, or sin, can only be understood in terms of a sensational crime story. This was the only way, then, which Eliot could find at the time in order to 'take such emotions as observation can confirm and give them artistic form'. The form is the one we saw, the one taken from the music-hall, which seemed the most easily understood by the wider modern audiences. 'I've gotta use words when I talk to you', says Sweeney, and what better words could he find than those which followed the syncopated music-hall rhythms of the 'twenties? The syncopation by which Amiens' song in *As You Like It* ('Under the greenwood tree') becomes

> Under the bamboo
> Bamboo bamboo
> Under the bamboo tree . . .

is in itself a comment on the fragmentary character of modern life.

But what is the emotion that this form tries to convey? Futility, vague foreboding, or, as Miss Gardner says,[2] horror and boredom? I think that the fundamental feeling of *Sweeney Agonistes* is the sense of sin, sin intended in its fully Christian and Scriptural meaning: the sin of Samson forsaking his people for earthly pleasures. Having to use words comprehensible to Godless people (for so Eliot seems to consider his contemporaries), the poet can only mention a sordid murder and nightmares. But Sweeney, for all his crudeness, is conscious

---

[1] The quotations from *Sweeney Agonistes* are taken from the *Collected Poems*, cit., pp. 117–32.

[2] H. Gardner, *The Art of T. S. Eliot*, cit., *passim*; see especially chap. IV, pp. 78 ff.

of evil: he is the cannibal who will eat the missionary; but is capable of comforting a murderer as sinner to sinner:

> I'd give him a drink and cheer him up.

The religious symbolism of *Sweeney Agonistes* will, I think, appear more clearly if we set side by side Sweeney's words

> I've been born, and once is enough.
> You don't remember, but I remember,
> Once is enough.

and those at the end of another poem which Eliot must have written shortly afterwards, *Journey of the Magi* (the *Sweeney* fragments appeared in 1926 and 1927 and the *Journey of the Magi* in 1927):

> I had seen birth and death,
> But had thought they were different; this Birth was
> Hard and bitter agony for us, like Death, our death . . .
> I should be glad of another death.[1]

And this theme of the identification of birth and death, on the material and the spiritual plane, is a fundamental one in Eliot's later poetry. It inspires all the Ariel poems and is treated most fully in the second of the *Quartets, East Coker,* which has been defined the most personal in subject of Eliot's later poems and is based on the double motto 'In my beginning is my end—In my end is my beginning'. In this poem the lines occur:

> Whisper of running streams, and winter lightning,
> The wild thyme unseen and the wild strawberry,
> The laughter in the garden, echoed ecstasy
> Not lost, but requiring, pointing to the agony
> Of death and birth.[2]

Here I take the rapid images listed as all expressions of the moment of ecstasy and illumination, we could say of revelation, 'the still point of the turning world'—finally, the mystic experience abolishing time. The remembrance (the echo) of such

---

[1] *Collected Poems,* cit., p. 108.   [2] *Four Quartets,* London, 1944, p. 20.

moments sharpens the agony of life in time, death and birth, which are identical, since being born in time is a sort of death to the condition of timelessness. It is at this point that the poet adds:

> You say I am repeating
> Something I have said before. I shall say it again.

It is indeed something Eliot had said many times before. But it is interesting to note that this theme, the identification of life and death and the sense of sin, is openly expressed for the first time in *Sweeney Agonistes*, though it was adumbrated in the earlier poem, *The Hollow Men*, to which we shall go back later. We may ask why the author has preferred to present it for the first time in dramatic rather than in lyrical form. Is it for mere chronological reasons, since the fragments were written just before his official 'conversion', and in spite of the absurdity of linking spiritual development to official dates (the date of Eliot's entrance into the Church of England was 1927) the importance of such a public pronouncement on the part of a man who had written poems like *The Hippopotamus* and *Mr. Eliot's Sunday Morning Service* should not be underrated. There is no doubt that it must reflect a deep (and presumably slow) spiritual and philosophical evolution. *Sweeney Agonistes* was written during the last phase of this evolution. We should therefore reverse our previous question: Eliot did not deal with this problem incidentally while writing the fragments, but wrote *Sweeney* in order to deal with it. He did not write *Sweeney* because he wanted to experiment in the dramatic form, but because the dramatic form seemed to be the fittest to convey his particular emotion.

The reason for this should be clear: in the previous poems he had to deal with static emotions, to represent conditions of the outer world and of the mind as objectively seen and felt. The tension in *The Waste Land* is given by the intensity of the feeling, not by a conflict in it: there may be uneasiness, obscure premonition, in it, but not strife. The poet expresses the horror and the vacuity of life without acceptation but without trying to fight it. A formula is suggested (give, sympathize, control) to reach 'the Peace which passeth understanding', and there is a hint of the poet's endeavour to put it into effect. But certainly these are in no way 'events', which are essential to the theatre; Eliot in fact wrote in *The Possibility of a Poetic Drama* [1]: 'The *Agamemnon* or *Macbeth* is a statement, but a statement of events.' *Sweeney Agonistes* too was meant to deal with events, not so much external ones (though the allusion to murder and the elusive figure of Pereira, connected perhaps with the knocking at the door at the end of the second fragment, may indicate some kind of external action) as inner action or development. [2] It is significant enough that Eliot revived in his melodrama some of the 'characters' which appeared in his earlier poems, such as 'apeneck' Sweeney, modern man in his most repulsively materialistic form, the haunter of bawdy houses in *Sweeney among the Nightingales* and *Sweeney Erect*, the man in his bath in the last stanza of *Mr. Eliot's Sunday Morning Service* (the bath is a Sunday rite replacing for modern man baptism and church going), the pleasure seeker who in his motor goes to Mrs. Porter in the Spring, in *The Waste Land*. The action, the events in the melodrama were to be, I think, the change of heart and of mind in this character who, coming from the world of the waste land, realizes first the significance of sin, and through it other and deeper facts. This should already appear in the second fragment published by Eliot: in the first place Sweeney is conscious that 'Death is life and life is death'.

And we should not forget the character of Doris. She is not just the partner of Dusty in a comedy duet: she was the cool-headed girl in *Sweeney Erect*:

> (But Doris, towelled from the bath,
> Enters padding on broad feet,
> Bringing sal volatile
> And a glass of brandy neat.) [3]

---

[1] *The Sacred Wood*, cit., p. 65.

[2] Eliot's own statement of his aim in writing *Sweeney Agonistes* is quoted later in this essay, see p. 138.   [3] *Collected Poems*, cit., p. 43.

And here she is the friend of both the mysterious Pereira and the tormented Sweeney, she says: 'I'll be the missionary. I'll convert you!'; *she*, finally, draws the two of spades, the 'coffin', which gives her a sense of premonition. In other words she seems to be in some way predestined, but to what it is difficult to guess. Perhaps a glance at *The Cocktail Party* will shed some light on this point. But it is too early to deal with that play. I want only to say here that there are good reasons for believing that the figure of Doris must have been important for Eliot at the time: in the *Chapbook*, n. 39 (1924), he had published three poems, under the title *Doris's Dream Songs*.[1] As the title implies, they are poems of a completely abstract character, and one of them has since been incorporated in *The Hollow Men*. Doris, then, was a live character in Eliot's mind, and a character capable of vision though unconscious; and we shall see the importance of *The Hollow Men* in the development of Eliot's more specifically religious poetry.

The existence of these two characters, so much more developed than the sketchy human types of the earlier poems, is a proof of Eliot's determination to represent and solve in a stage action the inner conflict of a modern man in his realization of higher values outside his everyday experience. The two fragments are attempts to establish the 'objective correlative' of the emotion produced by this realization. It is too frequently forgotten that Eliot was discussing a play, *Hamlet*, when he wrote his by now famous definition:

> The only way of expressing emotion in the form of art is by finding an 'objective correlative'; in other words, a set of objects, a situation, a chain of events which shall be the formula of that particular emotion.[2]

And he proceeds to explain that *Hamlet's* artistic failure is due to the fact that 'Hamlet (the man) is dominated by an emotion

---

[1] The poems and the different versions of *The Hollow Men* are reproduced in the appendix to D. E. S. Maxwell, *The Poetry of T. S. Eliot*, cit., pp. 213-17.

[2] *Hamlet* (1919); now in *Selected Essays*, cit., p. 145.

which is inexpressible, because it is in *excess* of the facts as they appear'. As Miss Bradbrook acutely suggested, this essay 'is a document more revealing of Eliot's own difficulties than of Shakespeare's: it might stand for instance, in part at least, as a commentary on *Sweeney Agonistes*'.[1] The fragmentary state of the Aristophanic melodrama is perhaps due to the realization of the impossibility of matching the emotion with the particular dramatic form chosen: the jingling rhythms derived from the music-hall cannot support the emotional weight with which they are charged—Eliot is still working in that allusive and concentrated technique which he had developed in his earlier work, while his subject required the sedate and repetitive patterns of meditation and slowly developing thought. But there is more in the essay on *Hamlet* which is interesting in view of Eliot rather than of Shakespeare; Eliot writes:

We must simply admit that [in *Hamlet*] Shakespeare tackled a problem which proved too much for him. Why he attempted it at all is an insoluble puzzle. . . . We need a great many facts in his biography; and we would like to know whether, and when, and after or at the same time as what personal experience, he read Montaigne II, xii, *Apologie de Raimond Sebond*.[2]

As Mr. Isaacs has remarked,[3] we would ask of Eliot a similar question. But we are more fortunate with him than with Shakespeare since we know that by 1919 (the date of the essay) *he* had read the *Apologie*. In a long and cogent argumentation on sceptical lines, demonstrating the weak and abject state of man, and how impossible it is for him to know God by means of his reason, Montaigne reaches a Christian conclusion: the possibility of knowing God through His grace; but the essay is mainly concerned with the condition of man, his uncertainty and helplessness, the state of permanent confusion in which he lives his shadow life. It was natural that

[1] M. C. Bradbrook, *T. S. Eliot,* cit., p. 51. [2] *Selected Essays,* cit., p. 146.
[3] *The Background of Modern Poetry,* London, 1951, p. 45.

such an attitude should appeal to the Jacobean writers, in an age in which man was fast losing faith in his own powers, while the new science 'called all in doubt'. And it was natural that it should have appealed to a poet like Eliot, so deeply conscious of the inner affinity between that age and ours. Other—and very many—texts have been brought forward as comments on Eliot's poems; but I think it will not be useless to add to them *An Apologie of Raymond Sebond*.[1]

It may, for instance, throw some light on *Gerontion*, written presumably at the same time as the essay on *Hamlet*. *Gerontion* is the monologue of the old man who 'did not fight', the weak soul 'driven to a sleepy corner'—Montaigne says:

The soule by reason of her trouble and embecility, as unable to subsist of her selfe, is ever, and in all places, questing and searching comforts, hopes, foundations and forraine circumstances, on which she may take hold and settle her selfe.[2]

He speaks of the condition of human reason, a permanent prey to uncertainty ('All things produced by our owne discourse and sufficiencie, as well true as false, are subject to uncertaintie and disputation'[3]) and adds:

With our weaknes we corrupt and adulterate the very essence of truth (which is uniforme and constant) when fortune giveth us the possesion of it. What course soever man taketh of himselfe, it is Gods permission that he ever commeth . . . to confusion.[4]

The consciousness of this confusion appears in lines like the following from *Gerontion*, dealing with history:

She gives when our attention is distracted
And what she gives, gives with such supple confusions
That the giving famishes the craving.[5]

Gerontion, who still considers Divinity (Christ) as the tiger,

---

[1] All quotations from Montaigne are from the Florio translation in the 'Modern Library' edition, New York.

[2] Montaigne-Florio, ed. cit., p. 497.

[3] *Ibid.*, p. 498.

[4] *Ibid.*, p. 498.

[5] *Collected Poems,* cit., p. 38.

as something formidable, but alien, cannot but despair in his own powers, having realized how ineffectual they are and being unable to surrender himself to faith:

> I that was near your heart was removed therefrom
> To lose beauty in terror, terror in inquisition.
> I have lost my passion: why should I need to keep it
> Since what is kept must be adulterated? [1]

Compare Montaigne: 'with our weaknes we corrupt and adulterate the very essence of truth.' Eliot goes on:

> I have lost my sight, smell, hearing, taste and touch:
> How should I use them for your closer contact?

His senses have failed Gerontion—Montaigne demonstrates at length in his essay the fallacy of sensory impressions.

It seems to me then that *Gerontion* expresses an attitude very similar to that of Montaigne's *Apologie*; this does not prove that Eliot has drawn directly from it—he seems rather to have accepted or recognized Montaigne's scepticism toward man's powers. But he was not ready yet, at the time of writing *Gerontion*, to accept Montaigne's religious orthodoxy. *The Hollow Men*, for all its air of repetition and meaningless jingle, is a great step in the direction of the latter. Here again a comparison with the *Apologie of Raymond Sebond* can provide useful pointers to an interpretation of the poem—though its imagery is very far from being restricted to the content of the essay, and I fully recognize the importance of the elements drawn from Conrad's *Heart of Darkness* pointed out by Miss Helen Gardner and Miss Elizabeth Drew.[2] But we could say that *The Hollow Men* moves on from the position of the epigraph prefixed to *Gerontion*, a passage of *Measure for Measure*:

> Thou hast nor youth nor age
> But as it were an after dinner sleep
> Dreaming of both.

---

[1] *Ibid.*, p. 39.
[2] H. Gardner, *The Art of T. S. Eliot*, cit., and E. Drew, *T. S. Eliot, the Design of His Poetry*, cit.

The Shakespearian lines themselves may have been influenced by Montaigne who wrote: 'Our vigilancie is more drouzie, then sleepe it selfe: . . . our dreames of more worth then our discourses' [1] and 'When we dreame, our soule liveth, worketh, and exerciseth all her faculties, even, and as much, as when it waketh; . . . we wake sleeping and sleep waking'.[2] In *The Hollow Men,* as in the two poems of a more personal concrete tone which are so strictly linked with it (*Eyes that last I saw in tears,* and *The wind sprang up at four o' clock* [3]) human life is described as 'death's dream kingdom' or the 'twilight kingdom', and contrasted with 'death's other kingdom', the Kingdom to be entered after physical death.[4] In this way the identification is repeated: human life = dream, and two more are added: human life = death = twilight. And Montaigne can explain this as well:

Euripides seemeth to doubt, and call in question, whether the life we live be a life or no, or whether that which we call death be a life. . . . And not without apparance . . . death possessing what ever is before and behind this moment and also a good part of this moment.[5]

Here then are death's kingdoms,—and the passage could stand also as a comment on Sweeney's words beginning:

> He didn't know if he was alive
> and the girl was dead
> He didn't know if the girl was alive
> and he was dead . . .[6]

and on the final chorus of the 'Agon':

---

[1] Montaigne-Florio, cit., p. 513.   [2] *Ibid.,* p. 540.

[3] In the 'Minor Poems' group of the *Collected Poems,* cit., pp. 143–4. The second was one of *Doris's Dream Songs,* mentioned above.

[4] Miss Gardner (*op. cit.,* p. 111) makes a distinction between 'death's dream kingdom', defined by her as 'the world of illusion, of imagination and reverie', and the 'twilight kingdom'= human life. It seems to me instead that the identification of the two results from the very line she quotes from *Ash Wednesday,* VI, 'the *dream*crossed *twilight* between birth and dying'.

[5] Montaigne-Florio, cit., p. 471.   [6] *Collected Poems,* cit., p. 131.

You dreamt you waked up at seven o'clock and it's foggy and
    it's damp and it's dawn and it's dark
. . .
And perhaps you're alive
And perhaps you're dead.[1]

The twilight kingdom is another image of the shadow existence
of man. To quote again Montaigne:

We have no communication with being; for every humane
nature is ever in the middle between being borne and dying;
giving nothing of it selfe but an obscure apparance and
shadow . . .[2]

And further on, in a long excerpt from Plutarch:

Time is a fleeting thing, and which appeareth as in a
shadow, with the matter ever gliding, always fluent, without
ever being stable or permanent; to whom rightly belong these
termes, *Before* and *After*.[3]

With this help we can perhaps see better the meaning of the
fifth and last movement of *The Hollow Men*. It begins with a
childish rhyme representing the perpetual meaningless flow of
life on earth, and goes on to say that 'the Shadow' prevents us
from reaching any real achievement. The Shadow, then,
which falls 'between the idea and the reality, between the
motion and the act, between the potency and the existence' . . .
is time, life in this world.[4] Two statements break the list of
the achievements which time prevents: 'For Thine is the
Kingdom', and 'Life is very long'. I believe that the second
is an equivalent of the first: real Life is not our shadow-life
(Montaigne defines it as 'a twinckling in the infinit course of an
eternall night'[5]) but is the one which is 'very long', is the

---

[1] *Ibid.*, p. 132.   [2] Montaigne-Florio, cit., p. 545.   [3] *Ibid.*, p. 546.

[4] While writing these lines Eliot might have remembered also the passage
from *Julius Caesar* which I quote later in this essay: 'Between the acting of a
dreadful thing And the first motion, all the interim is Like a phantasma, or a
hideous dream.'

[5] Montaigne-Florio, cit., p. 471.

Kingdom, and is God's. This seems to me to be the sense of the next three broken sentences:

> For Thine is
> Life is
> For Thine is the [1]

The equation between life and Kingdom is obvious in the very omission of the latter term. The same break after 'is' is found in *Sweeney Agonistes* where, after a song stressing the vacuity of life in time, the hollow round of 'morning-evening-noontide-night', Doris remarks:

> That's not life, that's no life
> Why I'd just as soon be dead.
> *Sweeney:* That's what life is. Just is
> *Doris:*   What is?
> What's that life is?
> *Sweeney:*   Life is death. [2]

Here the meaning is reversible: temporal life is but 'death's dream kingdom', and death of the body is real Life. In this light also the last lines of *The Hollow Men* assume a positive value:

> This is the way the world ends
> Not with a bang but a whimper. [3]

On one level they seem to stress the vacuity of temporal life (the world), but on the other they suggest that death is no final destruction, but is a birth, the first sound of a newborn creature.

The transition from *Gerontion* to *The Hollow Men* is, then, the transition from an absolute scepticism, which cannot find comfort in a faith, and rather dreads it (Christ, the tiger, 'springs in the new year. Us he devours') to a scepticism which applies only to human reason ('headpiece filled with straw'), while acknowledging another kind of life, a faith. I think that Montaigne has helped us to see this evolution. And the essay

[1] *Collected Poems,* cit., p. 90.   [2] *Ibid.,* p. 129.   [3] *Ibid.,* p. 90.

quoted could be illuminating also in respect to many themes of Eliot's later poetry.

But to revert now to *Sweeney Agonistes* and to drama, which is the subject of this essay: *The Hollow Men* shows that the struggle to reach faith is practically ended, though the faith at the time was only a faint hope of beatitude ('Multifoliate rose/Of death's twilight kingdom/The hope only/Of empty men' [1]). After the conquest, *Sweeney Agonistes* sets out to retell the struggle—a real *Agon,* a strife and a debate with oneself and with the world. It will have been noticed that all the passages which are most revealing of the symbolic value of Sweeney's attitude are to be found in the second fragment, called the *Agon,* rather than in the first, the *Prologue,* a mere statement of prevailing conditions. The dramatic form is not only justified, but necessary. Eliot then was dealing with matter susceptible of dramatic treatment. Why was the melodrama left in its unfinished state? The poet had injected into his music-hall rhythms the full force of an intense spiritual experience, so that the silly songs frequently become ritual formulae charged with philosophical or religious allusions. It is once again the Metaphysicals' way of joining together triviality and serious thought, contrasting elements which confer an extreme concentration and intensity on the writing. But can this intensity be maintained for a considerable period of time? The dramatic form cannot support the strain: it needs a certain elaboration, a continuous clarification of ideas and meanings, which is at the opposite pole from the Metaphysical instantaneous synthesis of contrasting ideas, with no apparent transition. *Sweeney* then is drama only in intention; but in fact it is poetry, and significant poetry, containing the seeds of much of Eliot's later work. We could even say that from this moment on he has only developed, deepened and clarified the themes contained in the poetry written between 1924 and 1930; this does not mean that he has monotonously repeated himself to satiety: he has added much and found ever new expressions

[1] *The Hollow Men,* IV, *Collected Poems,* cit., p. 89.

of his beliefs. It is the beliefs that are firmly rooted and immutable.

I have already spoken of the element of ritual (especially ritual repetition) which entered the Sweeney fragments, fused with the vacuous repetitiousness of music-hall songs. It is an element which asserted itself with particular vigour in that part of Eliot's poetry extending from the *Ariel Poems,* through *Ash Wednesday, Coriolan* and the two religious plays, to *The Family Reunion.* The poet's interest in it can be seen even in such early poems as *The Hippopotamus* or *Mr. Eliot's Sunday Morning Service,* but there with an impious ring. It appears in *The Waste Land,* but in brief flashes: repetition would have disturbed the taut elliptical style of the poem; it becomes more deliberate in *The Hollow Men,* though keeping a vacuous ring —the ritual of the nursery rhymes precedes that of prayer, 'For Thine is the Kingdom'. Profane imagery is ritualized by the insistent rhythms of *Sweeney Agonistes,* but there the full potentialities of these repetitions and formal enunciations, contrasting with the earlier concentration of image and thought, are realized. Ritual is at the basis of dramatic poetry: in his *A Dialogue on Dramatic Poetry,* written in 1928, the speaker E., who seems to be the mouthpiece of the author, says:

I say that the consummation of the drama, the perfect and ideal drama, is to be found in the ceremony of the Mass. I say . . . that drama springs from religious liturgy, and that it cannot afford to depart far from religious liturgy.[1]

And in the course of the discussion the 'essential relation of drama to religious liturgy' is stated in these terms:

We crave some liturgy less divine, something in respect of which we shall be more spectators and less participants . . . The more fluid, the more chaotic the religious and ethical beliefs, the more the drama must tend in the direction of liturgy.[2]

This statement, whether restricted to drama, to which it originally referred, or intended as applicable also to the rest of

[1] *Selected Essays,* cit., p. 47.   [2] *Ibid.,* p. 49.

poetry, carries several implications, particularly revealing in respect of Eliot's poetics:

(1) It obviously accounts for Eliot's next plays, the liturgical setting of *The Rock* and *Murder in the Cathedral*.

(2) It explains Eliot's conception of 'classicism'—we must remember that in 1927 he described himself as an Anglo-Catholic in religion, a royalist in politics and a classicist in literature. And the reference to liturgy is meant as a call for form; liturgy imposes that form and order which Eliot calls classical.

(3) It indicates the reasons for the subtle changes in the 'sound' of Eliot's poetry—and by sound I mean the way his verse sounds when read either aloud or silently.

I shall have to go back again to the first two points when discussing the later plays; so, for the time being, I shall be content to enlarge on the third. In the excellent first chapter of her book already quoted, Miss Gardner has illustrated very clearly the development of Eliot's diction and prosody, pointing out the change which took place with *The Hollow Men* and which she exemplifies from *Sweeney Agonistes*. Nothing could be added to her thorough and sensitive exposition of the metrical change; but I should like to point out that it was necessarily accompanied by a change in the very ring of the reader's voice, as conditioned by the verse-rhythms. The tone of Eliot's poetry has always been essentially unemphatic, avoiding melodramatic accents and sudden accelerations. The abrupt and fragmentary character of the earlier poems up to *The Waste Land* is set out more vividly by the fact that he has imposed on the poems an even, monotonous tone. The voice of the reader must be quiet, undramatic—there will be breaks and failings in the speech, but they will be only the reflections of an inner uncertainty. The final impression is one of deadness and emptiness. It is the monotony of despair:

> 'On Margate Sands.
> I can connect
> Nothing with nothing.
> The broken fingernails of dirty hands.

My people humble people who expect
Nothing.'
          la la
To Carthage then I came

Burning burning burning burning
O Lord Thou pluckest me out
O Lord Thou pluckest

     burning ¹

But with *The Hollow Men,* into this tense and even tone there
emerges a new affirmative ring. Whispers again and subdued
voices, but the speech is not so broken, the rhythm is firmer.
This new characteristic (the difference is that existing between
a sigh of final renunciation and a sigh of hope) gives to the
sound itself of the poems an increasing assurance. The uni-
formity and quietness of the reader's voice is now due not to a
sense of emptiness but to the knowledge of speaking not to
other men but to a deity, or of debating with oneself matters
which cannot stand an abrupt approach. It is, then, the
monotony of prayer—fully developed in the *Ash Wednesday*
sequence, with its ritual repetitions and invocations: with the
end of the third movement of *The Waste Land,* quoted above,
we can compare the end of the third movement of *Ash
Wednesday*:

Blown hair is sweet, brown hair over the mouth blown,
Lilac and brown hair;
Distraction, music of the flute, stops and steps of the mind over
     the third stair,
Fading, fading; strength beyond hope and despair
Climbing the third stair.

Lord, I am not worthy
Lord, I am not worthy
     but speak the word only.²

---

¹ *The Waste Land*—III: *The Fire Sermon,* ll. 300–11.
² *Collected Poems,* cit., p. 97.

We shall have to read both passages with the same even, unemphatic tone. But the first will sound like the disconnected monologue of a spirit engaged in a desperate search, of which he cannot see the outcome in spite of glimpses into an extratemporal dimension. The sense of dejection is brought out by the dead rhythm, the regularity of the stress-beats in spite of the metrical fragmentariness. In the passage from *Ash Wednesday* instead the accentual freedom itself relieves the monotony of the uniform enunciation: the effect is not of tiredness but of meditation, and the repetition at the end, which was the helpless call of a dying man in the first quotation, acquires here its full liturgical value of penitential formula and invocation.

The passages of the *Dialogue on Dramatic Poetry* already quoted are significant enough—drama is conceived as a lay liturgy, and liturgy, as we saw, means form. The Unities contribute to form; of them Eliot says:

I believe they will be found highly desirable for the drama of the future. For one thing, we want more concentration . . . A continuous hour and a half of *intense* interest is what we need.[1]

(the italics are Eliot's). But it was just because of its intensity that *Sweeney Agonistes* was left as a fragment. It would be unbearable and unpracticable to maintain a whole play at the same high tension of the two brief scenes. This is, I believe, why Eliot, still thinking to a certain extent in dramatic terms, reverted again to poetic monologues, where such complex intensity could be sustained. In the *Ariel Poems* he repeated the formal structure used in *Prufrock* and in *Gerontion*: *The Journey of the Magi*, *A Song of Simeon* and *Marina* are monologues by one and the same character—an old man. As in *Sweeney Agonistes* Eliot had infused new and deeper life into a character which had personified in *Poems 1920* and *The Waste Land* the most abject materialistic aspects of modern life, so in the *Ariel Poems* he revives, with a new content, the character of the Witness, Gerontion or Tiresias in *The Waste Land*. In the early

[1] *Selected Essays*, cit., p. 58.

poems he had been the witness of the fragmentariness, inconclusiveness and spiritual poverty of modern life. In the *Ariel Poems* the same old, tired man becomes the witness of higher mysteries. He is the man who has seen Birth and Death, in *The Journey of the Magi* (1927) and is

> no longer at ease here, in the old dispensation,
> With an alien people clutching their gods.
> I should be glad of another death.[1]

He is Simeon in *A Song of Simeon* (1928), who says:

I am tired with my own life and the lives of those after me,
I am dying in my own death and the deaths of those after me,
Let thy servant depart,
Having seen thy salvation.[2]

He is old Pericles, in *Marina* (1930), who exclaims in finding his long lost daughter

> let me
> Resign my life for this life, my speech for that unspoken,
> The awakened, lips parted, the hope, the new ships.[3]

The old man Gerontion, who had lost his passion and his senses since he could nowhere find certainty, the blind Pagan seer Tiresias, who '*sees* the substance' of *The Waste Land*, bearing witness to its sordidness and vacuity, becomes in these later poems the Witness to Godhead, the Christian prophet, tired only because he has realized that this life is death, and desiring the death which is life. To see in this evolution of the 'character' just the evolution of the author—to identify the two— would be an unwarranted assumption. Though the monologues reflect Eliot's thought, he is separated from the speakers, who are to be considered as truly dramatic characters, detached enough from the writer to be able to have a life of their own, and to be symbols as well as living creatures. The symbolic value of the figure of the old man is fully realized in his last

---

[1] *Collected Poems*, cit., p. 108.   [2] *Ibid.*, p. 110.
[3] *Ibid.*, p. 114.

appearance in Eliot's work: in the first chorus of *The Rock*
(1934) the Chorus leader says:

> . . . I perceive approaching
> The Rock. Who will perhaps answer our doubtings.
> The Rock. The Watcher. The Stranger.
> He who has seen what has happened
> And who sees what is to happen.
> The Witness. The Critic. The Stranger.
> The God-shaken, in whom is the truth inborn.
>   *Enter the* ROCK *led by a* BOY.[1]

The Rock is of course, in the words of the best-known
Concordance to the Bible, 'a figure and type of Christ', or
more specifically here, since the play was written to raise funds
for the City Churches, it is the spiritual leadership provided by
the Church of Christ ('and upon this rock will I build my
church'). The symbol of the Rock is another proof of the inner
consistency of Eliot's images developing through the years. The
long passage between lines 331 and 358 of *The Waste Land* is
a series of variations on the theme of the absence of water in the
spiritual wilderness implied in the title of the poem:

> Here is no water but only rock
> Rock and no water and the sandy road
>   . . .
> If there were water we should stop and drink
>   . . .
> If there were only water amongst the rock
>   . . .
>   If there were water
>   And no rock
>   If there were rock
>   And also water
>   . . .
>   But there is no water.[2]

The reference is to the 'evil place' in Numbers xx, which is 'no
place of seed, or of figs, or of wines, or of pomegranates; neither

[1] *Collected Poems,* cit., p. 158.   [2] *Ibid.,* pp. 74-5.

is there any water to drink'. The passage implies also that Eliot, though conscious of the Biblical events, could not see, in the contemporary wilderness, at the time of writing *The Waste Land,* any Moses who could strike the water out of the rock. But using the same symbol in *The Rock* Eliot openly affirms that he has found his Moses, the spiritual leader, in the doctrines of the Church he has embraced in the meantime. The symbol is maintained, continued and at the same time reversed. The 'Rock', who 'enters led by a boy', by resuming some of the essential recurring figures and images in Eliot's poetry (the Gerontion figure and the stony ground of *The Waste Land*) and by showing their transformation into an avowed symbol of orthodox Christianity, has also the value of a visible embodiment of Eliot's own spiritual change. And perhaps Mr. Maxwell is right in seeing in the Rock another impersonation of Eliot's Coriolanus, who, the critic thinks, represents the spiritual leader whom the poet considered lost and betrayed in his early poems (*A Cooking Egg,* line 11, *The Waste Land,* line 416), and whose advent he invoked in the *Coriolan* sequence (written 1931–2).[1] The Rock is the spiritual leader looked for and finally found, and the quotation from Shakespeare's *Coriolanus,* v, ii, mentioned by Mr. Maxwell (The worthy fellow is our general: he is the rock, the oak not to be wind-shaken) does seem connected with the passage of *The Rock* quoted above. In this way also the political leader fuses with the religious leader in this complex symbol.

The very complexity of the meaning of this figure in the religious pageant, destroys the Rock as a dramatic character and stresses the non-dramatic quality of the whole play. Even the statement that Eliot was trying his hand in it at the treatment of choric poetry is only partly true. The choruses have such a deliberate function of mere comment on and elucidation of ideas and abstract principles that no trace of dramatic life can be found in them. For this reason *The Rock* cannot be related to Eliot's essays on poetry and drama. He himself dis-

[1] D. E. S. Maxwell, *The Poetry of T. S. Eliot,* cit., p. 133.

claims responsibility for the structure of the pageant and for most of its dialogue. The interest of *The Rock* is rather in the fact that it provides in many cases clearer statements of ideas and beliefs than most other poems by Eliot. The need for direct communication of thought to a simple minded audience has induced the poet to illustrate and elaborate themes which had appeared in his previous poems and were to form the substance of the later *Quartets*. In the first chorus, for instance, the theme of the desert, so permanent in Eliot's poetry, is explained in full, while in the seventh the significance of the moment of revelation is made clear. *The Rock* may be taken as a key to most of what Eliot has written before or since, and it would be very useful to examine his other works in the light of the statements contained in it.

It would seem, then, that since—roughly—1927 Eliot's poetry has been exclusively concerned with one main theme (his religious belief) and a few secondary ones mixed and contrasted with the main theme: the condition of man in history and in respect to Godhead and the relation of time and eternity (time and the moment). Indeed, the poetry of *The Rock* is so obviously and honestly undramatic that the appearance of the Workers and the Unemployed in the first chorus comes as a shock and sounds alien to the general tone of the work. It reveals the fleeting influence of Auden's use of some ideas expressed earlier by Eliot himself. Auden obviously had in mind Eliot's statement on the significance of ballet when he wrote his *Dance of Death,* but was exploiting the liturgical quality of this fusion of dance, mime and poetry for political debate. Eliot in turn utilized in *The Rock* Auden's treatment of the social theme, but it was unconvincing and the choruses survive only as statements of belief and discussions of principles in dignified and pliable verse forms. Eliot himself must have been aware of this since he never republished the 'libretto' of *The Rock* and instead included the choruses in his collected poems; and in his most recent discussion of poetic drama he completely ignores this first incursion into the field of religious drama. He considers that his first play was *Murder in the Cathedral* (1936), but hastens to state that in writing it he was evading the real issues. This is perhaps true since he had been looking for a form of verse drama acceptable to modern audiences and able to express a wide range of subjects, plots or in one word, contents. This was considered by the poet as the main issue confronting the verse playwright and obviously *Murder in the Cathedral*, by the very occasion of its performance, did not face it squarely, and had to assume instead a very special form which could not be applied to other subjects or presented without preparation to the ordinary theatre-goer.

At this point what interests us is actually Eliot's attitude on the theoretical plane. He implies that there must be some kind of form or formula applicable to a whole section or *genre* of literature. This position is in full contrast with the prevailing attitude in the criticism of this century according to which each single work of art poses peculiar problems of its own and is an individual creation, unconnected with pre-established rules. Eliot instead, though never mentioning rules, insists on the necessity of finding some scheme more universally valid. It is at this stage that one realizes the full extent of Eliot's statement: 'I am a classicist in literature'. The word lends itself to so many interpretations, that here we should try to see clearly the different connotations that classicism has had for Eliot throughout his career. Eliot issued a warning in *After Strange Gods* (1934) where, speaking of 'romanticists' and 'classicists' he said:

These names that groups of writers and artists give themselves are the delight of professors and historians of literature, but should not be taken very seriously. . . . No sensible author, in the midst of something that he is trying to write, can stop to consider whether it is going to be romantic or the opposite.[1]

But six years earlier he had stated that he was a classicist, and that shows that the word had a meaning for him; and in two essays written as early as 1923 he had already been discussing

[1] Quoted in T. S. Eliot, *Points of View*, London, 1941, pp. 40-1.

that meaning.[1] In *The Function of Criticism,* questioning
Middleton Murry's identification of the classical principle with
Catholicism, the principle of unquestioned spiritual authority
outside the individual, Eliot wrote:

The difference [between Classicism and Romanticism]
seems to me rather the difference between the complete and the
fragmentary, the adult and the immature, the orderly and the
chaotic.[2]

And in his review of *Ulysses* there is a more definite attempt at
a definition of his idea of classicism:

We agree, I hope, that 'classicism' is not an alternative to
'romanticism', as of political parties, ... on a 'turn-the-
rascals-out' platform. It is a goal towards which all good
literature strives, so far as it is good, according to the possibilities of its place and time. ... In using the myth Mr. Joyce
is pursuing a method which others must pursue after him. ...
It is simply a way of controlling, of ordering, of giving a shape
and a significance to the immense panorama of futility and
anarchy which is contemporary history. It is a method already
adumbrated by Mr. Yeats ... [and] for which the horoscope
is auspicious. ... It is, I seriously believe, a step towards
making the modern world possible for art, towards order and
form.[3]

It appears then that by classic Eliot meant at that time just
the fully mature, the perfect work of art, which would of necessity have had its form, though perhaps a very new and original
one. Form is not intended as a pre-established scheme, as it
was for instance for the Augustans or the classicists of the previous ages, but is a new creation, the final expression of a
tradition, and one which, of course, by its very novelty, would

[1] Eliot's debt to Hulme's view of classicism, pointed out by Matthiessen (*op.
cit.,* p. 71), is examined by Nemi D'Agostino in his essay 'Gli anni di
tirocinio di Thomas Stearns Eliot', in *Belfagor,* VIII, n. 1 (Jan. 1953), pp. 16–
50, which is the most illuminating study I have read on Eliot's formative years.

[2] *Selected Essays,* cit., p. 26.   [3] *Ulysses, Order and Myth,* cit.

modify the tradition itself. Now, this definition of classicism has nothing to do with the usual opposition of classic and romantic, but it fits Eliot's particular kind of poetry, his search for a really new order in forms for which the world literary tradition was essentially raw material to be absorbed and re-expressed.

Another statement by Eliot, only three years later, shows a certain evolution in his consideration of the subject, and appears particularly significant since it came not long before the proclamation of his being a classicist. Here are the relevant words, quoted by Matthiessen:

I believe that the modern tendency is towards something which, for want of a better name, we may call classicism. . . . There is a tendency,—discernible even in art—toward a higher and clearer conception of Reason, and a more severe and serene control of the emotions by Reason. If this approaches or even suggests the Greek ideal, so much the better: but it must inevitably be very different.[1]

We may remark here two essential facts. First: the insistence on Reason, which reminds us of the classicism of the Age of Reason, the Eighteenth century; but Eliot's idea of Reason, with a capital R, is complicated by the fact that, for a firm believer like him, it must agree and nearly identify itself with religious faith. And the 'severe and serene control of the emotions' will be the result of the two concurring forces of reason and religion—a detachment which is expressed by St. John of the Cross in the sentence chosen by Eliot as the second epigraph to *Sweeney Agonistes*:

Hence the soul cannot be possessed of the divine union, until it has divested itself of the love of created beings.[2]

It is hardly necessary to remind the reader that St. John of the Cross remained one of the sources of Eliot's inspiration in his later works, and his prevailing influence on the *Four Quartets* has been pointed out by all the commentators. But also the first

[1] Matthiessen, *op. cit.*, p. 91.   [2] *Collected Poems*, cit., p. 117.

epigraph to *Sweeney Agonistes,* from the *Choephoroi,* is very interesting when considered in connection with his reference, in the passage quoted, to 'the Greek ideal'. This 'Greek' strain is the second point I wanted to make. Eliot's conception of the theatre, while based on Elizabethan texts, has always taken into account also the Greek models. This becomes clearer and clearer in the later phase of his development. The hint at the Unities in his *Dialogue on Dramatic Poetry,* quoted before, is significant enough. But even *Murder in the Cathedral,* a strictly Christian play, can be taken as evidence of it.

In spite of the fact, stressed by Eliot himself, that *Murder in the Cathedral* was a special play for a special audience, the author was adopting even in this case an obviously 'classicistic' attitude. He was thinking not so much, as he later stated, of *Everyman,* but of Greek drama and its rules. The unity of time is broken, but that of action is preserved. And the use of the choruses is strictly modelled on that of Greek tragedy. Instead the element which should connect *Murder in the Cathedral* back to *Sweeney Agonistes,* and the modern taste for sensational crime stories, has remained merely external, in the final choice of the title and in the hidden reference to Conan Doyle's *The Musrave Ritual.*[1] The use of this source (note the word 'ritual' in the title) is indeed too deliberate to be more than an intellectual game, somewhat in the taste of Charles Williams' novels of religion and black magic—and it could hardly have been intended as an appeal to those wider audiences which *Sweeney Agonistes* was meant to attract. *Murder in the Cathedral* is a fully vital work in its kind, but there is no doubt that Eliot's preoccupation in writing it was religious, and the form it took approached his classical ideal.

It is not surprising in view of these ideas of classicism that Eliot's preoccupation with form should become more exclusive. It was a matter not only of finding a particular form to express a particular world of feeling (in this case form would

---

[1] See the correspondence in *The Times Literary Supplement,* Jan. 19 and 26, and Feb. 23, 1951.

have been identified by Eliot with what he called 'the objective correlative'); it was a matter of establishing a form valid for more than one work and possibly for more than one author. The process was a slow one and the study of Eliot's interest in drama shows this very clearly. Perhaps the conventions and limitations of the stage made the poet realize that a stricter form was needed to communicate with an unprepared audience, and especially to hold their attention. In a letter to Ezra Pound, quoted by Mr. Isaacs, we find a very direct statement of this:

1. You got to keep the audience's attention all the time.
2. If you lose it you got to get it back QUICK.
3. Everything about plot and character and all else what Aristotle and others say is secondary to the forgoin.
4. But IF you can keep the bloody audience's attention engaged, then you can perform any monkey tricks you like when they ain't looking, and it's what you do behind the audience's back so to speak that makes your play IMMORTAL for a while.
If the audience gets its strip tease it will swallow the poetry.
5. If you write a play in verse, then the verse ought to be a medium to look THROUGH and not a pretty decoration to look AT.[1]

This very principle implied the solution of problems of a strictly technical nature in the construction of the work. The importance of construction, of—in journalistic jargon—the 'technical know-how' of playwriting, determined the conception of an existing set of rules, valid for more than one play at a time.

It is at this stage that Eliot's classicism takes a new turn. Once he has recognized the validity of the same principles for different works his position does not differ very much from that of the eighteenth-century classicists. It is a position which would fit Middleton Murry's definition of Classicism, to which Eliot had objected thirty years ago: the principle of unques-

[1] J. Isaacs, *An Assessment of Twentieth-Century Literature*, p. 159.

tioned authority outside the individual. In fact, Eliot can now say that

the poet with ambitions of the theatre must *discover the laws*, both of another kind of verse and of another kind of drama.[1]

The words I have italicized are particularly significant. It is not a matter of invention, but of discovery, meaning that the laws of composition are already there. And actually in the whole preface from which this sentence is quoted there are so many *must's* with reference to the work of the modern verse playwright that they look like a whole set of established rules such as were the foundation of classicistic writing. It must be remembered that in *The Use of Poetry and the Use of Criticism* Eliot had made a distinction between laws and rules with reference to the dramatic Unities, which he considered as laws of nature rather than rules invented by man.[2] But this only confirms the classical conception of abstract ideal models of perfection to which the work of art should try to conform and by which it should ultimately be judged. Classicism thrown out through the window comes in through the door.

The importance of Eliot's interest in the theatre should now be clear. The drama taught him to think in terms of established forms, to think, rather, of establishing new forms of a permanent character by discovering the hidden laws of composition. His interest in the theatre has, in the last analysis, resulted in his turning from a revolutionary conception of classicism to a traditional one. And that is also apparent in his lecture *What is a Classic?* (1945) where, apart from any assessment of value, Pope, a neoclassic in the historical and narrow sense of the word, is considered as the English poet nearest to the ideal of the 'relative classic', since he 'realizes the genius of the English language of a particular epoch'. This conception of the 'genius of the language' as the measure of a poet's

[1] Preface to S. L. Bethell, *Shakespeare and the Popular Dramatic Tradition*, London, 1944.

[2] *The Use of Poetry and the Use of Criticism*, London, 1933, p. 45.

classical quality, reveals Eliot's interest in the form of expression as such, and shows how near he is to the formal classicism of the eighteenth century.[1]

In *The Family Reunion* (1939) the problem of finding a form is also paramount. There is first of all the obvious device of modelling the play on the Greek drama. It is not the approach used by the modern French playwrights (or for that matter by Eugene O'Neill) who deliberately gave a new twist to the ancient myths: keeping even the mythological names, they wanted to emphasize the connection, they wanted their audiences to assume from the very start that their characters were literary creations acquiring little by little new individual personalities. Eliot instead tried to follow the reverse process by starting from characters who were supposed to belong to ordinary life in modern times and making the audience realize that their plight was the same as that of Greek heroes. The result is that while in the first case we have abstract types gradually humanized, in Eliot we have everyday characters dehumanized. There are other things which show how much the poet was preoccupied with the question of form, so that he tried deliberately to fuse elements which other dramatists had successfully used to create a poetic atmosphere. So alongside the pattern of the Greek drama there is a hint of the technique used by O'Neill in *Strange Interlude*. The lines given to the

[1] The connection between Eliot and Augustan classicism has been discussed by D. E. S. Maxwell (*The Poetry of T. S. Eliot,* cit.). But a further contribution to the subject has been provided by Irène Simon, who in her article 'Echoes in "The Waste Land"' (*English Studies,* XXXIV, n. 2, April 1953, pp. 64–72) examines afresh the passage of *A Game of Chess* I dealt with in a previous chapter of this book, pointing out a series of analogies with Pope's *The Rape of the Lock.* Mlle Simon's analysis is particularly interesting since it reveals Eliot's early approach to Augustan poetry. As I see it, in *The Waste Land* Eliot takes advantage more or less consciously of the mannerisms, in diction, incident and 'decor', of the eighteenth-century poet to add to the artificiality of the atmosphere he is creating. In other words, Eliot uses for his own purposes the 'artificial' element in Pope's style and aesthetic principles. Twenty years later, instead, Eliot's own aesthetic principles have evolved to the point that he has reached an attitude towards classicism very close to Pope's.

characters which form the chorus in *The Family Reunion* are an obvious compromise between the Greek model and O'Neill's device. As for the question of language and metre, Yeats seems to have been the main inspiration, and in fact Eliot acknowledges his debt to Yeats' last play, *Purgatory*. A comparison between the first lines of this and some lines of *The Family Reunion* shows that the debt is not only metrical. Here is *Purgatory*:

> Half-door, hall door,
> Hither and thither day and night,
> Hill or hollow, shouldering this pack,
> Hearing you talk.[1]

And in *The Family Reunion*:

> To and fro, dragging my feet
> Among inner shadows in the smoky wilderness,
> Trying to avoid the clasping branches
> And the giant lizard.[2]

Yeats had always been in Eliot's mind. We are told that he was taken by Pound in 1917 to see a performance of *The Hawk's Well* and that was the time when he first began to envisage the possibility of the revival of poetic drama. Yeats' play must have given him the idea of the importance of symbolism on the stage, an idea obviously still operating in *The Family Reunion*. But he realized that the form Yeats was working with at the time, based on the Japanese Noh plays, was unsuitable as a means of communication with larger audiences. (Yeats himself seemed to have been aware that his plays for dancers were perhaps more suited for performance in a studio or drawing-room than in a public theatre.)[3] We saw that Eliot thought at first of the music-hall as a means of contacting

[1] W. B. Yeats, *Purgatory* (1939), now in *Collected Plays*, 2nd ed., London, 1952, p. 681.

[2] *The Family Reunion*, London, 1939, p. 108.

[3] See the first stage direction of *The Resurrection*, in Yeats' *Collected Plays*, cit., p. 579.

the wider public. But the attempt to transfer symbolism into music-hall patterns in *Sweeney Agonistes* could not be realized. In *Murder in the Cathedral* he did not even think of addressing normal theatre-goers. But he had not given up his idea of communicating with the public at all levels. In 1933 he had written:

I believe that the poet naturally prefers to write for as large and miscellaneous an audience as possible. . . . I myself should like an audience which could neither read nor write . . . The ideal medium for poetry, to my mind, and the most direct means of social 'usefulness' for poetry, is the theatre. In a play of Shakespeare you get several levels of significance. For the simplest auditors there is the plot, for the more thoughtful the character and conflict of character, for the more literary the words and phrasing, for the more musically sensitive the rhythm, and for auditors of greater sensitiveness and understanding a meaning which reveals itself gradually.[1]

And he went on explaining that in *Sweeney* he had just tried to address this miscellaneous audience:

My intention was to have one character whose sensibility and intelligence should be on the plane of the most sensitive and intelligent members of the audience; his speeches should be addressed to them as much as to the other personages in the play—or rather, should be addressed to the latter, who were to be material, literal-minded and visionless, with the consciousness of being overheard by the former. There was to be an understanding between this protagonist and a small number of the audience, while the rest of the audience would share the responses of the other characters in the play. Perhaps this is all too deliberate, but one must experiment as one can.[2]

The Family Reunion is in fact the second experiment in the same direction. The music-hall has been discarded as incapable of bearing the tension, and a much more complicated and com-

---

[1] *The Use of Poetry and the Use of Criticism*, cit., p. 153. [2] *Ibid.*, pp. 153–4.

posite scheme has been substituted for it. We saw the main elements which went into its making. The resulting mixture is in fact intended to appeal to the audience on its different levels. But this conception of levels had taken in the meantime also another significance. They were not only levels of understanding on the side of the audience: they were levels of communication and expression on the side of the author. The idea is clearly stated for the first time in the famous passage of the essay on *Marston* (1934):

It is possible that what distinguishes poetic drama from prosaic drama is a kind of doubleness in the action, as if it took place on two planes at once. . . . In poetic drama a certain apparent irrelevance may be the symptom of this doubleness; or the drama has an underpattern, less manifest than the theatrical one. . . . [In Marston's *Sophonisba*] in spite of the tumultuousness of the action . . . there is an underlying serenity; . . . we perceive a pattern behind the pattern into which the characters deliberately involve themselves; the kind of pattern which we perceive in our own lives only at rare moments of inattention and detachment, drowsing in sunlight.[1]

These statements are of capital importance for Eliot's whole theory of poetic drama, and for the understanding of his work from this time onwards. Since then Eliot himself has repeated them again and again in his critical writings and in his poetry. In many of his lectures and articles on verse-drama, till his recent *Poetry and Drama* (1951), which summarizes his previous ones, Eliot has actually stated that the fundamental justification of the poetic-dramatic form is its exclusive ability to capture these 'hidden patterns which we perceive in our lives only at rare moments of inattention and detachment'. This is clarified in the concluding pages of *Poetry and Drama*:

It seems to me that beyond the namable, classifiable emotions and motives of our conscious life, when directed toward action—the part of life which prose drama is wholly

[1] *Selected Essays*, cit., pp. 229 and 232.

adequate to express,—there is a fringe of indefinite extent, of feeling which we can only detect, so to speak, out of the corner of the eye and can never completely focus; of feeling of which we are only aware in a kind of temporary detachment from action. There are great prose dramatists—such as Ibsen and Chekhov—who have at times done things of which I would not otherwise have supposed prose to be capable, but who seem to me, in spite of their success, to have been hampered in expression by writing in prose. This peculiar range of sensibility can be expressed by dramatic poetry, at its moments of greatest intensity. At such moments we touch the border of those feelings which only music can express.[1]

Here then, for Eliot, is the real function of poetry in the theatre, and here, obviously, is the reason for the composite construction of *The Family Reunion*: to convey and communicate a new level of consciousness.

From the liturgical conception of drama, expounded in his *Dialogue on Dramatic Poetry* (1928) Eliot has passed to that of the 'planes of reality'. This definition has been given currency by Prof. Tillyard's lectures in 1936 on *Shakespeare's Last Plays*. Prof. Tillyard's illustration of the different planes of reality represented at one and the same time in Shakespeare's so-called romances is deservedly well known. In these plays Shakespeare seems to be thinking on two levels at once: that of ordinary life and the 'feeling of seeing life distanced'. This feeling, says Prof. Tillyard speaking of *Cymbeline*,[2] is conveyed by the 'unearthly music' of Shakespeare's lines, for instance in the scenes in the Welsh mountains. It is this same quality that Eliot is pursuing in his later poetry plays. In this respect the unconscious references to *Cymbeline* in *The Waste Land,* which I have pointed out in a previous chapter of this book, seem particularly significant.[3] As an example of a different type of reality which pervades the consciousness of one character and is 'alien

[1] *Poetry and Drama,* Cambridge (Mass.), 1951, pp. 43–4.
[2] E. M. W. Tillyard, *Shakespeare's Last Plays,* London, 1938, p. 74.
[3] See pp. 60–70 of the present book.

to that of any other person's and set against it' Tillyard quotes
Brutus' lines in *Julius Caesar*:

> Between the acting of a dreadful thing
> And the first motion, all the interim is
> Like a phantasma, or a hideous dream.[1]

I said before that these lines might have been in Eliot's mind
at the time of writing *The Hollow Men*:

> Between the motion
> And the act
> Falls the Shadow [2]

But the Shakespearian quotation takes us back as well to *The
Family Reunion*. Is not Harry's condition very similar to
Brutus'? Between the first motion and the acting of something
great (not in this case dreadful) his world is indeed phantasma
or dream: 'One is still alone', he says, 'in an over-crowded
desert, jostled by ghosts,' [3] or

> The things I thought were real are shadows and the real
> Are what I thought were private shadows.[4]

The 'war of phantoms' in which Harry has been wounded is
the interim between the first vague apprehension of a different
level of life (of which the other characters of the play, except
Agatha, are unaware) and the moment of action, his decision
to face and meet his fate; the other level is in fact that of fate,
awkwardly represented in *The Family Reunion* by those obvious
intruders from Greek tragedy, the Eumenides. The problem
confronting Harry is, in other words, that of sin; the Eumenides
are the sense of sin haunting him till he discovers that the feeling is not negative or destructive, but is rather positive—a
heightened consciousness which may finally lead him to salvation through atonement. I should repeat here, then, what I said
in an earlier part of this essay: the feeling behind *Sweeney
Agonistes* is at the root of all later work by Eliot. It is expanded

---

[1] Tillyard, *op. cit.*, p. 66.
[2] *Collected Poems*, cit., p. 90.
[3] *The Family Reunion*, cit., p. 30.
[4] *Ibid.*, pp. 106–7.

in his poems to cover the whole range of his religious beliefs, but in his plays it is essentially restricted to the theme of the sense of sin and atonement, since this theme is of itself dramatic and it finds its natural expression in the dramatic form. Harry then is one aspect of Sweeney, the man who, in the general blindness of the wastelanders, has a sense of sin, and therefore a greater degree of consciousness. One of the epigraphs prefixed to the Aristophanic melodrama when compared with the later play makes obvious the connection between Sweeney and Harry. The first epigraph to *Sweeney Agonistes* is from the *Choephoroi*: 'You don't see them but *I* see them: they are hunting me down, I must move on.' The words are repeated by Harry in *The Family Reunion*:

> *You* don't see them, but I see them.[1]

The theme of both plays is stated in this sentence: the awareness of something beyond the common level of human feelings and actions. What in *Sweeney* was expressed in a very cryptic and concentrated form appears in *The Family Reunion* more openly. Apart from the physical presence of the Eumenides on the stage, the main characters in the play are exclusively concerned with their spiritual problems, identical with those of Sweeney, but expressed in terms which Eliot tried to make comprehensible for normal audiences of drawing-room plays, rather than for those of the music-hall. The analogy with the *Oresteia* is intended as a pointer to the overtones of meaning (the other level) which the text implies.

If the central theme of *The Family Reunion* is that of sin and atonement in an Unbelieving world, it is obvious that also other recurrent motifs in Eliot's poetry and thought must have entered the picture, though more superficially. Miss Helen Gardner has already pointed out the close affinities between this play and the *Four Quartets*. Her words cannot be improved upon; the *Four Quartets,* she says,

are poems on one theme, or rather on different aspects of the

---

[1] *The Family Reunion*, cit., p. 25.

same theme, and they are closely linked with *The Family Reunion,* which is a dramatic treatment of the subject. The theme can be variously defined. . . . It might be called the relation of time to eternity, or the meaning of history, or the redemption of time and the world of man. *The Family Reunion* emphasises the idea of redemption, for Harry is seeking salvation and release from his sense of guilt. . . .[1]

In Christian terms, the emphasis in the play is on sin and purgation, while in the poems it is on the broader issues—time and eternity, as Miss Gardner puts it. The latter theme is present in *The Family Reunion* especially in the scene where the Eumenides appear, giving a greater depth to the whole drama. Miss Gardner stresses particularly the recurrence in the Quartets and in the play of the motif of the rose-garden, an image which has been examined by many critics.[2] The image is linked with Eliot's intuition of the moment of illumination or, to use the Christian terminology, of Revelation. Miss Gardner refers, to illustrate her point, to the chorus of *The Rock* where the poet speaks of 'the moment in time and of time . . . but not like a moment of time'. (As I said, *The Rock* can provide a commentary on much that may appear obscure in Eliot's poetry.) But what interests me at present is the fact that what in *The Family Reunion* is called 'the moment of clarity' (the moment of Harry's decision, or conversion, or Revelation, as it could be defined) is expressed in *The Dry Salvages* in the lines:

> For most of us, there is only the unattended
> Moment, the moment in and out of time,
> The distraction fit, lost in a shaft of sunlight . . .[3]

This is not only an obvious reference to the garden image (as Harry says to Agatha, 'you walked through the little door/And I walked to meet you in the rose-garden') but it also recalls

[1] H. Gardner, 'Four Quartets', in *Penguin New Writing,* 29, London, 1947, p. 127.

[2] See especially L. Unger, *T. S. Eliot and the Rose Garden,* now in *T. S. Eliot, A Selected Critique,* ed. L. Unger, New York, 1948, p. 374 ff.

[3] *Four Quartets,* cit., pp. 32–3.

what Eliot said about 'the other pattern' which can be found in certain poetry plays: 'the kind of pattern which we perceive in our lives only in rare moments of inattention and detachment, drowsing in sunlight'. For the poet the shaft of sunlight stands for the sudden illumination, the momentary intuition of things beyond the ordinary human world. Now, we must remember that Eliot based his argument in favour of poetic as opposed to prose drama on the fact that the poetry allows for this new pattern, this different level of consciousness. But I think that there is a fallacy in the argument. By its very momentary quality, the revelation must be only a flash of extraordinary intensity: how can it become a real 'pattern', a permanent overtone to a whole play? The fundamental weakness of Eliot's later plays is in the fact that they are meant to be for the most part build-ups for the moment of revelation. This explains also the pains Eliot has taken to find a prosody as close as possible to common speech, hardly distinguishable from it when the play is performed. The audience should be unaware of the fact that they are listening to poetry, but get instinctively accustomed to the rhythm, so that, when the 'moment' comes —the moment that, according to the author, can be expressed only in poetry—they don't feel too sharply the transition from the ordinary level to the more intense one.

We are confronted then with something very different from the 'double level' of, for instance, Shakespeare's last plays. There, there was indeed a higher pattern running through the play as a whole and appearing again and again in the lines at different stages in the progress of the action. In *The Family Reunion,* and even more in *The Cocktail Party,* there are only odd flashes lost in a mass of serviceable verse. This very concentration on so few poetic flashes unbalances the structure of the plays and impoverishes their poetic vitality. At the same time it is a fact that in *The Family Reunion* Eliot has achieved complete mastery over a very individual verse-form, in which the rhythms of common speech reach a kind of nobility through subtle variations and intensifications, without the exhibitionism of Fry or Charles Williams, or that of Auden, or even Eliot himself in *Murder in the Cathedral*. The question, to which we cannot yet reply, is whether this unassuming prosody is really more acceptable to the audience and more able to communicate with them than the deliberately poetic language of the other verse-playwrights. The question is important enough when we consider that communication with the audience has always been the main concern of Eliot as a dramatist. So much so that he seems to have considered more and more his playwriting as a kind of missionary work in a Godless world.

The need for communication of a more direct kind is indeed the reason for such a play as *The Cocktail Party*. Eliot tells us that also in this case he had in mind a Greek model: *Alcestis*.[1] The choice is significant: *Alcestis* is not a regular tragedy; it is the fourth play which traditionally followed the great tragic trilogies, providing comic relief and a happy ending to the ritual tragic cycles. Eliot then seems to have gone back to the idea of the need of light entertainment for a modern audience, if they are to swallow the thought contained in the play. As in *Sweeney Agonistes* he had tried to communicate with the music-hall audiences, so in *The Cocktail Party* he addresses the theatre-goers who have decreed the success of Mr. Noel Coward or Mr. Terence Rattigan. The Greek model, as Eliot says, is in no way as closely followed as in *The Family Reunion*; it is treated only as a starting point, as an invisible understructure which provides, more for the author than for the audience, a level of deeper meaning. Once again the Greek drama is interpreted in Christian terms: Hercules becomes the Saviour not from physical but from spiritual death. And once again the Christian symbolism is in a lay setting. The Saviour is a psychoanalyst, the highest spiritual authority in a world of unbelievers. But in this case the disguise of the religious meaning of the play is thinner than usual; Mr. Arrowsmith has pointed out the wealth of religious allusion in the very language of *The*

[1] *Poetry and Drama,* cit., pp. 38–9.

Cocktail Party,[1] and certainly even the most superficial reader cannot miss the Christian implications of a sentence like 'Work out your salvation with diligence'. There is no doubt that the author has aimed at revealing more directly to the unprepared audience his real meaning. In order to do so he has not only inserted obvious and open allusions to religious ideas in the text, but has tried as well to use, especially at the beginning, that modish contemporary jargon which he had experimented with in *Sweeney*. The echoes in rhythm and fashionable mannerisms from the early unfinished play are clear. For instance:

> *Celia:* She's such a good mimic.
> *Julia:*   Am I a good mimic?
> *Peter:* You *are* a good mimic. You never miss anything.
> *Alex:* She never misses anything unless she wants to.[2]

But the analogies with *Sweeney Agonistes* are not limited to these formal echoes: side by side with the 'modern' story and with the elements from *Alcestis* there runs another parallel stream of meaning and even plot, which tried at first to find expression in *Sweeney*.[3] This will appear if we consider one of the most criticized parts of *The Cocktail Party*, Celia's martyrdom in Kinkanja. We are reminded of Sweeney's words:

> *Sweeney:*   I'll carry you off
>   To a cannibal isle.
> *Doris:*   You'll be the cannibal!
> *Sweeney:* You'll be the missionary!
>   You'll be my little seven stone missionary!
>   I'll gobble you up. I'll be the cannibal.[4]

---

[1] W. Arrowsmith, 'The Cocktail Party', in *Hudson Review*, III, 3, Aug. 1950, pp. 411–30.

[2] *The Cocktail Party*, London, 1950, p. 9.

[3] I am deeply indebted to Prof. Salvatore Rosati, the author of the excellent Italian translation of *The Cocktail Party*, for pointing out to me the connection between this play and *Sweeney Agonistes*.

[4] *Collected Poems*, cit., p. 126.

What was meant as a symbol in *Sweeney* has become part of the actual 'story' in *The Cocktail Party*. The allusion is prepared from the first act in a mood closer to that of the *Fragments of an Aristophanic Melodrama*. During the meaningless chitchat at the first cocktail party, so close to *Sweeney's* apparently pointless jingles, the brother of a fashionable lady is mentioned, and Julia says of him that he was 'not feeble-minded: He was only harmless', and was 'the only man I ever met who could hear the cry of bats'. The following dialogue with Celia ensues:

> *Celia:* But how do you know he could hear the cry of bats?
> *Julia:* Because he said so. And I believed him.
> *Celia:* But if he was so . . . harmless, how could you believe him?
> He might have imagined it.
> *Julia:*   My darling Celia,
> You needn't be so sceptical. I stayed there once
> At their castle in the North. How he suffered!
> They had to find an island for him
> Where there were no bats.[1]

I think that this bit of conversation, which fits in so well with the drawing-room small talk—the meaningless entertainment—of the first act, may take on a quite different value when we remember, in the light of the rest of the play, that Julia is one of the 'Guardians', the seers, the ministers of grace who prepare the salvation of the other characters, and that Celia will turn out to be the predestined being, endowed with full clarity of vision beyond the merely human range. Julia therefore knows and believes in the ability of the 'harmless' gentleman (a madman for the common humanity devoid of vision) to hear the cry of bats. And is not this mysterious voice, audible only to one person, something like Harry's sensation in *The Family Reunion,* at the moment when he is about to see the Eumenides?

[1] *The Cocktail Party,* cit., pp. 11–12.

> Do you feel a kind of stirring underneath the air?
> Do you? don't you? a communication, a scent
> Direct to the brain . . .[1]

The gentleman in Julia's story is Harry, the man with a deeper
consciousness, and is therefore also a prefiguration of Celia, a
creature with the same gift. And his end in an island is the end
predicted to Doris in *Sweeney Agonistes* and the end of Celia in
Kinkanja. There is a subtle humour in the choice of the bats
as the equivalent of the Eumenides: the implication being of
course that the ordinary people consider that those endowed
with a higher vision have, as the popular saying is, 'bats in
the belfry'.

The Cocktail Party, then, resumes and re-expresses in a more
direct way the content of *Sweeney.* Sir Henry Harcourt-Reilly,
the psychoanalyst, is Sweeney, the character, in Eliot's words
already quoted, 'whose sensibility and intelligence should be on
the plane of the most sensitive and intelligent members of the
audience'. We remember that Sweeney is not only sensitive and
intelligent in himself: he also tries, like Sir Henry, to help
others who are still in the dark but susceptible to salvation
since they feel strongly their sense of sin. Sweeney says of the
man who 'did a girl in':

> He used to come and see me sometimes
> I'd give him a drink and cheer him up.[2]

In the same way the psychoanalyst receives Celia in *The Cocktail Party* and helps her to realize the meaning of her feelings
under the level of ordinary consciousness. This same function
was partly performed in *The Family Reunion* by Agatha, but
with less deliberation. Harry there was the converted sinner,
like Celia in *The Cocktail Party,* but he was also Sweeney,
since his conversion had come essentially from his own consciousness: he was partly converted before the beginning of the
play. It is more difficult to find a character corresponding to
Celia in *Sweeney Agonistes,* but the allusion to the cannibal isle

---

[1] *The Family Reunion*, cit., p. 109.   [2] *Collected Poems,* cit., pp. 130–1.

can give us a hint: Doris, who does not come to life because of
the fragmentary condition of the play, was meant, I believe, to
be the equivalent of Celia. In *Sweeney* Doris's part is full of pre-
monitions of death—e.g. the 'coffin' in the fortune-teller's game.
Besides we saw that Doris existed before *Sweeney Agonistes* in
Eliot's mind, as the dreamer in those visionary songs which
contributed so much to the making of *The Hollow Men*. The
character therefore must have had in the author's mind a much
deeper significance than the one which appears in the *Sweeney*
fragments. Doris was meant to attain that higher or deeper level
of consciousness which Celia—a mere doll at the beginning of
The Cocktail Party—reaches in the course of the play.

Eliot's plays, then, are all based on the same situation and
deal with the same characters. The development is in the
direction of a more and more open statement of his aims.
Actually with many artists this need to declare their message,
the message implied rather than stated in their earlier work,
seems to make itself felt more urgently at a certain stage of their
careers. There is a sort of fear of not being understood, and a
feeling of the extreme importance of the things they have to say,
that induces them to have recourse to obvious examples. In *The
Cocktail Party* the content of thought so powerfully expressed in
the elliptical forms of Eliot's previous poetry, including the
great cycle of the *Quartets,* is popularized to such a point as
to be unable to avoid the ridiculous in scenes like that of the
toast or the awkward disclosure of Celia's end. Obviousness is
achieved at the expense of intensity, and the author still fails
to convince us of the dramatic (meaning theatrical) vitality of
the situation he has chosen as the subject of all his plays.

Fry: The Popular Theatre

WHEN we survey the work of that generation of pioneers which should, as Eliot said, break the ground for the re-establishment of poetry drama, it appears that the most successful practitioner of the revival is surely Christopher Fry. Successful also in the commercial sense, since his plays are popular both in the West End theatres and on Broadway, and are actually sought as 'vehicles' for the best-known Shakespearian actors. We can take him, therefore, as a writer in direct touch with the wider public, in contrast with the authors we have seen up to now, catering for restricted audiences.

Fry seems to have taken quite a different path from the one followed by Eliot, who had written:

How would people to-day speak if they could speak in poetry? They cannot be translated to a fairyland where they may talk appropriately in verse; they must on your stage be able to perform the same actions, and lead the same lives, as in the real world.[1]

This led of course to the unobtrusive though extremely skilful diction of *The Cocktail Party*, and to its realistic setting. Any passage from one of Fry's plays may be chosen to show the difference. Here is one:

---

[1] Preface to S. L. Bethell, *Shakespeare and the Popular Dramatic Tradition*, cit., p. 8.

> Now you, for instance,
> Still damp from your cocoon, you're desperate
> To fly into any noose of the sun that should dangle
> Down from the sky. Life, forbye, is the way
> We fatten for the Michaelmas of our own particular
> Gallows. What a wonderful thing is metaphor.[1]

This is very far from the Eliot of *Sweeney Agonistes*:

> That's all the facts when you come to brass tacks:
> Birth, and copulation, and death.
> I've been born, and once is enough.
> You don't remember, but I remember,
> Once is enough.[2]

or of *The Cocktail Party*:

> Oh, it isn't much
> That I understand yet! But Sir Henry has been saying,
> I think, that every moment is a fresh beginning;
> And Julia, that life is only keeping on;
> And somehow, the two ideas seem to fit together.[3]

The three quotations are all statements about life. But in the early 'melodrama' Eliot is boldly fitting the language of an uncultured person to an easy tune in order to express a philosophy of disillusionment; he strikes home more forcibly because of the deep charge of feeling the hearer detects behind the vulgarity of its expression (and we have already seen in the previous essay what this feeling was). In the last quotation the poet moves with nearly Jamesian caution, in a verse rhythm which is as close as possible to that of analytic prose. Instead, there is no risk of missing the fact that Fry writes in verse: his language, the marked though extremely varied rhythms and the elaborate imagery, are far from unobtrusive. In Eliot, even fairly developed images are weighed down by the serious content of

---

[1] C. Fry, *The Lady's Not for Burning*, London, 1949, p. 3.
[2] T. S. Eliot, *Collected Poems*, cit., p. 127.
[3] T. S. Eliot, *The Cocktail Party*, cit., p. 166.

thought, which checks the flight of the metaphor. His two *dicta* about life have a direct appeal to the speculative powers of the mind; instead, what first strikes the hearer, in the case of Fry's definition, is its outer form, and there is hardly time to think of the meaning. In the lines quoted above Fry directs our attention still more deliberately to the formal characteristics of his writing with the final sentence: 'what a wonderful thing is metaphor'. It is a sincere though ironical comment on his style: he joyfully rediscovers not so much the power of metaphor, as its external beauty, and is obviously playing with it for his own pleasure.

We may ask at this point: how did he reach this attitude while the other major poet playwright was taking just the opposite direction? The fact is still more puzzling since Fry, like Eliot, wrote his first full-length plays for religious institutions. But perhaps a link can be found through a verse-playwright who is too frequently ignored: Charles Williams. Getting hold of the structure prepared by Eliot's *The Rock* and *Murder in the Cathedral*, Williams grafted on to it, in his religious plays, a freer, half-roguish strain in diction and symbolism, balanced by an insistence on the openly musical elements of poetry. Eliot used anachronism (the speeches of the Knights in *Murder in the Cathedral*, the chorus of the unemployed in *The Rock*) to emphasize the actuality of the past and to establish a direct communication with his audience. Williams adopted the same principles: in his notes for an address after a performance of his *Seed of Adam* in 1937, he expressed them in his own way:

I had . . . abolished Time and Space. I was prepared to bring in anyone. . . .[1]

The play itself, written so shortly after Eliot's *Murder in the Cathedral*, bears a close resemblance to its model: its free articulation of action through a variety of verse patterns melting into each other would hardly have been possible without

[1] See the appendix to C. Williams, *Seed of Adam and Other Plays,* ed., A. Ridler, London, 1948, p. 95.

Eliot's experiments. Alliteration and internal rhymes are freely used:

> *Adam:* Dullards of darkness, light's lazybones,
> poor primitives of our natural bareness,
> where's your awareness? will moans and groans
> for gold of brawn or brain regain
> the way to the entry of Paradise? up!
> shut your eyes, will you? or make a play
> for your leisure, and a treasure of your idleness? You,
> have you nothing better to do
> in our world but to play hide and seek with oblivion?
> Say, say something, say
> *who are you?* I will tell you, tell you what you knew,
> I am Adam.[1]

But here the playwright seems to be interested mainly in impressing upon his audience the fact that what they are hearing is outside their everyday experience. He does not choose a form which may permit the abolition of time and space, but adopts a form which of itself *will* abolish them. Form has therefore for Williams a more active role, it is no longer essentially functional, and its increased importance is reflected by the way in which attention is constantly drawn to it. The choice of the words, the elaborate rhythmic pattern, and the ease with which they fit the flow of natural speech, testify to the achieved mastery of technique. Here, surely, is something like the writing of Fry; and indeed, Eliot's influence reached Fry filtered through Williams' dramatic experiments. Diction acquired a still greater importance when Fry began writing comedies instead of religious plays. Williams had introduced a new undercurrent of humour in religious pageants and masques, mainly through the extravagance of language; but at the same time he had stuck to their fundamental symbolic pattern, and the individualization of each symbol provided him with sets of clearly differentiated characters. Fry, in transposing the verse

[1] C. Williams, *Seed of Adam and Other Plays*, cit., p. 4.

play into lay comedy, renounced the symbolism, and the characterization practically disappeared along with it. Even the speech from Williams' *Seed of Adam* quoted above (though there are better examples to be found) shows an individual speaker affirming his personality. Here instead is the self-portrait of Thomas Mendip, the hero of Fry's *The Lady's Not for Burning*:

Richard: Name
          And business.
Thomas: Thomas Mendip. My well-born
          father,
          If birth can ever be said to be well, maintains
          A castle as drafty as a tree. At every sunset,
          It falls into the river and fish swim through its
          walls.
          They swim into the bosom of my grandmother
          Who sits late, watching for the constellation of
          Orion
          Because my dead grandfather, she believes,
          Is situated somewhere in the Belt.
          That is part of the glory of my childhood.[1]

And this is the normal way in which all characters express themselves, but the wit, though varied, is not individualized, and there is no attempt to make them speak in keeping. We could say, then, that character is substituted by wit. It is worth while inquiring into the origins or at least the precedents of Fry's wit, since this word is fairly elusive. For instance one definition of it may be the one given by Dr. Johnson with reference to the Metaphysicals ('the most heterogeneous ideas yoked by violence together'). But there is also the wit consisting merely in punning and playing on words, or that of rhetorical antithesis, or of elaborate conceit.

I propose at this point to enter into a fairly detailed analysis of the origins of Fry's wit, taking as terms of reference Elizabethan or rather Shakespearian texts. It is well to stress that I

[1] *The Lady's Not for Burning*, cit., p. 2.

have no intention of putting Fry on the same plane as the Elizabethan and Jacobean poets I shall mention. My analysis concerns only some stylistic elements and formal devices, not the intrinsic aesthetic value of the poetry discussed.

Mr. Marius Bewley, in *Scrutiny*,[1] severely castigated a critic for having compared Fry's verse to Marlowe's, and found a more fitting parallel between Fry and the verse-dramatists of the beginning of our century, like Gordon Bottomley and Lascelles Abercrombie. Questionable as this opinion may be, it is certain that the comparison with the sensuous quality of Marlowe's poetry is out of the question. Fry's verse is far from the early Elizabethans'. He himself remarks, of the verse plays written between the Elizabethan period and our own:

What seems most constant is a paralysing memory of Shakespeare, a kind of Oedipus complex with Shakespeare as mother, which made even the mature poets curl up as in a womb as soon as they wrote for the stage. And what is most odd, it is a pre-Shakespearian womb they curl up in. Ignoring one of the greatest gifts that Shakespeare gave, the development of blank verse into a flexible speech rhythm, they go the rounds of their iambic pentameters as though the Master had written nothing after *A Comedy of Errors*.[2]

After expressing surprise that Eliot 'should have been, and evidently still is afraid of the shadow of blank verse on the stage', Fry concludes:

This doesn't mean that I think that a poet dramatist should learn his speech-rhythms from Shakespeare. He should learn them from the voices about him. . . . But we shouldn't be alarmed if our own speech falls naturally into cadences familiar in the past.[3]

In this way Fry establishes a direct relation between his art and even his technique and the drama of Shakespeare's age.

Stylistic comparisons with Fry's comedies are naturally not

[1] *Scrutiny*, vol. XVIII, n. 1, June 1951, pp. 78 ff.
[2] C. Fry, 'Poetry and the Theatre', in *Adam International Review*, XIX, 1951, nos., 214–15, p. 3.   [3] *Ibid.*, p. 8.

to be looked for in Shakespeare's histories and later tragedies. Let us take first a passage from a comparatively early play, *Romeo and Juliet,* where Shakespeare has recourse to a fairly far-fetched simile and metaphoric imagery.

> O, she doth teach the torches to burn bright!
> It seems she hangs upon the cheek of night
> Like a rich jewel in an Ethiop's ear;
> Beauty too rich for use, for earth too dear.[1]

I have chosen these lines because they reveal Shakespeare's wit at its most earnest: it is the first glimpse Romeo gets of Juliet, and we are meant to take his words seriously as revealing his change from the academic display of love for Rosaline to the deep onrush of real feeling for Juliet. The lines ring true, but the imagery remains formal, with that jewel in the Ethiope's ear which comes straight from the repertoire of exotic similes in Euphuistic writings. The last line, for all its sincerity and beauty, is the exact and perfect application of a rhetorical figure, and as nobly rhetorical is the exclamative sentence at the beginning. The passage could be taken therefore as an example of mature Euphuism, where the intensity of feeling is reached through an extremely formal rhetorical language.

Now, in Fry the imagery is as dazzling as in the early Shakespeare, but it is founded on a greater concentration of metaphors rather than on lengthy similes. The simile of the gallows, in the first Fry passage quoted, is lengthy, but is continually broken by supplementary images taken from surprisingly incongruous objects. And, paradoxical as they appear, these objects are more commonplace than the jewel or the Ethiope's ear. The rhetorical exclamations and conventions of Romeo's speech are absent in Fry. And another substantial difference must be noted: Romeo's language suits Romeo's character to the point of identifying him as an individual, and the same could be said of Mercutio, the Nurse, old Capulet or Juliet. They all use the same witty or conceited style, but each

---

[1] *Romeo and Juliet,* I, v, ll. 46 ff.

of them has a distinct personality, being made to act conse-
quently and to have a meaning beyond his or her language; in
Fry instead, as we have seen, the life of the whole play is merely
verbal and there is no attempt to differentiate characters. Indeed
it is practically impossible to assign isolated speeches to any
particular speaker.

There are then clear differences between Fry's technique and
the early Shakespeare's, both in the quality of wit and in the
degree of characterization. It is interesting to turn, to find a
closer stylistic analogy between the two, to Shakespeare's late
romances, where, as S. L. Bethell rightly remarks, the characters 'are less important as persons than as symbols, and what
they are is much less important than what they say'.[1] In the
Winter's Tale Shakespeare once again enhances the resplendent
beauty of the heroine by the blackness of the Ethiope:

> I take thy hand, this hand
> As soft as dove's down and as white as it,
> Or Ethiopian's tooth, or the fann'd snow, that's bolted
> By the northern blasts twice over.[2]

Here again is a serried array of metaphors and similes with the
touch of extravagance characteristic of wit, but it is a far cry
from the style of Romeo. The formal image of the splendour of
the jewel on the negress is replaced by a rapid flashing of teeth;
not a whole sentence but two words are sufficient to convey the
image of gleaming whiteness—and the other similes, though
accumulated, are in themselves extremely concentrated: the
snow 'bolted . . . twice over' is assimilated to flour, adding another implicit comparison of whiteness, though not overtly
mentioned. The images this time are very concrete, many of
them everyday, and their expression is elliptical, in direct contrast with the formal completeness and balancing of contrasting
parts we saw in *Romeo and Juliet*. The rhythm of the lines is no
longer varied only by the changes in stress pattern: it is altogether freer and more flexible, following the natural stressing of

[1] S. L. Bethell, *The Winter's Tale: A Study*, London (1948?), p. 23.
[2] *Winter's Tale*, IV, iv, ll. 373 ff.

normal speech, and at the same time seconding the alternation of images. In other words, Shakespeare has left the abstract conceits of the Euphuistic convention at the close of the sixteenth century, and has passed to the concentrated and concrete conceits characteristic of the Donne phase of Mannerism.

In his preface to *Cymbeline,* Granville-Barker spoke of a 'new Euphuism' in Shakespeare's last plays, a Euphuism of imagination rather than expression.[1] This can be considered a good working definition, provided we take Euphuism to mean 'conceit' or rather 'wit'. Indeed, in the late Shakespearian plays, punning, rhetorical devices and elaborate similes have largely disappeared, to be replaced by a more concise and varied diction. On the other hand it has been noticed again and again how 'unrealistic' these plays are, and how crammed with impossible adventures. The plots are absurd, and show no attempt at logical consistency. The characters are hardly individualized, except in the most external and schematic way, and there is no differentiation in their way of expressing themselves. Finally, the scenes are set on the 'sea-coast of Bohemia', or an 'island full of noises', and there is a deliberate disregard for time and space. In the same way in Fry's plays we are transferred to fairylands outside space and time (nobody can be deceived into believing in the modern English mansion of *Venus Observed,* or the fifteenth-century market town of *The Lady's Not for Burning*), and the characters are vague: it hardly matters who is speaking lines which are constantly ingenious.

But still more important is a comparison of styles. Very seldom in Fry we find the straightforward play on words which was so common in Shakespeare's early comedies. He may play with the rhetorical questions and exclamations of the early Shakespeare, like:

> But, soft! what light through yonder window breaks?
> It is the east, and Juliet is the sun!—[2]

---

[1] H. Granville-Barker, *Prefaces to Shakespeare, Second Series,* London, 1930, p. 288. [2] *Romeo and Juliet,* II, ii, ll. 2–3.

But here is the result, a description of Jennet's entrance in *The Lady's Not for Burning*:

> *Nicholas:* Humphrey, poppin,
> Draw back the curtains. I have a sense of daylight.
> *Humphrey:* It seems we're facing east.[1]

Fry knows that the hearer will immediately think of Juliet; the lines are therefore in part a nod from the author to the audience and in part a borrowed evocation of beauty. Perhaps this is too obvious (or too like a music-hall song) to satisfy a very exacting taste, but from the exclusively technical point of view Fry is concentrating a Shakespearian simile in an elliptical form: it is implied, not stated.

This use of implication instead of full statement has been recognized as one of the distinctions between the Metaphysical poetry and that which preceded it; and, with its frequent jump of logical links, it is also a feature of modern poetry. But it is too often forgotten that Shakespeare too was tending to concentrate the imagery in the same way in his last plays. The passage quoted from the *Winter's Tale* may provide, in its last two lines, an example of concentration of metaphor in its highest form. And for his later use of elliptical imagery, we can compare the diluted description of Clarence's dream in *Richard III*:

> Methought I saw a thousand fearful wrecks,
> A thousand men that fishes gnaw'd upon;
> Wedges of gold, great anchors, heaps of pearl,
> Inestimable stones, unvalu'd jewels,
> All scatter'd in the bottom of the sea.
> Some lay in dead men's skulls; and in those holes
> Where eyes did once inhabit, there were crept,
> As't were in scorn of eyes, reflecting gems,
> That woo'd the slimy bottom of the deep,
> And mock'd the dead bones that lay scatter'd by.[2]

---

[1] *The Lady's Not for Burning*, cit., p. 68.
[2] *Richard III*, I, iv, ll. 24 ff.

with Ariel's song:

> Full fathom five thy father lies,
> Of his bones are coral made;
> Those are pearls that were his eyes;
> Nothing of him that doth fade
> But doth suffer a sea-change
> Into something rich and strange.[1]

The feeling of wonder in the line 'Those are pearls that were his eyes' is due to our ignorance of the logical transition. This passage has been extremely popular with modern poets, and has even been interpreted as a definition of poetry and its function. It is one of the fundamental leit-motifs of *The Waste Land,* and it recurs even in Eliot's criticism.[2] We saw it remembered by Stephen Dedalus during his walk on Dublin strand in *Ulysses,*[3] and even Eugenio Montale, the Italian poet who shows himself to be most aware of the development of contemporary world poetry, introduces it into one of his mature poems.[4] The fact is that, even before the critics revived a keen interest in Shakespeare's last plays, they seemed to be favourites of the most 'revolutionary' poets. In Eliot this is testified not only by the echoes from *The Tempest,* but by a poem like *Marina,* or even the presumably unconscious recollection of scenes from *Cymbeline* in *The Waste Land,* which I have illustrated in a previous essay. We could quote also Auden's *The Sea and the Mirror,* or Dylan Thomas' *A Winter Tale.* The critics' tendency, and apparently the poets' also, has been to read a more or less strict symbolic meaning in the last plays, the expression of Shakespeare's last phase of thought. I will not discuss this belief, but I want to say that in my opinion what largely (and more or less consciously) attracted the attention of the modern

---

[1] *The Tempest,* I, ii, ll. 396 ff. The comparison was suggested by H. W. Wells, *Poetic Imagery Illustrated from Elizabethan Literature,* New York, 1924, p. 101.

[2] T. S. Eliot, *The Use of Poetry and the Use of Criticism,* cit., p. 146.

[3] See pp. 81–3 of the present book.

[4] In the poem *Il ramarro, se scocca . . .,* in *Le Occasioni,* Turin, 1940, p. 49.

creative writers to Shakespeare's romances, was their stylistic quality.

We noticed that in them there is a resurgence of the taste for romance of the Arcadian type. But at the same time the diction, which we should expect to find extremely mannered, appropriate to such plots, yet appears very different from that of the early plays. It is a mannerism which would have been impossible before the development now known as Metaphysical poetry, a change of technique as well as of thought and mood. Of course, even Lyly's far-fetched similes are complicated or modified by the association of homely and familiar imagery, to reach, in the happiest moments, that 'fusion of the colloquial and the cosmic, of levity and seriousness' which is acknowledged as a characteristic of Metaphysical poetry; and a prefiguration of Metaphysical imagery may be found in Shakespeare's problem plays and great tragedies. But it is particularly interesting to our purpose to note the difference in intensity and structural importance of this kind of imagery between the middle and the last group of Shakespeare's plays. While, for example, in *Troilus and Cressida* the images, expressed in this synthesizing language, are all contributing to create a definite atmosphere and a unique intellectual tension, in the *Winter's Tale* or even in *The Tempest* they appear more loosely scattered, so that instead of achieving a dramatic concentration of feeling and mental power they create indefinite intellectual overtones, giving an unexpected dimension of depth to the most artificial plots. Conceit passes therefore from the Elizabethan paradoxical rhetoric, which was essentially a brilliant decoration of serious thought and feeling, through the Donne type, where a forceful synthesis of thought and feeling is directly expressed in concentrated imagery, to the 'last plays' phase, where the content of thought is in its turn a sort of decoration superimposed onto a slight and even inconsequential narrative.

The modern English poets, as it seems to me, seized eagerly upon this unification of sensibility (in Eliot's words), or the yoking together of heterogeneous ideas (according to Dr. Johnson), which had been most effectively achieved by the major Metaphysical poets. This led them to take a new interest also in Shakespeare's last tragicomedies where, beyond the violent concentration of symbol and vision compassed by Donne, there appears, in a similar form, a more elusive symbolism and a more restful vision; where, in other words, the decorative possibilities of intellectual symbols were revealed. Fry, in spite of his frequently reducing it all to a superficial game, is an example of the result of this new approach: his witticism and his style of repartee announce his closeness, in the technique of dialogue and of scene construction, to Wilde (the culmination of another mannerism, of a new preciosity); his connection with (and departure from) Eliot has been seen through Charles Williams; his plays show that, having absorbed these two recent influences, his technique has evolved towards a stage akin to that of Shakespeare's last plays. Again I must remind the reader that the operative word here is technique, and I am in no way attempting an appraisal of absolute values, or to place on the same artistic plane a popular verse-playwright and the greatest of English poets.

Apart from the paradoxical tone, in which the lesson of Wilde's comedies is very clear, there appears in *A Phoenix Too Frequent, The Lady's Not for Burning,* and *Venus Observed,* an undercurrent of elusive symbolism, which perhaps is due only to their luxuriance of both far-fetched and familiar imagery couched in a highly fantastic and at the same time colloquial language. But it may well be, in the words of Georges-Albert Astre, 'la réapparition du comique métaphysique qui est, en fait, le sens très aigu de l'absurde de la condition humaine quand elle se confronte à la création divine; mais sans que cet absurde retentisse au delà de l'humour'.[1] It may be, too, the

---

[1] G.-A. Astre, *Christopher Fry et la résurrection du poème dramatique,* in *Critique,* n. 44, Jan. 1951, p. 25 (reprinted in *Adam International Review,* XIX, nos. 214–15 (1951), pp. 20–3). Astre comments: 'Aristophane et Shakespeare connurent parfaitement cette attitude.'

application of Fry's statement: 'Comedy is an escape not from truth but from despair: a narrow escape into faith . . . to affirm life and assimilate death and persevere in joy.'[1] The danger is that the escape should become that of pure form, and I do not know that Fry has avoided it. 'What a wonderful thing is metaphor' conveys a feeling very close to that expressed in *The Importance of Being Earnest*, when Algernon comments on a witticism of his (and not a very good one at that): 'It is perfectly phrased! And quite as true as any observation in civilized life should be.' One may suspect that everything is solved on the verbal and technical plane, which prompts such *tours de force* as this:

> There isn't any reason
> Why a sentence, I suppose, once it begins,
> Once it has risen to the lips at all
> And finds itself happily wandering
> Through shady vowels and over consonants
> Where ink's been spilt like rivers or like blood
> Flowing for the cause of some half-truth
> Or a dogma now out-moded, shouldn't go
> Endlessly moving in grave periphrasis
> And phrase in linking phrase, with commas falling
> As airily as lime flowers, intermittently,
> Uninterrupting, scarcely troubling
> The mild and fragile progress of the sense
> Which trills trebling like a pebbled stream
> Or lowers towards an oath-intoning ocean
> Or with a careless and forgetful music
> Looping and threading, tuning and entwining,
> Flings a babel of bells, a carolling
> Of such various vowels the ear can almost feel
> The soul of sound when it lay in chaos yearning
> For the tongue to be created: such a hymn
> If not as lovely, then as interminable,
> As restless, and as heartless, as the hymn
> Which in the tower of heaven the muted spheres

---

[1] 'Comedy', in *The Adelphi*, New series, vol. 27, n. 1, Nov. 1950.

With every rippling harp and windy horn
Played for incidental harmony
Over the mouldering rafters of the world,
Rafters which seldom cared to ring, preferring
The functional death-watch beetle, stark, staccato,
Economical as a knuckle bone,
Strict, correct, but undelighting
Like a cleric jigging in the saturnalia,
The saturnalia we all must keep,
Green-growing and rash with life,
Our milchy, mortal, auroral, jovial,
Harsh, unedifying world,
Where every circle of grass can show a dragon
And every pool's as populous as Penge,
Where birds, with taffeta flying, scarf the air
On autumn evenings, and a sentence once
Begun goes on and on, there being no reason
To draw to any conclusion so long as breath
Shall last, except that breath
Can't last much longer.[1]

This is indeed the last phase of Mannerism, approaching stylistically that frenetic movement enclosed in strict rhetorical patterns which was characteristic of the Borrominian phase of Baroque. It can be seen how closely the movement of the passage quoted approaches Crashaw's *Musicks Duell*:

The humourous strings expound his learned touch,
By various Glosses; now they seeme to grutch,
And murmur in a buzzing din, then gingle
In shrill tongu'd accents: striving to bee single.
Every smooth turne, every delicious stroke
Gives life to some new Grace; thus doth h'invoke
Sweetnesse by all her names; thus, bravely thus
(Fraught with a fury so harmonious)
The Lutes light *Genius* now does proudly rise,
Heav'd on the surges of swolne Rapsodyes.
Whose flourish (Meteor-like) doth curle the aire
With flash of high-borne fancyes: here and there

---

[1] *Venus Observed*, London, 1950, pp. 62-3.

Dancing in lofty measures, and anon
Creeps on the soft touch of a tender tone:
Whose trembling murmurs melting in wild aires
Runs to and fro, complaining his sweet cares
Because the pretious mysteries that dwell
In musick's ravish't soule hee dare not tell,
But whisper to the world: thus doe they vary
Each string his Note, as if they meant to carry
Their Masters blest soule (snatcht out at his Eares
By strong Extasy) through all the sphaeres
Of Musicks heaven; and seat it there on high
In th' *Empyraeum* of pure Harmony.
At length (after so long, so loud a strife
Of all the strings still breathing the best life
Of blest variety attending on
His fingers fairest revolution
In many a sweet rise, many as sweet a fall)
A full-mouth *Diapason* swallowes all.[1]

Crashaw in fact is the only English poet for whom nobody has questioned the appropriateness of the epithet 'Baroque'. The movement of the two passages is very similar but not quite identical, for in Crashaw we can detect a greater balance, a sense of symmetry and conclusion. This is indeed the distinction between late Mannerism and full Baroque, and to make it clearer we could perhaps look at what was happening in Shakespeare's time.

What I should like to call Manneristic poetry in the theatre developed from the Euphuism of the early Shakespearian plays, through the metaphysical concentration of Chapman, and of Shakespeare's major tragedies, to the later Shakespearian technique which we have already discussed. These three stages are obviously representative of three phases in the general mental attitude of the audiences which accepted them. Apart from the strictly political events, which have been, if anything,

[1] I am indebted to Prof. Praz for pointing out the similarity between Fry's passage and Crashaw's (*Musicks Duell*, ll. 127 ff.).

over-emphasized by the critics, they mirror at first the last stage of humanism, when faith in the ability and individuality of man was already dwindling, and rhetoric was used to conceal doubt, while the need for an imaginative release was creating the Marlowe superman; in the second place there came (partly as an aftermath of recent scientific discoveries and of religious upheavals) the realization of the loss of faith in man, and the feeling of shock, of frenetic revolt and violent discussion of all accepted values; finally there is a time when the shock is superseded by a quieter struggle to reach some moorings, a feeling of overconsciousness which induced the most enterprising spirits to proceed with caution, with the elegance and agility of ropedancers, aware of the danger they are running and trying to overcome it by elegance and beauty. In this spirit, I think, the last plays of Shakespeare were written. From them it is a short step to early Baroque, where a less precarious sense of balance is achieved, by some through weariness and exhaustion, through the sheer physical need for rest, by others through the affirmation of new mental values and creeds. (The plays of Beaumont and Fletcher, where relaxation is found in its most common form—escapism, can be taken as representative of the first aspect of early Baroque; and Milton's *Comus,* setting down firmer beliefs, of the second.)

It is significant too, in respect of what has been said about the loss of faith in man as an individual, to note the progressive disappearance of character in the later Shakespeare and in Beaumont and Fletcher. As Prof. Mincoff noted speaking of the influence of D'Urfé on this famous pair of English playwrights, their plays are 'a gallery, not of portraits, but of emotional situations'; they had discovered that 'psychological interest could be achieved not only by the creation of individual characters and sharply drawn portraits . . . but by the play of emotions in a character conceived without any personality of its own'.[1] I will not go into this point now, but I will

[1] M. Mincoff, 'The Social Background of Beaumont and Fletcher', in *English Miscellany*, I, Rome, 1950, pp. 24-5.

only recall what has been said about lack of characterization in Fry.

Going back to him and to his box-office success, we find that the modern theatre audiences enjoyed, in the last years of the nineteenth century, all Wilde's preciosity of wit; at the same time, as the cracks in a world and society which seemed to have reached perfection became more visible, they accepted the disruptive criticism of Ibsen or Shaw. Between the two wars, when poets and critics, rediscovering Donne, had recognized the affinity of the early seventeenth-century intellectual crisis with that of our own time, the theatre audiences confirmed the diagnosis by flocking to a number of 'plays of ideas' where irony and pessimism soon became the leading motives. But after the second world war, swept by another wave of disillusionment and anxiety, the theatre-goers found themselves ready to accept not so much raw ideas and indictments of man, as some sort of release from their daily scepticism, some escape into legend and myth which would project the dreariness of the modern world, tired of its confused struggle, into a realm of beauty and lightness. And together with this, the reaction against scepticism brought back a religious sense which is not so much an exposition of definite creeds and dogmas, but is rather the expression of a more or less vague aspiration. The French critic quoted above writes:

En retrouvant à la fois le mythique et le sacré, notre époque s'arroge à nouveau le droit de badiner avec les dieux. Elle rencontre du même coup l'une des sources les plus profondes de la poésie dramatique, cette surimpression constante d'une destinée commune, toute contingente et empêtrée dans l'humanité, et d'un destin légendaire, rêvé, projeté sur un écran d'humanité. Et c'est une lourde erreur de croire que le sacré exclut le comique: s'amusent avec lui en parfaite familiarité ceux qui sont les plus croyants, ou les plus incroyants, donc vraiment libres.[1]

Certainly the way to Fry was paved by the French playwrights like Giraudoux, Cocteau and Anouilh, with their

[1] G.-A. Astre, *loc. cit.,* p. 25.

serious and ironical *badinage* with ancient myths. We could even suspect that Fry has deliberately fused their technique with Eliot's suggestion that the music-hall comedian was the best material with which to build the new poetry drama—but has done it in the way that Eliot most dreaded:

I am aware—Eliot wrote—that this is a dangerous suggestion to make. For every person who is likely to consider it seriously there are a dozen toymakers who would leap to tickle aesthetic society into one more quiver and giggle of art debauch.[1]

All the same, Fry is certainly sincere when he writes:

I know that when I set about writing a comedy the idea presents itself to me first of all as tragedy. . . . If the characters were not qualified for tragedy there would be no comedy, and to some extent I have to cross the one before I can light on the other. In a century less flayed and quivering we might reach it more directly; but not now unless every word we write is going to mock us.[2]

With a sense of tragedy, and aware of the anxiety of our age, he is determined to avoid the negative of irony and to reach beyond it to something positive: the joy of comedy and the security of religion. He seems to have achieved a remarkable balance between these two objectives in *A Sleep of Prisoners* (1951). His previous comedies could be taken as mere fireworks, displaying his deftness in steering clear, in a perpetual airy gaiety, of the rough edges of realism and serious thinking, though letting his audience clearly realize their existence. His obvious awareness of the tangle of complex problems which beset modern man added the thrill of danger to his act, and his graceful way of keeping perpetually though precariously balanced above those problems, gained him the applause due to a successful acrobat.

On the other hand, his previous religious plays were either technical experiments or occasional pieces of no great origin-

[1] T. S. Eliot, *The Sacred Wood*, cit., p. 70; see p. 109 of the present book.
[2] 'Comedy', in *The Adelphi*, cit., p. 28.

ality. Of the published ones, *The Boy with a Cart* (1938) is little more than a competent rendering of a medieval legend in the form of a miracle play; what humour there is, is rather of situation, exploiting fully the naivety of the story. *The Firstborn* (1946) is a much more ambitious attempt, this time at tragedy. The alternation of poetry and bathos as Fry struggled towards the polished form of his later plays can be seen in the following passage, which is representative of many in *The Firstborn*:

> Fowling,
> I clucked and clapped as the sun rose
> And up shot so much whistle and whirr
> I could only hold my spear and laugh.
> All the indignant wings of the marshes
> Flocking to the banner of Tuesday
> To avoid the Prince of Egypt.
> Off they flapped into the mist
> Looking about for Monday
> The day they had lived in peace: and finding nothing
> Back they wheeled to Tuesday.
> I had recovered myself by then and killed
> One that had the breast of a chestnut.
> At last he could feel the uninterrupted darkness
> Of an addled egg. I watched his nerves flinching
> As they felt how dark the darkness was.
> I found myself trying to peer into his death.
> It seemed a long way down. The morning and it
> Were oddly separate,
> Though the bird lay in the sun: separate somehow
> Even from contemplation.[1]

In *Thor, with Angels* (1948) Fry shows mastery of diction, but the play suffers from the limitations of the set form and occasion for which it was written, the Canterbury Festival of 1948.

A Sleep of Prisoners, a play to be performed in a church, should logically be classed with his other religious plays. And it is one of them, but with a difference. First of all, the scheme

[1] C. Fry, *The Firstborn*, Cambridge, 1946, pp. 22–3.

of the mystery or miracle play has been discarded: it is not only a play that can be performed in a church, it is a play that has the interior or a church as its permanent set. In this way Fry has achieved a compromise between the church play and the lay play. Instead of, like Eliot, introducing religion into a cocktail party, he has transferred the world as represented by four soldier-prisoners, into his church. This allows him to introduce the wit of the profane into the sacred precincts, where it is even heightened by contrast with the setting, while at the same time the audience is compelled to believe in the seriousness of his religious message. Fry's rendering of military swearing modified by his knack for verbal invention ('Too many pricking thistles in this straw' or 'Those bleating sheep can look after them-selves'[1]) is an example of his ability in emphasizing this contrast.

In the earlier Fry the lightness of touch transformed all serious issues into pure jokes, or at least exempted the hearers from taking them seriously. Instead, in the context of *A Sleep of Prisoners* one cannot ignore the implication of a passage like the following, although Fry's pleasure in the sound of words, tricks of alliteration, punning and mixing of the colloquial and poetic are as lively as ever:

Fish, fish, fish in the sea, you flash
Through your clouds of water like the war in heaven:
Angel-fish and swordfish, the silver troops . . .
And I am salt and sick on a raft above you,
Wondering for land, but there's no homeward
I can see.
God, have mercy
On our sick shoals, darting and dying.
We're strange fish to you. How long
Can you drift over our sea, and not give up
The ghost of hope? The air is bright between us.
The flying fish make occasional rainbows,
But land, your land and mine, is nowhere yet.[2]

---

[1] C. Fry, *A Sleep of Prisoners*, London, 1951, pp. 3 and 12.
[2] *A Sleep of Prisoners*, cit., p. 37.

The love of metaphor, which we saw as one of the happiest features of Fry's style in his comedies, assumes here a more complex form: indeed, the whole play can be considered as an extended metaphor of the condition of man and his relation to God, including in turn the separate metaphors of the four characters of the play, who are used allusively to represent man's passions and feelings. I am now speaking of characters, though earlier in this essay I have said how characterization had practically disappeared from Fry's plays. The fact is that at first sight the four figures appearing in *A Sleep of Prisoners* and identifying themselves with different Biblical characters seem more clearly defined than the poetical creations appearing in Fry's other plays. But a closer examination will reveal that the apparent deepening of the characterization takes place not through a more precise individualization, but through the projection into the past of the figures of the four soldiers. Once again they are not real characters, but rather human prototypes. Their link with the present is merely in the allusions to their temporary predicament as prisoners of war. But it is made clear that the condition of prisoner is only a metaphor for the prison of the flesh. In their dreams they re-enact the stories of Cain and Abel, David and Absalom, Abraham and Isaac, and the Fiery Furnace, and they do become the Biblical figures, abolishing time and space and also their own separate personalities, to represent merely Man before God.

The projection of the characters into the past is not of course a new invention of Fry's. As we saw, Eliot's Tiresias in *The Waste Land* is another figure containing all the past and the future. Charles Williams himself had introduced characters conceived as Chinese boxes containing one inside the other different figures from the past in his verse play *Seed of Adam*. In his notes already quoted we can see how simple his conception is:

I was prepared to bring in anyone. After all, the Nativity was a local event, besides being universal. Augustus and so on. How did we, if we did, bring in Augustus? How did we keep in Adam and keep out Augustus? Now remark this is a real technical difficulty . . . and then one of those admirable clicks happened and I said to anybody: 'Good God! Adam-Augustus, Augustus-Adam.' Admirable—*if* it could be done.[1]

Now, how did Fry solve the same technical difficulty that faced Williams, how did he bring in his group of Biblical characters to be identified with the four soldiers, our contemporaries? In his prefatory letter to the play Fry writes that *A Sleep of Prisoners* has

a complicated design where each of four men is seen through the sleeping thoughts of the others, and each, in his own dream, speaks as at heart he is, not as he believes himself to be. In the later part of Corporal Adams' dream the dream changes to a state of thought entered into by all the sleeping men, as though, sharing their prison life, they shared, for a few moments of the night, their sleeping life also.[2]

This conception is curiously near that of Joyce in *Finnegans Wake*. Surprising as the Fry-Joyce parallel may appear, both works adopt similar complicated dream structures. Their action (if it can be called so) is enclosed in the space of one night, but is crowded with the past of history and legend. The projection of the past into the present and vice versa is reached in both cases by means of the dream, which demolishes the barrier between consciousness and the subliminal world of thought and feeling which is revealed through the different personification each character assumes. Of course in *A Sleep of Prisoners* no figure possesses the unlimited Protean faculty of H. C. E. in *Finnegans Wake,* and the different impersonations of the four characters in Fry's play have each a precise religious meaning. But in both works full advantage is taken of the interest in the deeper levels of consciousness roused by psycho-

[1] C. Williams, *Seed of Adam,* cit., p. 95.
[2] C. Fry, *A Sleep of Prisoners,* letter to Robert Gittings.

analysis and in the release from conscious control brought about by sleep. (It is interesting to see how Eliot introduces a psychologist as the *deus ex machina* of *The Cocktail Party*, to establish the link and the contrast between the two ways of exploring man's inner life: religion and psychology.) The connection between Fry's play and *Finnegans Wake* is not only in the design of the two works, but also in more superficial features. Here, for instance, is how one of Fry's characters sinks from waking consciousness to dream consciousness:

> Who's that, fallen out? How many men?
> How many? I said only one.
> One was enough.
> No, no, no, I didn't ask to be God.
> No one else prepared to spell the words.
> Spellbound. B-o-u-n-d. Ah-h-h-h . . .
> It's old Adam, old, old, old Adam.
> Out of bounds. No one said fall out.
> What time did you go to bad?
> Sorrow, Adam, stremely sorrow.[1]

This verbal dissolution is intended as something more than Jabberwocky: not as just another amusing invention, but a transference of planes. It is as deliberate as *Finnegans Wake*. So too is the verbal concentration and ambivalence of

> What bastard language
> Is he talking? Are we supposed to guess?
> Police on earth. Aggression is the better
> Part of Allah. Liberating very high
> The dying and the dead. Freedom, freedom.[2]

Indeed this bastard language, generated by the union of opposites, is probably a conscious adoption of Joyce's technique, a vulgarization of it.

Returning to Fry's definition of his play, the emphasis on the 'complicated design' is particularly significant. His comedies

[1] C. Fry *A Sleep of Prisoners*, cit., p. 10.
[2] C. Fry, *A Sleep of Prisoners*, cit., p. 43.

give the impression of things put together scene after scene, caring mainly for the sentence, the line or the word, with only a vague preoccupation for the resulting structure. Instead, in *A Sleep of Prisoners* we find a methodical plan: it is an intellectual construction on a carefully worked out scheme. Fry seems to have acquired a new feeling for proportion, symmetry and balance of parts. Though the verbal decoration is still exuberant and whimsical, the emphasis is this time on the structural parts of the play. So much so that there are hardly any single lines or speeches that can be taken out of their context and even superficially impress the reader or the hearer: they are all subservient to the final impression of the play as a whole.

All the same, the final result retains that character of extravagant elegance and whimsical richness of detail that is to be found in Fry's previous plays. Fry is still a man belonging to an age of anxiety, and the formal balance reached in his last work is still precarious: his art is still the art of the funambulist. Only, the tendency to enclose the frenetic movement and the rhetorical exuberance of his writing in a balanced formal pattern seems to indicate that Fry is proceeding from a Manneristic form towards the quieter Baroque.

The Moment as a Time Unit in Fiction

~~~~~~

THE presence of the past is one of the fundamental motifs of Eliot's poetry—or we should rather say that Eliot's achievement is the full realization and expression of this presence, the consciousness of which is detectable in the work of writers of all times. Even before writing *The Waste Land* and *Gerontion,* Eliot had stated:

Tradition . . . involves, in the first place, the historical sense, which we may call nearly indispensable to anyone who would continue to be a poet beyond his twenty-fifth year; and the historical sense involves a perception not only of the pastness of the past, but of its presence. . . . This historical sense, which is a sense of the timeless as well as of the temporal and of the timeless and of the temporal together, is what makes a writer traditional. And it is at the same time what makes a writer most acutely conscious of his place in time, of his own contemporaneity.[1]

But in Eliot's later poetry alongside this awareness of the past there is a growing insistence on the expression of the moment when this awareness is realized. We have seen in a previous essay [2] how important the 'moment in the Rose-garden' became for Eliot. It is, as Mr. Unger has pointed out, the 'still point of

---

[1] 'Tradition and the Individual Talent', in *Selected Essays,* cit., p. 14.
[2] 'The Lotus and the Rose', see pp. 89-103 of the present volume.

the turning world': a timeless moment of illumination, a meeting of time and eternity:

> To be conscious is not to be in time
> But only in time can the moment in the rose-garden . . .
> Be remembered; involved with past and future.
> Only through time time is conquered.[1]

This idea of the moment as a fundamental unit containing life at its fullest, present, past and future, is a corollary to Eliot's earlier conception of the presence of the past. But he was neither the only writer nor the first to conceive this idea. In studying the 'lotus' symbol, which, together with the 'shaft of sunlight',[2] is another of the images used by Eliot to express his realization of the complexity and depth of life contained in the space of a single moment, we saw how Marcel Proust and D. H. Lawrence had already used it for the same purpose. For Proust the famous experience of the *madeleine* was an instant of extremely acute awareness which recalled a whole world of the past into the reality of the present, and sent him *à la recherche du temps perdu*. For Lawrence the moment meant an intensified realization of all his physical and mental potentialities. But they both lacked a deep historical sense, so that their moments of revelation are revelations of themselves, of the worlds of their own feelings and experiences. For Eliot, instead, with his strong sense of history and tradition, the revelation is that of historical and universal values. This universal view is at the root of a philosophical attitude, but the very unaccountability of the moment of revelation suggests a religious interpretation.[3] The same could certainly not be said of Ezra Pound, though he too, at about the same time, based on the moment his doctrine of Imagism:

---

[1] *Four Quartets*, cit., p. 10.

[2] See the essay 'Eliot and the Theatre', in the present volume, pp. 143–4.

[3] The religious and historical significance given to the moment is clearly stated in the seventh chorus of *The Rock* (*Collected Poems*, cit., p. 173).

The Moment as a Time Unit in Fiction

An Image is that which presents an intellectual and emotional complex in an instant of time.[1]

Pound was approaching the new realization of the importance of the moment from an aesthetic point of view, Proust from an individualistic and Lawrence from a sensuous one, while Eliot, influenced perhaps by their conceptions, finally reached a religious standpoint.

But, apart from these distinctions, what I intend to discuss is this new conception of time which originated in the heightened awareness of the intensity of the moment and of the momentary experiences. The acute preoccupation of the modern writers with time is now an acknowledged fact and even a commonplace of critical jargon. This has induced several authors who had only a dim apprehension of its real significance, to take advantage of the great general interest aroused in time and memory, and to play successful tricks with them. J. B. Priestley's time plays (in which he takes advantage of recent psychological theories on the subject) are an example of the cleverest form this tendency assumes; works like Hilton's *Lost Horizon* show how its magical suggestions can be commercialized. The extremely wide use of the flashback technique in films and even in plays, like Arthur Miller's pretentious *Death of a Salesman,* is significant too. Finally a story like Edmund Wilson's *Ellen Terhune* [2] shows how these suggestions can work on a fully mature critical mind which had also been influenced by Henry James' unfinished novel *The Sense of the Past.* But this is by the way.

The first to confront the problem with full consciousness in the narrative field of English literature were James Joyce and Virginia Woolf. As early as 1905 Joyce had built up his theory of the epiphanies [3] which he expounded in the first draft of *The*

[1] E. Pound, *A Few Don'ts by an Imagist* (1913).

[2] First published in *The Partisan Review*; now in *Memoirs from Hecate Country,* English edition, London, 1951, pp. 23–69.

[3] For all this part I am very much indebted to Theodore Spencer's introduction to *Stephen Hero* (Star editions, London, 1944, pp. 13–14) and to I. Hendry,

Portrait of the Artist as a Young Man, now published under the title of *Stephen Hero*:

> By an epiphany he meant a sudden spiritual manifestation, whether in the vulgarity of speech or of gesture or in a memorable phase of the mind itself. He believed that it was for the man of letters to record these epiphanies with extreme care, seeing that they themselves are the most delicate and evanescent of moments. He told Cranly that the clock of the Ballast Office was capable of an epiphany. . . .
> —Yes, said Stephen. I will pass it time after time, allude to it, catch a glimpse of it. It is only an item in the catalogue of Dublin's street furniture. Then all at once I see it and I know at once what it is: epiphany.—
> —What?—
> —Imagine my glimpses at the clock as the gropings of a spiritual eye which seeks to adjust its vision to an exact focus. The moment the focus is reached the object is epiphanized. . . .[1]

Stephen goes on expounding at some length Aquinas' theory of beauty, with its three qualities: integrity, symmetry and radiance. Having dealt with the first two, Stephen proceeds:

> —Now for the third quality. For a long time I couldn't make out what Aquinas meant. . . . But I have solved it. *Claritas* is *quidditas.* After the analysis which discovers the second quality the mind makes the only logically possible synthesis and discovers the third quality. This is the moment which I call epiphany. First we recognize that the object is *one* integral thing, then we recognize that it is an organized composite structure, a *thing* in fact: finally, when the relation of the parts is exquisite, when the parts are adjusted to the special point, we recognize that it is *that* thing which it is. Its soul, its whatness, leaps to us from the vestment of its appearance. The soul of the commonest object, the structure of which is so adjusted, seems to us radiant. The object achieves its epiphany.

Joyce's Epiphanies, reprinted in *James Joyce: Two Decades of Criticism,* cit., pp. 27–46.
[1] *Stephen Hero,* cit., pp. 188–90.

The Moment as a Time Unit in Fiction

In spite of the fact that the whole of this passage was rejected in the final version of the *Portrait*, there is no doubt that the revolution Joyce affected in the form of the novel owes much to the idea here expressed. The epiphanies, these sudden perceptions, in the space of a moment, of the total meaning and character of a scene, of a person, of a phrase, can be expressed only in a language which will be able to extract the full meaning of each word with all its implications, a language where the intensity of the experience is matched by the verbal intensity. In *Ulysses* Joyce refers again to his epiphanies, and speaks with good-humoured detachment of Stephen's youthful ideal:

Books you were going to write with letters for titles. Have you read his F? O yes, but I prefer Q. Yes but W is wonderful. O yes, W. Remember your epiphanies on green oval leaves, deeply deep, copies to be sent if you died to all the great libraries in the world, including Alexandria? [1]

The one-letter titles are in my opinion a further proof of the need Joyce felt for concentration, to reach the maximum intensity in the minimum space of time. But in *Ulysses* what in fact he tried to do was to extend through the length of a whole day the state of epiphany. The revolution in the novel brought about by the stream of consciousness technique—the attempt to follow moment by moment the mental processes in one or more characters—is due mainly to the fact that this technique introduced a new conception of time. Even at its most developed stage, even with Henry James, the psychological novel was dealing with a sequence of external events which, although brought about by very subtle reactions of the characters and often very subtly analysed, still respected the calendar and the clock. Instead, in books like those of Joyce or Virginia Woolf there are events, but they are important only in so much as they are thought of at a certain moment; what matters is the feeling or thought of the moment, not what is happening.

Virginia Woolf's works are a series of attempts to fix exactly

[1] *Ulysses*, cit., p. 37.

179

what she called the 'moments of being' in the 'incessant shower of innumerable atoms' which is life. Her aim and her struggle are summarized by Lily Briscoe in the very last sentences of *To the Lighthouse* (1927):

> She looked at the steps; they were empty; she looked at her canvas; it was blurred. With a sudden intensity, as if she saw it clear for a second, she drew a line there, in the centre. It was done; it was finished. Yes, she thought, laying down her brush in extreme fatigue, I have had my vision.[1]

We can compare this late restatement of aim and achievement with the well-known earlier theoretical affirmation:

> Examine for a moment an ordinary mind on an ordinary day. The mind receives a myriad impressions—trivial, fantastic, evanescent, or engraved with the sharpness of steel. From all sides they come, an incessant shower of innumerable atoms; and as they fall, as they shape themselves into the life of Monday or Tuesday, the accent falls differently from of old; the moment of importance comes not here but there; so that, if a writer were a free man and not a slave, . . . there would be no plot, no comedy, no tragedy, no love interest or catastrophe in the accepted style . . . Life is not a series of gig lamps symmetrically arranged; life is a luminous halo, a semi-transparent envelope surrounding us from the beginning of consciousness to the end. Is it not the task of the novelist to convey this varying, this unknown and uncircumscribed spirit, whatever aberration and complexity it may display, with as little mixture of the alien and external as possible? We are not pleading merely for courage and sincerity; we are suggesting that the proper stuff of fiction is a little other than custom would have us believe it.[2]

Compared with this, the already quoted passage from *To the Lighthouse* reveals a new awareness of the effort implied in fixing the 'moment of importance'. Virginia Woolf seems to feel how shattering is the impact of a moment in which the whole of life

[1] V. Woolf, *To the Lighthouse*, London, 1927.
[2] *Modern Fiction*, written April 1919, collected in *The Common Reader*, First series, London, 1925, p. 189.

at its most intense is enclosed. The 'extreme fatigue' of Lily Briscoe is the fatigue of Virginia Woolf in trying to render in words the moment of vision. She realizes that everything must be contained in the minimum time unit, but becomes increasingly aware of the impossibility of sustaining the tension. Ten years after *To the Lighthouse,* in the last chapter of *The Years,* she writes:

> There must be another life, here and now, she repeated. This is too short, too broken. . . . She hollowed her hands in her lap. . . . She held her hands hollowed; she felt that she wanted to enclose the present moment; to make it stay; to fill it fuller and fuller, with the past, the present and the future, until it shone, whole, bright, deep with understanding.
> 'Edward', she began, trying to attract his attention. But he was not listening to her. . . . It's useless, she thought, opening her hands. It must drop. It must fall. And then? she thought.[1]

Virginia Woolf's novels are a series of efforts to express, and hold, the moment of vision. She felt this effort as a necessity, or as a mission. But she felt as well, more and more, that the moment, as soon as expressed, would drop, would fall. The variety of techniques she used—so that each of her novels was greeted upon its publication with the adjective 'experimental'— witnesses to her endless search for the novel-form which would substitute the single time unit of the fleeting instant for the restful time sequence of days, months and years. She tried to follow Joyce, selecting an ordinary day rich in intense moments of vision (*Mrs. Dalloway*); she bridged together two extended moments years apart (*To the Lighthouse*); she looked for some sort of relaxation in *Orlando,* playing with moments of history; she thought that the right momentary intensity could perhaps be reached through a consistent use of the stream of consciousness technique (*The Waves*); she singled out a whole series of moments over a distance of years (*The Years*); she hoped to sustain the necessary intensity by making the action last only a

---

[1] V. Woolf, *The Years,* London, 1937, pp. 461-2.

few hours and mixing together the temporal and the timeless through the performance of a pageant (*Between the Acts*). But the perpetual changes in technique are evidence of the fact that, perfect as each single book may be, the final novel-form substituting the traditional one was never found. As she says in the passage quoted from *The Years,* the momentary vision cannot be sustained for long: 'It must drop. It must fall. And then?' This question is a question posed also to the modern writer of fiction who will (or, as it seems, must) adopt as his time unit the single instant of utter awareness.

The fact is that the consciousness of the intensity of what happens in the moment requires an extremely high tension in writing, which becomes unbearable to both reader and writer when sustained for any length of time. At its most successful the result is a *tour de force.* Joyce, to sustain it in *Ulysses,* had to make recourse to a whole immense symbolic structure. Actually I think that the more and more frequent recourse of modern writers to ancient myths (as the French dramatists' remodelling of the stories of Orpheus or Antigone, Eliot himself basing his plays on the *Oresteia* or *Alcestis*) is due not only to the wish to give a new version of the fundamental human situations, or to the pleasure taken in brilliant intellectual *divertissements,* but also to their need of a solid framework, strong enough to support such tension in writing.

After *Ulysses,* Joyce, who had always taken a great interest in the form of words, tried to reach a maximum of intensity by increasing to the utmost limits the pregnancy of the words used. He felt that the momentary impressions we receive are so extremely complex and compressed, that although the complexity could only be expressed in many words, the compression required few. In this way he bred and compounded new words to form the unrecognizable language of *Finnegans Wake*; in it the concentration of meaning is reached at the expense of clarity, and at the same time the book, by taking the form of a dream, assumes the right of expanding the moment indefinitely. The solution found seems to evade the problem which still confronts the modern writer who wants to introduce the new time unit into the narrative tradition.

I am speaking particularly of the prose writers, because poetry, as a matter of fact, has always dealt with deep momentary intuitions. To take a random example, Thomas Hardy himself had collected part of his poems under the title *Moments of Vision*; and William Blake (a main influence on Joyce) had written:

Every Time less than a pulsation of the artery
Is equal in its period & value to Six Thousand Years,
For in this Period the Poet's Work is Done, and all the Great
Events of Time start forth & are conciev'd in such a Period,
Within a Moment, a Pulsation of the Artery.[1]

Of course, the fact that this has been realized also by the novelist, that the new time unit has come as the most revolutionary discovery of the century in the field of prose literature, has given the poets as well a new insight into their own work. As we have seen, to Eliot the realization of the supreme importance of the world contained in a moment gave a sense of such intensity of feeling that it could be equated only with religious experience. On the other hand the quality of poetic intuition has given prose that lyrical pace which is so evident in Virginia Woolf and James Joyce; it has stressed the already existing tendency to approach the two literary media. In fact, prose and poetry had never been closer to each other, even in their rhythms, diction and technical devices.

But, as I said, for the novelist the problem remains: when the time unit is reduced to Eliot's moment in time and timeless, Joyce's epiphany or Virginia Woolf's moment of being, there is not much scope for development of plot and action. It is impossible to build up a narrative in the tradition even of the

---

[1] W. Blake, *Milton,* book I, in *Poetry and Prose of W. B.,* ed. G. Keynes, 4th ed., London, 1939, p. 413. I find that also Virginia Woolf was struck by Hardy's expression, 'moments of vision'; see V. Woolf, *A Writer's Diary,* London, 1953, p. 98.

most penetrating psychological novel. Psychology has in fact spent itself. The psychological analysis has moved from the character to the moment of being. It is no longer a question of individual psychology, but of the analysis of the interplay of persons and things and atmosphere within a moment, as apprehended by one individual mind—the author's—in a phase of heightened perception. So the characters become mere projections of the author, as for instance can be clearly seen in *The Waves,* where all six characters are different aspects of Virginia Woolf which she had tried to separate.

We may say that if *Ulysses* is indeed the novel to end all novels, this is not because of its extravagance in technique, but because it was the first novel in which the consciousness of the new temporal perspective appeared. The technical experiments of Joyce and Virginia Woolf, which at first dazzled the readers, had the effect of diverting attention from the fundamental fact that these experiments were the result of the new conception of time, and set the still open problem of the treatment of this new element in fiction.

No wonder that critics complain that today there is no generation of novelists comparable to those writing in the 'twenties. Philip Toynbee for instance writes: 'That the English novel has declined is unlikely to be disputed.' [1] It is very nearly impossible for a sensitive author to ignore the impact of the transference into the writing of prose of a temporal conception which had been limited for centuries to lyrical poetry; or to ignore the unbearable tension which it calls for in his writing. The very critic I have just mentioned seems paralysed by it when attempting the novel form. In his *Tea with Mrs. Goodman* [2] he boldly faces the problem of expressing the variety of individual reactions to each single moment of time; but the strain that this imposes on the form of the novel is such that the experiment can hardly be called successful. Contemporary novelists,

[1] P. Toynbee, 'The Decline and Future of the English Novel, in *The Penguin New Writing,* n. 23 (1945), pp. 127 ff.

[2] P. Toynbee, *Tea with Mrs. Goodman,* London, 1947.

then, work under very difficult conditions. Some of them have preferred to concentrate merely on the stylistic and technical side of their art. Others have tried to devise new narrative forms or to compromise with the past ones. This is what the most gifted contemporary prose writers are successfully doing.

Let us take for instance William Sansom. Sansom concentrates his attention on a single fragment of action and fixes it permanently as a timeless experience, emphasizing especially the visual side of it rather than the spiritual implications as Virginia Woolf tried to do. Sansom's by now famous sketch *The Wall* [1] is typical: it is a four-page description of the second during which the façade of a burning building collapses. The story has a tremendous impact; an impact which is increased several-fold by the absolute respect for the minimum time unit. Or let us take a longer story, *Through the Quinquina Glass*. There, a whole story is told as if perceived by sudden intuition during a magical suspension of the ordinary time sequence:

Through the quinquina glass the scene was sunless. The life had left it. . . . Something unearthly had happened. I had lowered the glass—yet the scene retained its lurid quality. . . . The green gloom persisted. . . . This story was coming to my lips with a peculiar fluency. . . . I was curiously sure of my words. The dull light of the quinquina glass alone illumined the scene. The air was breathless. [2]

A story with a fairly normal plot is given in this way a quality of timelessness, of a momentary intuition, acquiring a new and extraordinary intensity. But when the same plot is extended by the same author to ordinary novel length, though the writing is constantly highly-strung, the intensity is necessarily weakened. That is why the impact of *The Body* (1949), Sansom's novel which re-utilizes the plot of the earlier short-story, is much weaker: the story is no longer seen through the magic glass of an altered temporal perspective.

[1] W. Sansom, *Fireman Flower*, London, 1944, pp. 108–11.
[2] *Ibid.*, cit., pp. 8–9.

Other examples of this timeless quality can be found in the novels of Henry Green; in most of them the normal time sequence is eluded by isolating the characters in what have been defined 'emotional Black Holes of Calcutta':[1] a fog-bound railway hotel (*Party Going,* 1939), a castle in Ireland during the war (*Loving,* 1945)—places temporarily isolated from the rest of the world where the normal limits of space and time are abolished by their own narrowness. In his later books the temporal definitions are still vague: *Concluding* (1948) and *Nothing* (1950) are set in a near future, by no means utopistic, but rather projecting outside time a present realistically described. Though in Green's case the extratemporal quality of the novels is closer to Kafka's than Virginia Woolf's, there is in him that extreme attention to the stylistic and technical side of writing which is at the same time an approach to poetical diction and a way of adding to the intensity of expression.

The sense of a different temporal perspective has engendered a tendency to adopt an altered physical one as well. Characters and backgrounds are frequently seen from what appears to be a distorted angle. Joyce Cary's *The Horse's Mouth* (1944) is a case in point. The long novel is told by a Blakian artist, and his way of looking at things is obviously highly personal; this produces an alteration in the normal perspective in which facts, things and people are seen, with the result of giving a vision of the world from a new angle, an angle which—one cannot help feeling—is deliberately wrong. As startlingly unreal is the picture given in a book like Graham Greene's *Brighton Rock* (1938), a novel which at first sight seems modelled on obvious tough realistic schemes; but it is just the contrast between this sordid realism and the complex, subtle and abnormal psychology of the characters and their interreactions that produces the impression of an alteration in the balance of normal life. I believe that it is not mere chance that the director Carol Reed, in making films out of Greene's scripts (*The Fallen Idol, The*

[1] H. Reed, *The Novel since 1939,* London, 1946, p. 29. On Henry Green, see the next essay in the present book.

Third Man), nearly always held the camera at a slant: the slanting images grow naturally out of Greene's descriptions of persons and places that, for all their humanity and reality, undergo some sort of deforming violence, acting on the inner nature of men and making things, seen through their eyes, look different.

We can go back to Sansom for a final example: the physical slant given to the hero of his *Equilibriad* (1948) is the externalization of the change in the inner vision of the writer. The title of the book seems particularly well chosen, since it conveys one of the impressions left on the readers by so much of the best contemporary prose. There is about it a feeling of perpetual tension and alertness, even of fear: the authors are indeed afraid lest their words should loose that stylistic balance which is made the more essential when the world they represent, the physical and the psychical world and the world of time, seems to have lost its equilibrium.

This necessary caution may at times induce too much self-consciousness in the writers and hamper their freedom of expression—it may cause preciosity, but it leads as well to new achievements. It cannot be said that novel-writing is declining as a creative form of expression: it has undergone and is undergoing a process of readjustment. For the time being we can only assess which stage of this process each individual writer has reached.

The Abstract Art of Henry Green

THE process of literary creation is memory: memory of one's experiences, whether concrete and physical, (the memory of actual character and incident) or mental and spiritual (the memory of ideas and writings more or less consciously assimilated). By memory I do not mean the *recherche du temps perdu,* where the process is open and deliberate, but the less conscious, involuntary recollection of the innumerable elements which go to form a new work of art. That is why the search for similarities and echoes in thought or form with other authors can contribute to a more thorough understanding of a literary personality.

For instance, in his novel *Concluding* Henry Green describes a girls' dormitory at siesta time on a very hot day:

Panelling around the *walls* was enamelled in white paint, as also the bedsteads with pink covers, the parquet floor was waxed and *gold, two* naked *Cupids* in cold white *marble,* and life size, *held up* a slab of *green* above a basket grate, while white and brown arms were stretched into the tide of late afternoon *pouring by*; a redhead caught fire with sun like a flare and, out of the sun, *eyes,* opening to *reflected light,* like *jewels enclosed* by flesh *coloured* anemones beneath *green* clear water when these yawn after shrimps, disclosed great innocence in a *scene* on which no innocence had ever shone, where life and *pursuit* were fierce, as these girls came back to consciousness from the truce of a summer after luncheon before the business of the dance.[1]

It is one of the richest passages in Green's prose; one of those passages approaching the florid diction, the syntactic freedom and the sensuous imagery of poetry, which stud all his novels up to *Concluding*—unexpected flourishes of feeling, fanciful word-pictures departing from his more restrained style in the same way as a complicated stucco scroll will suddenly break out of the quiet and balanced form of an arch or balustrade in a seventeenth-century building. The impression it conveys is obviously of warmth and stillness as well as of richness; but the whole is suffused with a kind of dreamy haziness and un-reality, which mellows figures and contours, and this in turn gives a sense of uneasy expectation which suddenly strikes a sinister note in the image of the sea anemones. Let us now place side by side with it a passage of poetry:

> The Chair she sat in, like a burnished throne,
> Glowed on the *marble,* where the glass
> *Held up* by standards wrought with fruited vines
> From which a *golden Cupidon* peeped out
> (Another hid his *eyes* behind his wing)
> Doubled the flames of sevenbranched candelabra
> *Reflecting light* upon the table as
> The glitter of her *jewels* rose to meet it,
> From satin cases *poured* in rich profusion;
> In vials of ivory and *coloured* glass
> Unstoppered, lurked her strange synthetic perfumes,
> Unguent, powdered, or liquid—troubled, confused
> And drowned the sense in odours;
> . . .
> Huge sea-wood fed with copper
> Burned *green* and orange, framed by the *coloured* stone,
> In which sad *light* a carved dolphin swam.
> Above the antique mantel was displayed
> As though a window gave upon the sylvan *scene*

[1] *Concluding,* London, 1948, p. 109 (italics mine).

The change of Philomel, by the barbarous king
So rudely forced; yet there the nightingale
Filled all the desert with inviolable voice
And still she cried, and still the world *pursues,*
'Jug jug' to dirty ears.
And other withered stumps of time
Were told upon the *walls*; staring forms
Leaned out, leaning, hushing the room *enclosed.*[1]

Here, as we saw, Eliot (in *A Game of Chess,* the second part of *The Waste Land*) wanted to create a very similar atmosphere of richness and seclusion pervaded by a threatening sense of foreboding. In another essay [2] I have tried to point out the elements which went, (probably unconsciously) to the building of this passage: I showed how Shakespeare and Swinburne, Keats and Joyce, Dante and Coleridge had contributed to its structure and even to its diction. Now, as this process of assimilation and re-creation went on in Eliot's mind, so it must have done in Green's in whose memory the *Game of Chess* passage unconsciously loomed, while he was confronted with the problem of communicating to the reader the same sort of feeling Eliot had aimed at.[3] From the choice of words, colours and images it is obvious that the younger writer, during his formative years in the late 'twenties must have deeply felt the pervasive influence of the Eliot of *The Waste Land*; hardly any writer of his generation escaped it, and it is no wonder that this passage welled up again. But what matters is that the two authors seem to share a certain feeling about life: the 'cruel pursuit' shattering the state of quiet serenity.

And Green's recollection of Eliot is indicative too of a fundamentally poetic stimulus at the root of the novelist's prose: poetic, that is, not only in feeling—in the current meaning of the adjective when used of a prose work—but in form as well,

[1] T. S. Eliot, *Collected Poems,* cit., p. 64 (italics mine).
[2] See pp. 53–71 of the present book.
[3] This same Eliot passage might also have been recalled by Green in *Loving* (1945), p. 11.

or rather in that indivisible synthesis of form and feeling which is the essential of art. Description is the usual means by which a prose writer creates 'atmosphere'; a description which can be subtle, shaded and allusive. The poet instead, within his stricter medium, must create his atmosphere by using the more elliptical devices of image and symbol. The fact that Green has frequent recourse to images and even cryptic symbols, transferring into prose an essentially poetic technique, is significant of a trend of present writing, in which the two techniques have become practically interchangeable. An example of this association with poetry while writing prose can be found in an arresting mannerism used by the author most consistently in an early novel, *Living*. The definite article here is practically abolished in the text except in direct speech. It must be said that the device is tiresome and at times it seems to be done by mere mechanical revision, with resulting artificiality. Mr. Philip Toynbee [1] attributes this peculiarity to Green's 'aversion to looseness'. Perhaps this is true, as he was writing a novel about workers and aiming at a naked natural way of speaking. But the fact that he kept the articles while reporting the conversations of the Birmingham workers shows his intention of being strictly documentary and factual: recording other people's words seemed to him the only way of describing their lives with the utmost objectivity, since even description of their actions would impose his own interpretation. For this reason he stressed the difference between dialogue and narrative, restricting the latter to the status of notes and thereby emphasizing the importance of the former. The importance that dialogue has retained for Green can be seen in his latest novels, in which the comment is limited almost to the function of stage direction.

As for the abolition of the article, it is significant that the same device is largely used by Auden in the poems written at the same time as Green's *Living*. Auden too was deeply concerned with the life of the working class and was aiming at a

[1] P. Toynbee, 'The Novels of Henry Green', in *The Partisan Review*, XVI, n. 5, May 1949, pp. 487-97.

similar directness. Now, Auden had been inevitably influenced by the poetry of G. M. Hopkins, one of the greatest
poetical 'discoveries' of the 'twenties. Hopkins, in order to
render the fullness of his feelings with the greatest immediacy,
had frequently eliminated the minor connecting parts of speech,
as for instance the relative pronoun. How close Auden could
be to Hopkins can be seen in these lines from his very early
poetry drama with a strong social inspiration, *Paid on Both
Sides*:

> Not from this life, not from this life is any
> To keep; sleep, day and play would not help there
> Dangerous to new ghost; new ghost learns from many
> Learns from old termers what death is, where.[1]

In the same play there are also prose passages like this:

In Kettledale above Colefangs road passes where high banks
overhang dangerous from ambush. To Colefangs had to go,
would speak with Layard, Jerry and Hunter with him only.
They must have stolen news, for Red Shaw waited with ten,
so Jerry said, till for last time unconscious. Hunter was killed
at first shot. They fought, exhausted ammunition, a brave
defence but fight no more.

Auden obviously thought that by abolishing the definite
article he was achieving an essential factuality, capable of conveying that sense of actuality in the raw he needed to shock his
readers into realization of the urgency of immediate social problems. This literary device, which came to be known as Auden's
telegraphese, was rather startling at the time, and there is little
doubt that Green, a writer always interested in poetry, got it
from him. But the difference in the use of it between the two
authors deserves some consideration: Auden thought that con-
ciseness of this kind was a means of reaching complete realism
—confusing perhaps a rough press telegram style with plain
realistic reporting; Green instead saw that straight reporting

[1] W. H. Auden, *Collected Shorter Poems, 1930–1944*, London, 1950, p. 200.

required normal dialogue. At the same time he realized the potentialities of the device as a means of reaching in description the same effects that Impressionist painters had achieved in their landscapes: the simplification of natural forms heightening the emotional quality of the picture by concentrating on the really significant features. Indeed Green is less aiming at social reform than giving a social picture. It has the detachment of something seen from the outside, and in a frame. Green's Impressionism can of course be cheap at times, and may even resemble arty child talk, as in the following:

Evening. Was spring. Heavy blue clouds stayed over above. In small back garden of villa small tree with yellow buds. On table in back room daffodils, faded, were between ferns in a vase. Later she spoke of these saying she must buy new ones and how nice were first spring flowers.[1]

But it can also achieve a genuine lyrical as well as pictorial power:

Here pigeon quickly turned rising in spirals, grey, when clock in the church tower struck the quarter and away, away the pigeon fell from this noise in a diagonal from where church was built and that man who leant on his spade.[2]

It shows how Green can use with economy some typical devices of poetry; he invests a passage, which is at first sight just a quick pictorial image, with vague undertones which place it in a sudden deep perspective of feeling and meaning. One senses a hidden allusion in the sloping flight of the pigeon, the sound of bells, the leaning figure of the man. And the impression is strongly confirmed by the rest of the novel, and by the later novels of Green's where these images recur insistently, apparently carrying some sort of a message, never fully revealed. The pigeon, like other birds in Green's prose, reaches at times the intensity of a symbol, but lacks all precision of reference and consistency, two essential qualities of symbols. And indeed Green's are not symbols: they are rather those sudden

[1] *Living*, p. 11.   [2] *Living*, p. 199.

images recurring in the works of poets and marking the high points at which the strength of their feeling finds release in visual terms. Visual images without an abstract counterpart in the realm of thought or a definite reference to known facts or persons are the expression only of a mood, of a condition of the author's mind, so individual that it can be communicated only through this visual embodiment.[1] In a sense they themselves

[1] For further evidence of the closeness of Green's modes of expression to poetry compare this passage from *Living* (p. 45): '. . . "Yes it's a pleasure to be there of a Sunday afternoon. I'd say I saw quite seven from our street up there. And only a 6*d*. bus ride." "Ah, it's worth a tanner every time." "Yes it is. Yes we all went there last Sunday. Mr. Craigan said 'e'd like a bit of fresh air after all the hot weather we've been 'aving so we packed up and went. I cut steps of bread and cheese that we took with us, oh, we did 'ave a time "' with the pub. scene in *The Waste Land*, or *Sweeney Agonistes*, which antedated the publication of *Living* only by two years. Still closer to the pub. scene in *The Waste Land* is the following from *Caught* (1943, p. 58):

'She 'ad a terrible time 'aving it, really, but as I said to 'er in the 'ospital, I says, "you take a pull on yourself . . . I know things ain't been easy," I says, and she said to me, "Not a word against Ted, mum," . . .'

Again from *The Waste Land*, part III (*The Fire Sermon*), comes the river scene in *Living* (pp. 114–15):

'Sunshine was pale. So drifted into sleep. Yet came party from Maidenhead in launch up the river, men and women, a silver launch. Laughter came like birds from women in it. It came on slowly and he opened eyes and it went by, this laughter reaching . . . back to him and then in wide circle launch turned leisurely and came back past him and he thought why did they turn it there. Why did they turn it there he thought and then men on launch played dance tune from the wireless they had on it and it went on down with stream till he could see them no more but still hear them, then he could not hear them any more . . .

'Still flowed river Thames and still the leaves were disturbed, then were loosed, and came down on to water and went by London where he was going, by there and out into the sea.'

Here Eliot's river images fuse with the mechanical sound of the typist's gramophone, the music creeping upon the water, Elizabeth's pleasure barge and the narrow canoe on the Thames, which are all in this section of *The Waste Land*, to form Green's picture, a picture like Eliot's of lassitude and emptiness. And we should remember that the spectator of the scene, in *Living*, is one of Eliot's 'loitering heirs of city directors'.

become abstract. But he did not try to render this abstraction exclusive. It is true that there was in him a keen preoccupation with the means of expression used and, as in Eliot, there was the sense of the discovery of the beauty of rhythm in common speech and its repetitive pattern. Others had been experimenting in the same direction, and Gertrude Stein had tried to exploit all the effects of repetition, as it is so frequently found in common speech. But while she had tried to stress its incantatory power and to reach through it abstract and surrealistic effects (pure music), Green was trying instead to strike a balance between the realistic rendering of common conversation and the underlying secret rhythmical pattern which gives at times poignancy and musical beauty to the speech of the uncultured.

Eliot, Auden, Gertrude Stein: the young novelist was obviously keeping in touch with the most revolutionary tendencies in the literature of the 'twenties—and he was determined in his search for a way of expression which he could call his own and which would go beyond the results achieved by his predecessors. This determination can be seen in the fairly elaborate construction of *Living*: from a series of sketches giving a general view of the setting and characters, through a more precise interest in a single story, which becomes the leading thread uniting the separate figures in the book, figures which should render the real naked 'feel' of life. This complex construction— hidden behind what were meant as jotted down direct impressions out of a pocket book—gives the measure of Green's interest in the formal side of novel-writing, and of the self-consciousness of this writing.

That Green's main preoccupation has been with structure is shown by his next novel, *Party Going*, dated at the end 'London 1931–1938'—a long period over which his style had matured. This time he has chosen only a small group of characters within a strict unity of time and place. In this very unity one can detect a sign of Green's aspiration towards an abstract order. A fog-bound hotel at a London terminus becomes a set stage and by its very limitation acquires an extra-temporal quality. In it the different actors keep re-grouping and the dialogue maintains the importance it had in *Living*. But the very nature of the middle-class characters chosen gives to their speech, realistic as it is, a certain stylization, which contributes to confirm the abstract atmosphere of the novel. Green has not renounced the social element which was so strong in *Living*. But now it is expressed indirectly through the vacuity of the behaviour of these characters, the sense of utter uselessness in their attitudes. At the same time a feeling of threat, almost of siege, hangs over them and over the whole book. This emanates from the crowd of the less privileged eddying about in the station below:

Although all those windows had been shut there was a continual dull roar came through them from outside, and this noise sat upon those within like clouds upon a mountain so they were obscured and levelled and, as though they had been airmen, in danger of running fatally into earth. Clouds also, if they are banked up, will so occupy the sky as to dwarf what is beneath and this low roar, which was only conversation in that multitude without, lay over them in such a pall, like night coming on and there is no light when one must see, that these people here were obscured by it and were dimmed into anxious Roman numerals.[1]

This passage shows also Green's growing taste for elaborate imagery and mixed metaphor. In spite of the precious effects reached, this very style increases the general tone of instability. From time to time the author intervenes to establish the balance with neat recapitulations:

Now both Julia and Angela had kissed their young men when these had been cross, when Mr. Adams had made off down in the station and when Max had stopped chasing Julia to sit in his chair.[2]

The very baldness of these summaries serves to emphasize the futility of the actions described. They are the more necessary

[1] *Party Going*, pp. 175–6.   [2] *Ibid.*, p. 114.

because in spite of the time and place limits, the action does not develop in an orderly fashion; the complicated re-groupings of the few characters are completely casual, and the continuous exchanges between them follow no pattern. They are only kept together by the recurrence of vague symbols and allusions—a dead pigeon, the references to Embassy Richard who appears only on the last page—or by the repetition of the same incidents narrated by different people or even by the same person in a number of ways. Descriptive passages are much more developed at the expense of dialogue, and Green takes advantage of them to display the preciosity of his style. I insist particularly on this novel because in it the Manneristic character of his writing appears more clearly. In *Party Going* the preoccupation with style is so strong that the content is overpowered. In the following and better novels form is more fused with content; here instead it is easy to isolate and examine that style, already fully mature, which Green later used in *Caught, Loving* and *Back*. It is extremely artificial and ornate. Green is not afraid of using the most flamboyant rhetorical devices. When he is successful he reaches an intensity akin to that of the Metaphysical poets:

She lay on his shoulder in this ugly room, folded up with almost imperceptible breathing like seagulls settled on the water cock over gentle waves. Looking at her head and body, richer far than her rare fur coat, holding as he did to these skins which enfolded what ruled him, her arms and shoulders, everything, looking down on her face which ever since he had first seen it had been his library, his gallery, his palace and his wooded fields, he began at last to feel content and almost that he owned her.[1]

Here the Donnian echoes are obvious. But when he tries to

[1] *Party Going*, p. 226. The interpretation of the human body in terms of land-scape or of Donne's 'Newfoundland' is not uncommon in Green; e.g. in *Caught* (p. 117): 'The relief he experienced when their bodies met was like the crack, on a snow silent day, of a branch that breaks to fall under a weight of snow, as his hands went like two owls in daylight over the hills, moors, and wooded valleys, over the fat white winter of her body.'

couple this rich imagery with the involutions of a Jamesian style his prose can no longer support the strain.[1] In fact Green's writing can carry a good deal of precious ornamentation, provided it is light and elegant like rococo scroll-work:

> Aromatic steam as well from her bath salts so that if her maid had been a negress then Amabel's eyes might have shone like two humming birds in the tropic airs she glistened in.[2]

There is nothing functional about this decoration, but it suits well Green's lighter vein, in which he aims at giving a sort of hard transparence to his writing. He can achieve that precarious balance between frank sensuality and refinement found at its best in the novels of Firbank and the paintings of Fragonard. He himself is fully conscious that his style has all the brittleness of writing on glass. The following passage may be taken as symbolic of this quality—it is a framed picture of extreme elegance, utterly detached from reality, and outside time:

> The walls were made of looking-glass, and were clouded over with steam; from them her body was reflected in a faint pink mass. She leaned over and traced her name Amabel in that steam and that pink mass loomed up to meet her in the flesh and looked through bright at her through the letters of her name. She bent down to look at her eyes in the A her name began with, and as she gazed at them steam or her breath dulled her reflection and the blue her eyes were went out or faded.
>
> She rubbed with the palm of her hand, and now she could see all her face. She always thought it more beautiful than anything she had ever seen, and when she looked at herself it was

---

[1] Cp. *Party Going* (p. 144) 'It seemed to him she was not unlike ground so high, so remote it had never been broken and that her outward beauty lay in that if any man had marked her with intimacy as one treads on snow, then that trace which would be left could not fail to invest him, whoever he might be, with some part of those unvulgar heights so covered, not so much of that last field of snow before any summit as of a high memory unvisited, and kept.'

[2] *Party Going*, p. 154.

as though the two of them would never meet again, it was to bid farewell; and at the last she always smiled, and she did so this time as it was clouding over, tenderly smiled as you might say goodbye, my darling darling.[1]

Henry Green's style then reaches a balance which is not the classical one, and it is also far from the unrestrained outpour of feeling characteristic of romantic prose. It is marked by the consciously perilous control of the funambulist.

His next work is the so-called 'self-portrait' *Pack My Bag* (1940), which is rather a series of impressions of childhood and youth set down under the premonition of an early death in the approaching war. It gives revealing glimpses into his formative years and it contains passages of masterly writing which are perhaps the most precise he ever produced, but as a whole is unwieldly and stands rather as a notebook than as a work of art. In spite of the difference in method and stature, this book seems to have been written with an eye on Proust. The obvious concern with himself coupled with a desire not to give himself away cheaply, the precious style which throws a halo of sad beauty on personal trivia, the conscious transfiguration of memories, the 'genteel' rather than aristocratic attitude to life and society; all these are common in different degrees to Proust and Green. And besides, as far as it can be taken as a confession, *Pack My Bag* is a document of the terrible self-pity of the epicurean:

We who must die soon, or so it seems to me, should chase our memories back, standing when they are found, enough apart not to be too near what they once meant.[2]

There is detachment even in this self-pity, a fear of being too involved and of spoiling in this way the precious aesthetic stimulation that the very contemplation of one's own misery can give. Green is indeed an epicurean, a late heir of Pater's ideal, ready to catch the fleeting apparitions of beauty and to preserve them through a strict discipline, in spite of his being

---

[1] *Party Going,* pp. 171–2.   [2] *Pack My Bag,* p. 143.

aware of and his bitterly commenting on the sordidness of the surrounding world. Green actually looks for release in the vacuous atmosphere of night clubs:

> Going to what we now know as a night club in London with a friend is a serious thing. The band should be coloured, the room dark, we should be tired and not so sober as to be afraid to tell the truth but not so drunk as to be incapable of lying.[1]

This partiality for night clubs, with its implication of subtle and sincere aesthetic emotion gained through the very sense of their false luxury, is emphasized in Green's next novel, *Caught* (1943), where one of them is described at length. The mixed emotion roused by it is apparent in a passage like this, fusing bathos and pathos:

> The blues negroes played were to foreigners in a foreign land of the still farther south which, with simplicity, became everyone's longing in this soft evening aching room.[2]

It is again a form of precarious equilibrium, both emotional and stylistic. The last four words are in fact an example of the farthest point Green reached in contriving elaborate adjectival expressions; others, in the next few pages, are for instance 'with sea flower fingered hands', or 'the hyacinthine, grape dark fellowship of longing'. It is once again a transference into prose of a way of constructing images characteristic of poetry. But it should be noted that Green is generally careful, even when he adopts a poetic technique, to avoid the rhythm of poetry.

Caught is based on the author's experiences in the Auxiliary Fire Service during the blitz. As in *Party Going*, there is a small group of people thrown together in extraordinary circumstances, isolated, threatened, and under the strain of prolonged and indefinite waiting. The emotional impact of this waiting is the real subject of both books, as it is of *Loving*, his next novel. The three, as Mr. Henry Reed has said, are 'emotional Black

---

[1] *Pack My Bag*, p. 185.
[2] *Caught*, p. 107. In *Who's Who*, Green defines his 'recreation' as 'Romancing over the bottle, to a good band'.

Holes of Calcutta'.[1] When this suspense finally breaks into action, at the end of the book, the hero finds it impossible to recreate the experience, and breaks down in his attempted narration. 'The extraordinary thing is,' he says, 'that one's imagination is so literary.' [2] Action itself is only a temporary release from waiting and is, for Green, relatively unimportant. This attitude is very similar to that of Kafka, who hardly cared to give conclusions to his novels, since only the sense of expectation in them was real. Green's is not an imitation but rather a shared feeling of futility common to many sensitive writers in this century. This is what Mr. Walter Allen means by saying, with reference to *Party Going,* that it is 'so much more successful than anything the English disciples of Kafka have written'.[3]

The preoccupation with time is also present in *Caught,* where it assumes a new form. *Party Going,* as we saw, evaded a time-setting through the isolation of the characters; here, though the same feeling of isolation persists, the very fact of the war provides a clear indication of time. Green looks then for other means of evasion: practically in each chapter he devises new

---

[1] H. Reed, *The Novel since 1939,* cit., see p. 186 of this book.

[2] *Caught,* p. 174.

[3] W. Allen, 'Henry Green', in *Penguin New Writing,* n. 25 (1945), pp. 144–55. Actually in *Party Going* there is also at times a similarity in form with Kafka, as in the following (p. 59): 'She was in a long hall with hidden lighting and, for ornament, a vast chandelier with thousands of glass drops and rather dirty. It was full of people and those who had found seats, which were all of them too low, lay with blank faces as if exhausted and, if there was anything to hope for, as though they had lost hope. Most of them were enormously fat. One man there had a cigar in his mouth, and then she saw he had one glass eye, and in his hand he had a box of matches which now and again he would bring up to his cigar. Just as he was about to strike his match he looked round each time and let his hands drop back to his lap, his match not lighted. Those standing in groups talked low and were rather bent and there was a huge illuminated clock they all kept looking at. Almost every woman was having tea as if she owned the whole tray of it. Almost every man had a dispatch case filled with daily newspapers. She thought it was like an enormous doctor's waiting room and that it would be like that when they were all dead and waiting at the gates.'

ways of linking and alternating separate and non-parallel actions. The main devices are flash-backs, quick cuts, evocations very much in the form of fade-ins and fade-outs in films, and *montage* effects; but there is even at times a flash-back inside a flash-back: memory becomes a Chinese box and the sense of the present is so bound up with past and future that the temporal sequence is abolished.

Loving (1945), as I said, belongs to the same group of novels. The 'black hole' in which the characters (a group of servants and, in the background, their masters) develop their subtle and elusive emotional entanglements is an Irish castle, an island of peace during the war. What action there is in the novel revolves round the discovery by one of the servants of her mistress's unfaithfulness to her husband. This event becomes a permanent centre of reference, round which a whole sensual web of allusion and vague hints is spun. The evasion from time is here attempted by deliberately presenting the story as a fairy tale: 'Once upon a time an old butler . . .' it begins—and it ends with a pretty Valentine card: 'For what with the peacocks bowing at her purple skirts, the white doves nodding on her shoulders round her brilliant cheeks and her great eyes that blinked tears of happiness, it made a picture', and the usual formula: 'they were married and lived happily ever after'. This neatness of presentation should make also for constructive balance. But it is not so: the story instead winds its way through a maze of conversation. Green at this stage has acquired a complete mastery of the spoken word. He could reproduce ordinary speech with absolute perfection—and this ability is developed still further, as we shall see, in his later novels. But there is another feature of *Loving* worth attention: for the first time a Green novel has a hero, Raunce the butler. It will have appeared from what has been said that the choral nature of *Living* and the following novels prevented the predominance of a single figure. They were concerned instead with the interaction of characters, setting and atmosphere. But in *Loving* the figure of Raunce stands out and seems to achieve the quality of an all round portrait. However it should be noted that this fullness of representation is not obtained through a direct description or by showing in a logical sequence the different elements which go to form his character. It is rather a slow accumulation of differing and frequently contrasting characteristics, shown each in isolation. In other words the character is built up with the same technique of accumulation of independent details which Green had used to build up the industrial town life in *Living*. Not a consistent character then, but the separate reactions of an individual in different moments of time to his surroundings. Human personality is not as in the past the foundation of the novel: what matters is the individual reaction to the atmosphere which keeps changing through the subtle variations of psychological moments.

Constructionally *Back* (1946) differs from the previous novels. The action develops more definitely along traditional lines. The novel is carefully built up: a short story introduced in the exact middle of the book symbolically projects into the past events which instead in the novel itself are so strictly related to the post-war years. The central evasion into a pre-romantic setting contrasts with, and at the same time enhances, the shabbiness of the contemporary world in which the main action is set. Green's preoccupation with structure and form is more than ever present, not only in the elaborate parallelism of the two parts of the book, but also in the preciosity of the writing and its imagery. A frequent recourse to puns and complicated metaphors reveals the author's determination to create a lyrical climate in which the realistic narrative should have acquired a deeper poetical significance. The experimental quality of this writing is too obvious to be successful, but it can at times create a strange incantation. Very deliberately Green has constructed this novel on one main *leit-motif*: the word 'rose' and its sensuous appeal to the imagination. The figure of Rose, the dead heroine, is evoked with obsessive insistence by the rich and frequent imagery connected with the flower. Actually this motif had already appeared in previous novels;

Green's recourse to rose imagery was instinctive whenever he wished to evoke a sensuous atmosphere. In *Caught,* for instance, roses and rose colour are consistently the symbols of emotional crises. They are evoked in all love scenes and are also images of the pale reflections of London fires, which play havoc with the hero's imagination. Presumably Green uses them so deliberately in order to give a kind of stylization to those parts of his work which feeling should dominate. Where the barriers of detachment would be unacceptable, he substitutes another intellectual defence: stylization and conceit. But such conceits at times become comical through over-elaboration:

Mrs. Howells, with shaking fingers, put down the china tea-pot covered with pink roses her sister, Aggie, had given as a wedding present; which had reflected Brid's conception by that liquid rose flower light of a dying coal-fire twenty-one years back; which now witnessed Brid's return, deflowered, but married, and with the fruit, a child.[1]

This is Green's wit (in the seventeenth-century meaning of the word) at its worst. Conceits of a similar kind are frequent in *Back,* where he does not even hesitate to pun on the past tense of the verb 'to rise'. But the result here is more convincing, through the obsessive quality his writing reaches:

But as it was he went in the gate, had his cheek brushed by a rose and began awkwardly to search for Rose, through roses, in what seemed to him should be the sunniest places on a fine day, the warmest when the sun came out at twelve o'clock for she had been so warm, and amongst the newer memorials in local stone because she had died in time of war, when, or so he imagined, James could never have found marble for her, of whom, at no time before this moment, had he ever thought as cold beneath a slab, food for worms, her great red hair, still growing, a sort of moist bower for worms.[2]

Green's style reaches the extreme form of Mannerism, with all its excesses, like the taste for the macabre; but the magic he

[1] *Caught,* p. 78.   [2] *Back,* pp. 7–8.

created through the rarefied atmosphere of his earlier books is here maintained, transposed onto a verbal level.

After this *tour de force* in flamboyant Mannerism, the prose of *Concluding* (1948) seems restrained. But actually this novel is perhaps the best example of Green's skill as a funambulist. He has abolished time by placing his story in an indeterminate near future; has abolished the place connections by using as a set the isolated milieau of a girls' boarding school; and finally has abolished plot. The novel is in fact the minute chronicle of a day from dawn to night, in which several things happen; but none is really brought to a head; crises open, but are not solved; and in spite of the utter inconsequence of the events related, the book has a roundness and a finish, given by the slow passing of the hours, the rising of the sun and its late setting— a natural rhythm which could be repeated *ad infinitum,* but which is in itself concluded. From this structure the book acquires a new tension: the perfect formal polish contrasts with the sense of suspense, and produces a slight feeling of unbalance, of distortion, of disturbing though elegant deformation, emphasized even by the touches of actual description, like this:

> The panelling was remarkable in that it boasted a dado designed to continue the black and white tiled floor in perspective, as though to lower the ceiling. But Miss Edge had found marble tiles too cold to her toes, had had the stone covered in parquet blocks, on which were spread State imitation Chinese Kidderminster rugs. As a result, this receding vista of white and black lozenges set from the rugs to four feet up the walls, in precise and radiating perspective, seemed altogether out of place next British dragons in green and yellow; while the gay panelling above, shallow carved, was genuine, the work of a master, giving Cupid over and over in a thousand poses, a shock, a sad surprise in such a room.[1]

This chequered pattern, halved vision, broken perspective, is repeated again and again. The very structure of the sentences

[1] *Concluding,* pp. 11–12.

reflects the restlessness, the contortions and convulsions of the feelings and images they describe: no straight lines or plain statements—everything is swayed by fluctuation, not temporary and seeking a consummation, but self-sufficient and permanent. A bird-image (and they are very frequent in all Green's work) can give an idea of this feeling:

Then, as they came to where the trees ended, and blackbirds, before roosting, began to give the alarm in earnest, some first starlings flew out of the sky. Over against the old man and his grand-daughter the vast mansion reflected a vast red; sky above paled while to the left it outshone the house, and more starlings crossed. After which these birds came in hundreds, then suddenly by legion, black and blunt against faint rose. They swarmed above the lonely elm, they circled a hundred feet above, until the leader, followed by ever greater numbers, in one broad spiral led the way down and so, as they descended through falling dusk in a soft roar, they made, as they had at dawn, a huge sea shell that stood proud to a moon which, flat sovereign red gold, was already poised full faced to a dying world.

Once the starlings had settled in that tree they one and all burst out singing.

Then there were more, even higher, dots against paler pink, and these, in their turn, began to circle up above, scything the air, and to swoop down through a thickening curve, in the enormous echo of blood, or of the sea, until all was black about that black elm, as the first mass of starlings left while these others settled, and there was a huge volume of singing.[1]

Here Green is fully in the centre of that tradition of modern Mannerism—I should say Funambulism—to which most of the writers of the 'thirties and 'forties belong. Their terms of reference could be Gothic art, the Metaphysicals of the seventeenth century, or Rococo—in no case could they be compared with the art of writing of the full Renaissance, of the neoclassic 'Augustan' age or of the Victorian era. It is a style char-

[1] *Concluding*, pp. 176–7.

acterized by asymmetry, by the lack of precise focus and, when successful, by the capacity to achieve a new precarious balance in fleeting moments in spite of, or even *through,* the absence of a predetermined equilibrium. This is, I think, what Green succeeded, or nearly always succeeded, in doing. The titles of his books are interesting in themselves. They are meant as essential notes on the subjects of the books, and also like musical indications to keys. As such, they are self-explanatory, and *Concluding* is particularly significant: it is at first sight the most inconclusive of Green's novels for what concerns the conventional development of the plot. But, apart from the allusion to the uncertain 'conclusion' of the life of the old scientist, the main character of the book, the title reflects too on the perpetual and inescapable variety and inconsistency which the author feels to be the only real 'conclusion' man can reach.

Starting from this assumption it is only logical that after *Concluding* should come *Nothing* (1950). Nothing is the very essence of life and to reach and fix this essence in writing Green tries to make also his prose as essential as possible. Indeed, the most surprising feature of *Nothing* is the almost total absence of descriptive passages. As in *Living* and even more than there, the book is all told through dialogue. But there is a profound difference in the reason for the adoption of this technique in the two books. In *Living* dialogue was important as a means of presenting realistically the life of the working class; in *Nothing* conversation is all that survives of a society—the upper middle class—which is fast decaying. (Once again the novel is set in the future; the novelist wants, as before, to escape the boundaries of time.) Description is limited to brief stage directions at the beginning of each long and vain dialogue:

A fortnight or so later Mrs. Weatherby was with her son Philip in the sitting room of their flat.
'Dear boy' she was saying '. . .[1]

On this formal set stage the characters meet two by two for their

[1] *Nothing,* p. 28.

petty intrigues carried out in dialogues which acquire a rarefied brilliance through their very realism. It is not like the brilliant wit of the dialogues in some previous novels, and particularly *Party Going,* which made them the heirs of the Peacock-Firbank tradition of the 'conversation novel', or, on a lower level, the equals of Mr. Evelyn Waugh's books; the irony of the conversations in *Nothing* (and in the later *Doting*) is more pointed because they are not exercises in wit, but are as close as possible to reality. An emotional centre to the novel is provided this time not by a feeling of isolation and premonition, as in *Party Going, Caught* or *Loving,* but by the very formal business of a party. In the same way in *Concluding* the main episode was a dance. The external nature of this occasion is a key to the inner vacuity of feeling. What matters is the outer polish; this abolition of deeper values gives to *Nothing* a greater pungency, the peculiar nostalgia communicated by things which are so refined as to appear useless. This novel is indeed an extreme example of funambulism: the ability to sustain for the length of a whole book so immaterial a web of insinuations. As early as 1940 Green had defined the essential quality of prose writing in these words:

Prose is not to be read aloud but to oneself alone at night, and it is not quick as poetry but rather a gathering web of insinuations which go further than names however shared can ever go. Prose should be a long intimacy between strangers with no direct appeal to what both may have known. It should slowly appeal to feelings unexpressed, it should in the end draw tears out of the stone.[1]

By 1950 he had achieved his object, the greatest possible rarefaction of style. But the achievement is at the expense of the common human values, which the book seems to have abolished. The stone from which he wants to draw tears is identical with that which Barbara Hepworth has patiently and lovingly smoothed and freed from all earthly accretions, re-

---

[1] *Pack My Bag,* p. 88.

duced to an essential form of pure perfection. Green seems to have started from the idea, common to a large section of contemporary literature and art, that there is a world of 'unexpressed feelings', beyond the common human ones which have formed the material of earlier works of art—feelings of an exquisitely aesthetic nature. The nearly mathematical perfection in the relation and balance of the elements of composition, the consciousness of creating an unassailable formal structure, polished and compact, can actually give an intense pleasure and is capable of drawing tears through an indefinable emotion. The idea is fundamentally derived from the 'art for art's sake' theory at the end of last century, and in the field of the novel Henry James had intensely worked in this direction. But still, at the time, it was not conceived in its pure state: it was rather superimposed on the world of human feelings and values, which remained at the basis of all forms of literature. The figurative arts and music, instead, have been quicker in seizing upon it. While the Impressionists and the *Fauves* had only tried to impose a greater purity of form on a still fundamentally romantic material, the Cubists aimed at complete abstraction—a pattern of rigid geometrical figures creating abstract emotions through the intellect rather than the heart. And Schoenberg worked in the same direction in the musical field.

In this essay I have mentioned the Impressionists in connection with Green's earlier works. He too moved from them towards a more and more rigid conception of his obligation to absolute form; and the process seems to have been a conscious one. This is proved by his latest novel, *Doting* (1952), where the title itself alludes not only to the actions of some of the characters, but also to the author's attitude. Green now dotes on his chosen form, the novel, perfecting it more and more, giving to his writing a further polish and finish. The structure of the book is again that of dialogues with brief introductions, and the characters belong to the same social group as those of *Nothing*. But the author has imposed an even stricter order on his matter. The construction is carefully studied: at the beginning and at the end of the book all the main characters are presented together, while the rest of the novel is again a series of dialogues in which the characters are introduced in ever changing combinations. The precision and the near automatism of these changes emphasize the stylized abstraction of the book. The vacuity of the plot and the conversation corresponds to a perfect formal scheme, included as it is in the time limit of a school holiday, between the two parties given one for the homecoming and one for the end of the vacation of a boy (who incidentally is only an 'extra' among the actors in this comedy of manners). The sense of uselessness here is even greater than in *Nothing,* where the main character of the predatory woman is at least triumphant. Here she has held her group together for her last party, but this keeping up of appearances is the only achievement. They are back as nearly as possible to where they were before. The pessimism of the conclusion, the sense of failure and emptiness deriving from the chosen subject is perhaps the expression of a moral judgement.

But the emphasis is all on the aesthetic approach to the act of writing. The truth is that Green's recent work is based on a consistent vision of life as an inconclusive sequence of episodes to which the only order we can impose is of an aesthetic kind. In a very interesting article on *The Aesthetics of Nihilism*[1] Lienhard Bergel has convincingly illustrated how modern art is based on this vision of life—an essentially nihilistic conception which induces the artist to assume a position of 'dishuman' aloofness, to found his work on abstract mathematical principles rather than on human feelings. Bergel, though, demonstrates that even such a book as *Ulysses* does not belong with the nihilists, and is fundamentally human and 'old fashioned'. Perhaps in English literature Virginia Woolf was the only one to approach a more abstract view of life, when she resumed the whole process in the formula 'Tuesday follows Monday' and, as early as 1919, said that the task of the novelist

[1] In *Lo Spettatore Italiano,* VI, n. 2, Feb. 1953.

was that of conveying the 'varying, unknown and uncircumscribed spirit' which is life, 'a semi-transparent envelope which surrounds us from the beginning of consciousness to the end'.[1] The 'envelope' is art, the superimposed aesthetics which must absorb and annihilate reality.

But Green has succeeded in avoiding, or rather in gradually getting rid of, that deliberate lyricism in the language which marred the works of Virginia Woolf's followers. English writers were indeed too deeply steeped in a glorious narrative tradition based on reality and on the analysis of feeling, to easily accept the opposite principles of abstraction and formal precision. And in the 'twenties D. H. Lawrence was a further deterrent from an abstract attitude. Green himself, as we saw, had held at first a more romantic attitude, and before *Nothing* and *Doting* had also approached the other compromises between abstraction and romanticism adopted by less 'nihilistic' writers in the age of uncertainty between the two wars: I mean Expressionism and Surrealism. The first (a mild abstraction reached through the emphatic deformation of realistic data) can be seen even in the quoted passages of *Party Going, Caught* and *Loving*; Surrealism (nearly absolute abstraction achieved by creating a world of personal symbols) left its mark especially on *Back* and *Concluding*. But in *Nothing* and *Doting* to the romantic interpretation of Virginia Woolf's principles of composition he has substituted a classical one, building up a perfect structure, beautiful in its delicate sequence of scenes, held together by a constant rhythm—so that the final impression is similar to that of a Mozartian opera: a musical edifice made of elegant nothings, but endowed with a strangely pathetic poignancy. Still, a much apter musical equivalent could be found in Schoenberg, whose activity has run through the same phases: Romanticism, Impressionism, Expressionism, to reach the final stage in the atonal method, the affirmation of an abstract

[1] V. Woolf, 'Modern Fiction', collected in *The Common Reader*, first series, p. 189. The passage is quoted more fully in a previous essay in the present book, see p. 180.

classicism based on pure form. It is significant that the subject of Schoenberg's opera *Von Heute auf Morgen* (1928) closely resembles that of *Doting*: the temporary estrangement of husband and wife, and their reunion in a meaningless convention, a purposeless 'carrying on': as Virginia Woolf said, 'Tuesday follows Monday'. Schoenberg has been considered by Thomas Mann as the prototype of the abstract, nihilistic artist, basing his music on mathematical principles, completely isolating himself from reality and discarding human values. As Mr. Bergel has pointed out in the article mentioned above, the hero of Mann's *Dr. Faustus,* a composer modelled on Schoenberg, aims at the composition of a 'magical square', a perfect and perfectly empty musical construction. But was not this the ideal of Virginia Woolf? She went back to it more than once when speaking of music; for instance in *The Waves* (1931), here are Rhoda's impressions at a concert:

Let me see the thing. There is a square. There is an oblong. The players take the square and place it upon the oblong. They place it very accurately; they make a perfect dwelling-place. Very little is left outside. The structure is now visible; what is inchoate is here stated; we are not so various or so mean; we have made oblongs and stood them upon squares. This is our triumph; this is our consolation.[1]

This, then, is what the modern artist, Schoenberg or Green, is doing. But the emptiness of feeling is not so complete as critics have pretended. Their abstract reflection of the modern world *has* poignancy, due perhaps to despair—but despair is after all a 'human' feeling, and implies also a judgement of a society. Green's penetrating artistic consciousness enables him to reflect in his fiction the moods and the varying stylistic tendencies of his time.

[1] V. Woolf, *The Waves,* Albatross edition, p. 147.

Dylan Thomas: The Poetry of Vision

THE word 'organic' has been frequently mentioned in connection with the poetic world of Dylan Thomas: it has been said that his use of imagery is organically related to the ideas he wants to convey, instead of having a decorative function; and it has been observed that the poet is particularly attentive to the organic processes rather than to the outward aspects of nature, and renders them in his lines with singular evidence:

> The force that through the green fuse drives the flower
> Drives my green age; that blasts the roots of trees
> Is my destroyer.[1]

This is an early poem, but the same vigour is found in his more recent productions, for instance *In the White Giant's Thigh*:

> . . . Heard the lewd, wooed field flow to the coming frost . . .[2]

The organic development in nature has in fact a parallel in the very technique of his composition; his imagery follows a

---

[1] *18 Poems*, London, 1934, p. 13; now in *Collected Poems 1934–1952*, London, 1952, p. 9.

[2] First published in *Botteghe Oscure*, VI, Rome, 1950, p. 335; now in *Collected Poems*, cit., p. 177.

natural organic process of development which will bear comparison with the mysterious growth of a plant or a living creature. There is no better way of describing this process than in the words of Thomas himself, in a letter written several years ago to Henry Treece:

A poem by myself *needs* a host of images because its centre is a host of images. I make one image—though 'make' is not the word; I let, perhaps, the image be 'made' emotionally in me and then apply to it what intellectual and critical forces I possess—let it breed another, let that image contradict the first, make, of the third image bred out of the other two together, a fourth contradictory image, and let them all, within my imposed formal limits, conflict. Each image holds within it the seed of its own destruction, and my dialectical method, as I understand it, is a constant building up and breaking down of the images that come out of the central seed, which is itself destructive and constructive at the same time.[1]

It is very seldom that a poet appears so conscious of the mental process followed in composing his work. Such consciousness is more akin to the technical discipline of a musician, and it would be interesting to substitute, in the passage just quoted, the word 'theme' for the word 'image'. I think that it would become a fair description of the creative technique followed by the composer of a quartet or a symphony. And the musical parallel could be carried a step further remembering the set forms in which Thomas cast his poems. He devised new ones all the time, but always imposed on himself the rule of following them most rigidly in all their complicated pattern of rhyme, metre, rhythm and stanza. The equivalent could only be some kind of instrumental music, which imposes on the composer the same strict formal discipline (Thomas' 'imposed formal limits').

And indeed, going back to the structure and development of Thomas's imagery, the definition 'organic growth', implying

[1] H. Treece, *Dylan Thomas, 'Dog among the Fairies'*, London, 1949, pp. 47–8, note.

the transference into art of a nature-process, has been used with reference to Bach's compositions. Themes in Bach, images in Thomas, are allowed to grow out of each other as if following a natural process of generation, with its inevitability and consistency. This sense of a fixed static form within which all is perpetual movement, a movement of elements (lines in painting, planes in architecture, themes in music, images in poetry) springing one out of the other, is the main feature of Baroque art. And Thomas' poetry has noticeably some of the characteristics of Baroque: apart from the one just mentioned, there is in it the predilection for curious though balanced patterns, the predominance of the decorative invention which might at times run away with a whole poem. But all the same other important elements of Baroque art are lacking in it, and one especially which is fundamental: the final sense of repose, of balance and completeness which a Baroque work of art reveals when surveyed as a whole. In Baroque art the movement is all inside, contained in one harmonious structure. In Thomas instead the movement is the outcome of an unreconciled strife of conflicting elements, a continuous spiral of feelings and images which can never reach a point of repose. It is true that in the letter quoted above Thomas wrote also:

Out of the inevitable conflict of images—inevitable because of the creative, recreative, destructive and contradictory nature of the motivating centre, the womb of war—I try to make that momentary peace which is a poem. . . . A poem of mine is, or should be, a watertight section of the stream that is flowing all ways, all warring images within it should be reconciled for that small stop of time.[1]

He aims then at this moment of balanced calm, but it must be noticed that he speaks of a poem as a section of a stream, not as an independent whole, and implies in this way a perpetual motion rather than a static structure. Thomas himself, besides, acknowledged that in his earlier poems 'I was not

---

[1] H. Treece, *op. cit.*, p. 48.

successful in making a momentary peace with my images at the correct moment . . . the warring stream ran over the insecure barriers . . .'

It is better at this point to quote a whole poem by Dylan Thomas, a later one, *The Conversation of Prayers,* which is one of his most balanced and clearest works especially from the point of view of its form:

The conversation of prayers about to be said
By the child going to bed and the man on the stairs
Who climbs to his dying love in her high room,
The one not caring to whom in his sleep he will move
And the other full of tears that she will be dead,

Turns in the dark on the sound they know will arise
Into the answering skies from the green ground,
From the man on the stairs and the child by his bed.
The sound about to be said in the two prayers
For the sleep in a safe land and the love who dies

Will be the same grief flying. Whom shall they calm?
Shall the child sleep unharmed or the man be crying?
The conversation of prayers about to be said
Turns on the quick and the dead, and the man on the stairs
Tonight shall find no dying but alive and warm

In the fire of his care his love in the high room.
And the child not caring to whom he climbs his prayer
Shall drown in a grief as deep as his true grave,
And mark the dark eyed wave, through the eyes of sleep,
Dragging him up the stairs to one who lies dead.[1]

As in so much contemporary poetry, what first strikes the reader here is the form of the poem. The recurrent words create an intricate contrapuntal pattern. Inversion is used throughout to give a sort of double-twisted shape to the structure of the poem. For instance, the two human figures (the two

[1] First published in *Life and Letters,* July 1945; then in *Deaths and Entrances,* London, 1946, p. 3; now in *Collected Poems,* cit., p. 100.

'characters') in the poem, the child and the man, appear in this order in the first stanza (*the child going to bed and the man on the stairs*), but the order is reversed in the second: *the man on the stairs and the child by his bed*; they go back to the original order in line 12 (*shall the child sleep unharmed or the man be crying*), only to change places again in the next few lines (lines 14 and ff.: *the man on the stairs . . . and the child not caring*). The same inversion, which underlines the mysterious crossing and interchanging of the prayers, happens with single nouns and their attributive expressions: here is the word *prayers*: in the first stanza there is *the conversation of prayers about to be said,* but in the second it has become *the sound about to be said in the two prayers,* while in the third it goes back to the *prayers about to be said*; or let us take the *dying love in her high room* of the first stanza—in the second the inversion takes place (*the love who dies*), but in lines 15–16 we find *no dying but alive and warm . . . his love in the high room*. These inversions, and the recurrence at irregular intervals of the significant words *sleep, dead, dark, sound, grief, care* (and *not caring*), contribute toward the building up of a sinuous and always interlaced word- and image-pattern, which, for all its precision, is never symmetrical. To confirm this there are the only two verbs in the third person singular of the present tense: *turns* and *climbs,* recurring twice each. For their position in the poem (one in the second and third stanza, the other in the first and fourth) they seem to act as pivots on which the whole composition is hinged. And their choice is significant, as they imply rotation and upward movement; they are expressive therefore, of the physical shape itself of the poem.

The structural elements in it form an irregular spiral, which in visual terms could be represented by serpentine lines intersecting at irregular intervals and with no visible end or culmination. I have compared before Thomas' poetry to Baroque art, and found one of the essential characteristics of the latter lacking in it. Now the analysis of this poem should have suggested to which style it approaches: asymmetry, the serpentine and spiral design, the upward impulse, are all typical of the style which immediately preceded Baroque: Mannerism. Thomas' poetry is close to Mannerism also in mood—and we must remember that most of Donne's poetry and Shakespeare's last plays can be included in the Manneristic period.[1] In them as in Thomas there is the attempt to affirm new and evasive values, felt rather than possessed, the interest in the intellectual play with words and images, the sensuous apprehension of thought, the preciosity in expression, the concentration of meaning in elliptical and pregnant sentences.

Thomas can be taken as representative of the most complex and sophisticated development of contemporary poetry—the poetry of a time when no belief is firmly settled and the struggle to affirm or discuss it induces the authors on the one hand to intellectualize their work to the utmost (hence the charge of obscurity), on the other to concentrate their attention on the elements which appear most matter of fact and intellectually unquestionable: technical problems of writing, semantics, sound effects. Thomas' poetry is an outstanding example of this second tendency, the concentration on the outer elements of poetic composition, the dissection of words and their meaning in order to invest them with a new charge of significance. As Mr. Aivaz writes,

the transition from image to image is by way of the pun, the double meaning, the coined word, the composite word, the noun-verb, the pronoun with a double antecedent. And there is a larger machinery, verbal and syntactical: clauses that read both forward and backward; uneven images that are smoothed by incantatory rhythms, rhymes, word patterns, verse forms, by the use of commas instead of full-stop punctuation; wrenched platitudes and clichés, the shifted word or words suggesting the image to follow; cant, slang terms and formal, general, abstract wording juxtaposed in image after image.[2]

[1] On the 'serpentine' poetry of Donne and its influence on contemporary poetry, see M. Praz, 'Poesia inglese contemporanea', in *Aut Aut*, II, March 1951.

[2] D. Aivaz, 'The Poetry of Dylan Thomas', in *Hudson Review*, vol. III, n. 3, Autumn 1950, pp. 382–404.

But in this way a new freshness is given to hackneyed words, which seem to revive in their unfamiliar contexts:

> And from the first declension of the flesh
> I learnt man's tongue, to twist the shape of thoughts
> Into the stony idiom of the brain,
> To shade and knit anew the patch of words
> Left by the dead who, in their moonless acre,
> Need no word's warmth.[1]

As a first impression we could go so far as to say that Thomas' inspiration is fundamentally verbal. For him, as for the surrealists, there has been talk of verbal compulsion, and perhaps this may be true of some of his weakest poems:

> Every morning I make,
> God in bed, good and bad,
> After a water-face walk,
> The death-stagged scatter-breath
> Mammoth and sparrowfall
> Everybody's earth.[2]

This impression is strengthened by the limited use (especially in his earlier poems) of pictorial imagery. Colour for example is always used emblematically, red for Christ's blood, green for life force, etc. Perhaps it is the very rarity of naturalistic description which gives such emotional power to 'a room with a stuffed fox and a stale fern' in his poem in memory of Ann Jones [3] or to the sudden evocation in an adjective of 'star-gestured children', which occurs in a passage where he is stating with exceptional clarity his infatuation with words:

> Shut, too, in a tower of words, I mark
> On the horizon walking like the trees

---

[1] From *Love's first fever to her plague*, in *Collected Poems*, p. 21.

[2] *When I Woke*, in *Deaths and Entrances*, p. 40; now in *Collected Poems*, p. 134.

[3] *After the Funeral*, published first in *The Map of Love* (1939); now in *Collected Poems*, pp. 87–8. That the room of Ann Jones is an actual memory is proved also by the short story 'The Peaches', in *Portrait of the Artist as a Young Dog*, London, 1940.

The wordy shapes of women, and the rows
Of the star-gestured children in the park,
Some let me make you of the vowelled beeches,
Some of the oaken voices, from the roots
Of many a thorny shire tell you notes,
Some let me make you of the water's speeches . . .[1]

For Thomas then words have a substance of their own. Things are transformed into words, words which have almost a physical existence. 'Star-gestured children' is a perfect example of the natural object which is transformed into corporeal word. While star-gestured is descriptive of the uncontrolled movement of the child, the association is not between the child and the star in the sky, but with the star symbol in its emblematic significance. The alternation of noun and adjective in 'vowelled beeches' and 'oaken voices' emphasizes the identity for Thomas of word-sound and object. These incarnate words are his material.

The word incarnate is the basis of much of his religious symbolism. Creation for him is the work of words:

> In the beginning was the word, the word
> That from the solid bases of the light
> Abstracted all the letters of the void;
> And from the cloudy bases of the breath
> The word flowed up, translating to the heart
> First characters of birth and death.[2]

The whole of life, meaning the world of feeling and sensation, is for Thomas a translation into words of these two extremes of human experience, birth and death. They are constantly referred to in Biblical terms and acquire in this way a universal and eternal value. It has been noticed that the most insistent

[1] *Especially when the October wind* (*18 Poems*); now in *Collected Poems*, p. 16.
[2] *In the beginning* (*18 Poems*); now in *Collected Poems*, p. 22. Compare with the first lines of this passage Joyce's sentence in *Finnegans Wake*, 'amengst menlike trees walking or trees like angels weeping', discussed by Edmund Wilson in *The Wound and the Bow* (New York, rev. ed., 1947, p. 260).

religious symbols and metaphors recurring in Thomas' poetry come from the Book of Genesis and from the Crucifixion. This interest in the two Adams gives unity to Thomas' work and is the solid nucleus of his imagery. A large part of the impression of strength and power given by his poems is due to the fact that they are contained between these opposed yet united poles of Genesis and Crucifixion, birth and death. 'Thomas,' writes Mr. Huddlestone in a sensitive evaluation of his poetic world, 'begins by considering the physical cycle of man—birth, and copulation, and death';[1] but it will be noticed that the second term is by no means of equal importance with the other two. Actually Thomas' poems are rather deceptive with their apparently obsessive insistence on the sexual act. In fact this is never seen as an end in itself, as an exclusive theme for a poem: it is only the act of generation, the real 'entrance':

> Before I knocked and flesh let enter,
> With liquid hands tapped on the womb,
> I who was shapeless as the water
> That shaped the Jordan near my home . . .[2]

This is an allusion not so much to a pre-natal state, as to a state previous to conception. It is 'man-in-seed in seed-at-zero', as Thomas says in another poem[3] where the sexual act is described in military metaphors—man on the point of being generated, rather than man generating.

Before I knocked is an important poem also as the clearest statement of the identification of man with Christ, and of birth with death through the symbol of Christ. The allusion to 'the Jordan near my home' immediately connects the poet, or man, with Christ. This is further emphasized in the conclusion of

---

[1] L. Huddlestone, 'An Approach to Dylan Thomas', in *Penguin New Writing*, n. 35 (1948), p. 131.

[2] *Before I knocked* (*18 Poems*); now in *Collected Poems*, p. 7.

[3] *The seed-at-zero*, published first in *25 Poems*, London, 1936; now in *Collected Poems*, p. 42.

the poem, where the identification becomes substitution (the same exchange as in *The Conversation of Prayers*):

> You who bow down at cross and altar,
> Remember me and pity Him
> Who took my flesh and bone for armour
> And doublecrossed my mother's womb.[1]

The 'doublecrossing', while stressing the ambiguity of the central figure of the poem, man-Christ, is a punning reference to the crossing of the womb—birth, and the Crucifixion—death. This same connection is made as directly in the lines which immediately precede those quoted:

> I was a mortal to the last
> Long breath that carried to my father
> The message of his dying christ,

where a description of the physical act of procreation is expressed through imagery consistently connected with the Crucifixion. In this way a powerful synthesis of the two fundamentals of generation and death is achieved through the ambivalency of the diction used. It is another instance of the all-important function of diction, of the words used, in Thomas' poetry. We could say then that his poetry is motivated by the conflict and union of the two extremes of life—birth and death—and is dominated by the consciousness of the physical and intellectual power of the word.

Perhaps the only other artist who had relied so much on the sheer power of the word has been James Joyce. In fact, most of the critics of Thomas' poetry have mentioned this debt. This is a standard and fair judgement:

Thomas is Welsh, with all the Welshman's relish for words . . . has read his Bible, studied his Hopkins, and Joyce, and, possibly, Freud. So his poems are attempts to put his feelings into striking word-patterns, with incidental symbolism, some invention of words, and the devices of repetition, alliteration and assonance.[2]

---

[1] *Before I knocked*, cit., p. 8.
[2] C. L. Boltz, *Crown to Mend, A Letter on Poetry*, London, 1945, p. 134.

There is no doubt that the influence of Joyce exists in Thomas' general attitude to reality. They are both intensely subjective, and adolescent experience has the greatest importance for them. In *A Portrait of the Artist as a Young Man* and the *Portrait of the Artist as a Young Dog,* respectively, they regard the world from the vantage point of an adolescent mind. Both succeed in shocking the public to attention—in fact their ideas are conveyed through a series of shocks. To communicate their meaning they both rely largely on the very sound of words rather than on their dictionary value. Both contrive also an extreme concentration inside the word itself together with a large diffuseness in the number of words used. But here the connection ceases. For Joyce the realization of the power of words becomes more and more an exclusive interest in them, an obsession with their history and breeding. In *Ulysses* he was still using words as Thomas might, or for that matter Hopkins:

Listen: a fourworded wavesspeech: seesoo, hrss, rsseeiss, ooos. Vehement breath of waters amid seasnakes, rearing horses, rocks. In cups of rocks it slops: flop, slop, slap: bounded in barrels. And, spent, its speech ceases. It flows purling, widely flowing, floating foampool, flower unfurling.[1]

Opening instead *Finnegans Wake* we find

Sir Tristram, violer d'amores, fr'over the short sea, had passencore rearrived from North Armorica on this side the scraggy isthmus of Europe Minor to wielderfight his penisolate war: nor had topsawyer's rocks by the stream Oconee exaggerated themselse to Laurens County's gorgios while they went doublin the mumper all the time: nor avoice from afire bellowsed mishe mishe to tauftauf thuartpeatrick; not yet, though venissoon after, had a kidscad buttended a bland old isaac; not yet, though all's fair in vanessy, were sosie sesthers wroth with twone nathandjoe.[2]

Even here there is a complicated pattern of sound which in other passages of the book may reach a very high musical

[1] *Ulysses,* cit., p. 46.　　[2] *Finnegans Wake,* cit., p. 1.

quality. But obviously the writer is possessed by the daemon of association, whether philological or mnemonic. He is trying to give his words as many meanings as possible, and even more. The word is all important, but to reach this pregnancy it has to be continually dissected and reconstructed. The result is a violent deformation of language. In Thomas instead, what new word coinage there is utilizes existing English words and Anglo-Saxon roots. The concentration of meaning is reached mainly through the apparent strangeness or novelty of the associations. But these associations are emotional as well as intellectual, and never scholarly (as is mostly the case with Joyce). While Joyce creates new abstract words, Thomas, as we have already seen, gives a corporeal weight, a physical force to the known ones.

Keeping strictly to the peculiarities of diction, Thomas is no doubt nearer to Hopkins than to Joyce. The novelty of some of his words and expressions is given not, as in Joyce, by the mixing of different words into one, but rather, as in Hopkins, by the substitution of one of the terms in known compounds or expressions, as in

> The Atlas eater with a jaw for news [1]

or

> A springful of larks in a rolling
> Cloud [2]

comparable to Hopkins'

> . . . up above, what wind-walks! what lovely behaviour
> Of silk-sack clouds! has wilder, wilful-wavier
> Meal-drift moulded ever and melted across skies? [3]

There are of course many more similarities with Hopkins; the use of alliteration, assonance, adjectivation, and a complete dis-

---

[1] *Altarwise by owl-light* (*25 Poems*); now in *Collected Poems*, p. 71.
[2] *Poem in October* (*Deaths and Entrances*); now in *Collected Poems*, p. 102.
[3] G. M. Hopkins, *Poems*, cit., *Hurrahing in Harvest*, p. 30.

regard for grammatical parts of speech. But this has been often said and fully illustrated.[1] It has been especially emphasized that both Thomas and Hopkins are Welsh, and their particular relish for the sound of words has been attributed to this. On this point it is useful to notice how most of the writers who attempted stylistic innovations in English prose and poetry were not of English origin. Henry James, Ezra Pound, T. S. Eliot, Joseph Conrad, James Joyce, W. B. Yeats and Hopkins: these, with the exception of Conrad, were English speaking from birth, but perhaps the co-existence in their countries and consciousness of different local languages or idioms heightened their sensitivity to the form of English. Possibly this consciousness of form led them to give greater value to it, so that their care for and interest in the structure of the poem or novel begins with their care for the structure of the sentence.

Going back to the relation of Thomas to Hopkins, one fact must be made clear: Hopkins aimed at creating a completely new poetic rhythm based on the stresses of common speech. In one way therefore he was approaching the prose form, but at the same time he emphasized the poetic character of this writing in the diction. It is through the diction that he aims at a concentration of thought and expression, which could not be reached in prose. Now, in Thomas instead, there is no attempt at loosening the rhythm. He uses a variety of metres but is not a metrical innovator. His diction has the same characteristics as Hopkins, but he is counting more on the psychological associations of the words and images which he uses. Another difference between the two lies in the fact that, while in Hopkins images have a very strong visual basis, in Thomas the stress is all on the intellectual side. Hopkins' concreteness is frequently of a pictorial kind, while Thomas tends rather to give concreteness to his intellectual images through the use of corporeal words which do not *represent* objects but are objects themselves, are each a solid unit held together by the mental associations it evokes in the reader. Hopkins, working by

[1] See for instance the book by Henry Treece mentioned above.

accumulation, adds adjective to adjective, picture to picture, as in *The Windhover*, or in:

Cloud-puffball, torn tufts, tossed pillows | flaunt forth, then
    chevy on an air-
built thoroughfare: heaven-roysterers, in gay gangs | they
    throng: they glitter in marches.[1]

Thomas relies instead on the intellectual associations even in nature descriptions:

My images stalk the trees and the slant sap's tunnel,
No tread more perilous, the green steps and spire
Mount on man's footfall,
I with the wooden insect in the tree of nettles,
In the glass bed of grapes with snail and flower,
Hearing the weather fall.[2]

Even when Thomas seems to be drawing directly from Hopkins, the difference will appear from the contexts in which similar lines figure. In the following passage by Thomas:

Never until the mankind making
Bird beast and flower
Fathering and all humbling darkness
Tells with silence the last light breaking . . .[3]

there is a definite echo from 'the widow-making unchilding unfathering deeps' in *The Wreck of the Deutschland*,[4] and perhaps the 'womb-of-all, home-of-all, hearse-of-all night' in *Spelt from Sibyl's Leaves*.[5] But once again Thomas presents images appealing not to what we see but to what we know,

---

[1] *That Nature Is a Heraclitean Fire . . .*, in *Poems*, cit., p. 67.

[2] *I, in my intricate image* (*25 Poems*); now in *Collected Poems*, p. 36.

[3] *A Refusal to Mourn the Deaths, by Fire, of a Child in London* (*Deaths and Entrances*); now in *Collected Poems*, p. 101.

[4] G. M. Hopkins, *Poems*, cit., p. 15.

[5] *Ibid.*, p. 51.

while the two similar images quoted from Hopkins are part of contexts where the pictorial element prevails:

Wiry and white-fiery and whirlwind-swivellèd snow
Spins to the widow-making unchilding unfathering deeps . . .

and

Earnest, earthless, equal, attuneable, | vaulty, voluminous, . . .
    stupendous
Evening strains to be time's vàst, | womb-of-all, home-of-all,
    hearse-of-all night.
Her fond yellow hornlight wound to the west, | her wild
    hollow hoarlight hung to the height
Waste;

It should be noticed however that in his most recent work Thomas has acquired a more definitely visual quality, so that we find in *Over Sir John's Hill*:

Over Sir John's hill,
The hawk on fire hangs still;
In a hoisted cloud, at drop of dusk, he pulls to his claws
And gallows, up the rays of his eyes the small birds of the bay
And the shrill child's-play
Wars
Of the sparrows and such who swansing, dusk, in wrangling
    edges.[1]

This is pictorial in the same generous way as *The Windhover*. On the other hand we must not forget that the young Hopkins himself had at times a view of natural things not objectively pictorial, but conceived in strictly personal anthropomorphic terms. These jottings in his notebook, presumably of 1866, when he was about twenty-two, show how he related natural objects to the human body:

Drops of rain hanging on rails, etc., seen with only the lower rim lighted like nails (of fingers). Screws of brooks and

---

[1] First printed in *Botteghe Oscure*, IV (Rome, 1949); now in *Collected Poems*, p. 167.

twines. Soft chalky look with more shadowy middle of the globes of cloud on a night with a moon faint or concealed. Mealy clouds with a not brilliant moon. Blunt buds of the ash. Pencil buds of the beech. Lobes of the trees. Cups of the eyes. Gathering back the lightly hinged eyelids. Bows of the eyelids. Pencil of eyelashes. Juices of the eyeball. Eyelids like leaves, petals, caps, tufted hats, handkerchiefs, sleeves, gloves. Also of the bones sleeved in flesh. Juices of the sunrise. Joins and veins of the same. Vermilion look of the hand held against a candle with the darker parts as the middles of the fingers and especially the knuckles covered with ash.[1]

This can be compared with Thomas' studies of his hand and arm:

> When once the twilight locks no longer
> Locked in the long worm of my finger . . .[2]

> My hero bares his nerves along my wrist
> That rules from wrist to shoulder . . .[3]

Or with some of his cosmological visions:

> From the divorcing sky I learnt the double,
> The two-framed globe that spun into a score;
> A million minds gave suck to such a bud
> As forks my eye . . .[4]

> One bough of bone across the rooting air,
> The substance forked that marrowed the first sun . . .[5]

> Dawn breaks behind the eyes . . .
> Night in the sockets rounds,
> Like some pitch moon, the limit of the globes; . . .
> The film of spring is hanging from the lids . . .

---

[1] *The Note-Books and Papers of G. M. Hopkins*, ed. H. House, cit., p. 53.
[2] *When once the twilight locks no longer* (18 Poems); now in Collected Poems, p. 4.
[3] *My hero bares his nerves* (18 Poems); now in Collected Poems, p. 10.
[4] *From love's first fever to her plague* (18 Poems), now in Collected Poems, p. 21.
[5] *In the beginning* (18 Poems); now in Collected Poems, p. 22.

The secret of the soil grows through the eye,
And blood jumps in the sun . . .[1]

All these quotations are from poems included in Thomas' first collection, *18 Poems,* published in 1934; it is unlikely that he had access to Hopkins' notes, extracts from which were published apparently for the first time only in *The Criterion* for October 1935. This goes to prove that the similarities we have noticed with the Hopkins' passage are not due to a direct literary influence of the earlier poet, but to the kinship of feelings and impressions in the two poets as young men.

If the connection between Thomas and Hopkins is mainly in the diction and technique, that between Thomas and Donne (another of the references *de rigueur* when speaking of Thomas) is mainly in the quality of the images employed. I have already insisted on the intellectual character of Thomas' imagery—and this is of course a first connection with Donne. Mr. Huddlestone remarked that Thomas' imagery 'has an emotional impact similar to Donne's intellectual impact'.[2] The fact is that in Donne there is as much emotional as intellectual power, so that Thomas at his best, when he succeeds in expressing a sustained intellectual content in his poetry, is directly in the line of the Metaphysicals. In Thomas for instance there is the same tendency as in Donne to use metaphors taken from contemporary technical or scientific inventions, and the more recent gramophone, cinema, propeller and periscope take the place of Donne's telescope and compasses. In both poets there is a visible pleasure in the sound of the technical vocabulary. This can be seen in the film terminology of *Our eunuch dreams* in *18 Poems* or *Then was my neophyte* in *25 Poems,* or in this image, from a gramophone:

---

[1] *Light breaks where no sun shines (18 Poems);* now in *Collected Poems,* pp. 24–5.
[2] L. Huddlestone, article quoted, p. 132. Perhaps Thomas was more influenced by the Welsh metaphysical poet Henry Vaughan than by Donne; see the passages from Vaughan quoted by Thomas himself in his radio-talk 'Welsh Poets' (1946); now in *Quite Early One Morning,* London, 1954, pp. 140–2.

Turn the sea spindle lateral,
The grooved land rotating, that the stylus of lightning
Dazzle this face of voices on the moon-turned table,
Let the wax disk babble
Shames and the damp dishonours, the relic scraping.
These are your years' recorders. The circular world stands still.[1]

Here the metaphor is extended, as in Crashaw and the later
Metaphysicals, who worked their images out with that completeness which is required by the amplitude of Baroque. But
more frequently Thomas introduces these metaphors in passing, using them as intellectual foci for his complex imagery,
which reaches through them a more marked compactness and
concentration. Here is an example in a context which may
recall also Donne's preoccupation with the decay of flesh after
death:

The dry Sargasso of the tomb
Gives up its dead to such a working sea;
And sleep rolls mute above the beds
Where fishes' food is fed the shades
Who periscope through flowers to the sky.[2]

And perhaps an affinity of conception may be discovered between Thomas' interest in Genesis and Crucifixion, and the
identification of the two Adams with himself, and the following lines of Donne's:

We thinke that *Paradise* and *Calvarie*,
   Christs Crosse, and *Adams* tree, stood in one place;
Looke Lord, and finde both *Adams* met in me;[3]

There is of course a substantial difference in the use of religious
or Biblical imagery in the two poets. In Donne it may be
employed in peculiar contexts, and even at times associated, (as

[1] *I, in my intricate image (25 Poems)*; now in *Collected Poems*, p. 37.
[2] *When once the twilight locks no longer (18 Poems)*; now in *Collected Poems*, p. 5.
[3] *Hymne to God my God, in my sicknesse*, in *The Poems of John Donne*, ed.
H. J. G. Grierson, Oxford, 1933, p. 337.

in Thomas) with sexual allusions or mechanical and scientific inventions, but it always asserts itself in the end as the real foundation of thought. In other words, religion stays as the basis of the poetry, though the Manneristic style in which the poet naturally expresses himself creates startling associations for it. With Thomas instead the religious symbolism, though expressed in a similar Manneristic style, is only a metaphorical means of expression of the poet's personal thought; it contributes to the creation of that personal myth which seems to be the real aim of his poetry. Donne in his later phase (after the earlier intellectual gropings) reached a point of religious belief —and this passage onto a more solid spiritual ground is mirrored in his style which, from Mannerism, reaches toward the more rounded solidity of Baroque. Thomas instead is striving to affirm an individual vision in which the religious element is only incidental, and is employed as a useful imaginative contribution. Even the ritualism of some of his more recent poems (e.g. *Ceremony after a Fire Raid*) is not an effort in the direction of church ritual, but it is used to create a personal legend, to enclose in a hieratic atmosphere a new myth.[1]

As Francis Scarfe remarks, 'it would be ridiculous to claim Thomas for any church. It is sufficient to note to what entirely different uses T. S. Eliot and Dylan Thomas have put the Bible for purposes of poetry.'[2] There is no more striking example of this difference than the image suggested to both poets by the sight, during the war, of raiding aeroplanes, scattering fire. Both associated them with the Biblical dove, but the result of the association is widely divergent. Eliot, in *Little Gidding*, in the section containing open allusions to his fire watching during the London blitz, speaks of the dawn

[1] These words seem to run counter to what Thomas himself states in his note to his *Collected Poems* (these poems . . . are written for the love of Man and in praise of God), and to the opinion of critics. But I think my argument is made clear in the following paragraphs.

[2] Francis Scarfe, *Auden and After*, London, 1942, pp. 101–17.

After the dark dove with the flickering tongue
Had passed below the horizon of his homing . . .[1]

and in a later section the image is taken up again:

The dove descending breaks the air
With flame of incandescent terror
Of which the tongues declare
The one discharge from sin and error.
The only hope, or else despair
    Lies in the choice of pyre or pyre—
    To be redeemed from fire by fire.[2]

For him, then, the image of a flaming dove suggested by an enemy plane leads to a vision of the descent of the Holy Ghost, bringing the Pentecostal fire. The idea of death is transformed into that of purification.

Here instead is the context in which Thomas has included the same image suggested by the enemy plane:

Into her lying down head
His enemies entered bed,
Under the encumbered eyelid,
Through the rippled drum of the hair-buried ear;
And Noah's rekindled now unkind dove
Flew man-bearing there.
Last night in a raping wave
Whales unreined from the green grave
In fountains of origin gave up their love,
Along her innocence glided
Juan aflame and savagely young King Lear . . .[3]

This could be taken as a typical example of the polivalency of Thomas' imagery, and also of the gusto with which he tries to complicate it, exploiting all its potentialities in order to extract

[1] T. S. Eliot, *Four Quartets,* cit., p. 38.
[2] *Ibid.,* p. 42.
[3] *Into her Lying Down Head (Deaths and Entrances)*; now in *Collected Poems,* p. 113.

the maximum effect. At first he plays on the fairly obvious contrast between the war-bringing enemy aircraft and the dove, a messenger of peace. The language itself emphasizes the formal character of the antithesis (*rekindled now unkind*). In the next line, while on one side *man-bearing* makes the image of the aircraft more evident, on the other it introduces a complex double-meaning. There is in it a hidden reference to the Conception of the Virgin, with the Holy Ghost traditionally represented as a dove, man-bearing, the bringer of Christ, man-God. As usual with Thomas, the idea of conception introduces a whole host of sexual images obviously connected with psycho-analytical symbols, till the image of the dove is identified with *Juan aflame* (this adjective connects back to the flames of the Holy Ghost and the fire of the aircraft); the Biblical reference is in this way related to an act of rape, introducing a further antithesis and at the same time identifying religious and Freudian symbols. Eliot, from the same starting point, presents one consistent religious interpretation of the dove symbol, the dove of the Pentecost, while Thomas mixes the Old and New Testament doves and further transforms them into symbols of a personal Mythology.

This indicates a difference not only in beliefs, but also in literary technique and style. At its first appearance the dove-aircraft image is presented by Eliot in an elliptical enough form —it is already intellectualized, containing an emblematic element which fully affirms itself at its second appearance, in the fourth section of the poem. The image, with its surprising union of apparently heterogeneous elements, obviously belongs with the conceits of the seventeenth-century Metaphysicals. It may be taken as an example of Manneristic or early Baroque intellectual mood. But its treatment is restrained: Eliot's going back to it, clarifying in the second passage its symbolic meaning, is evidence of a preoccupation with structure and balance. The second presentation of the image is direct, without decorative or supplementary imagery: it goes straight to its purpose, treating a fundamentally Baroque conception, rich in the element of surprise, with classical sparingness and severity. It appears that Eliot, starting from a position similar to the Mannerism of Donne, has reached, in his later poems, togethe with his new firmness of belief, a sense of structural symmetry which is no longer Manneristic but Baroque. We must remember that there are two sides also to seventeenth-century Baroque; the more flamboyant one, represented in literature by poets like Crashaw, and the classical one of Milton. Eliot seems to be following this second road of 'classical Baroque', as is witnessed by his verbal restraint and, in his critical writings, by his preoccupation with the rules and principles of composition—and finally by his 'change of mind' on Milton.[1]

For Thomas I have already spoken of Mannerism (the contemporary form of which I have called in the previous essays Funambulism), and his treatment of the image that now interests us tends to confirm it. It is not resumed and developed in Eliot's orderly way: it is instead subjected to the action of other images, and re-emerges indirectly, utterly transformed, to be immediately re-absorbed by a new wave of fresh images. There is development, but not balance. We could say then that while Eliot is proceeding from Mannerism to the classicistic form of Baroque, Thomas has still all the Manneristic taste for the 'serpentine' form of construction, the wavy line of development, which implies a basic unity of conception but does not seek structural solidity, squareness and symmetry. Indeed, in other poems by Thomas, as for instance *Vision and Prayer*,[2] one could detect an aspiration toward formal symmetry, but the partiality for intellectual flourishes, for rich and contrasting images still prevails. If, then, he tends towards the formal balance and repose of Baroque, it is the most flamboyant expression of it that he approaches, what could be called, in opposition to 'classical', the 'romantic' aspect of this style, as represented in Herbert and Crashaw. It should be clear by now that when I use the terms Mannerism or Baroque, I do not mean that the

---

[1] See the essay on Eliot's theatre in the present volume.

[2] First published in *Deaths and Entrances*; now in *Collected Poems* 137–48.

poets I am dealing with belong altogether with their seven-teenth-century predecessors; I use the terms only as approximate and provisional working definitions of stylistic characters, to show a parallel development of style in different periods. It is indeed to stress this parallelism that I have used throughout this essay the definition 'Mannerism' instead of 'Funambulism' with reference to contemporary writers.

The different treatment of images we have just noticed reflects not only on what we could call the stylistic affiliations of the different authors, but also on their position in the main current of English poetical tradition. Dr. Leavis, speaking of Hopkins in his *New Bearings on English Literature,* has distinguished two main trends in poetry, one represented by the works of Shakespeare, Donne, Eliot, and the later Yeats, the other by those of Spenser, Milton and Tennyson.[1] It appears at once that Thomas is closer to the first group—with the necessary qualifications of course that each single poet requires. His language, in spite of word play and unusual sentence

---

[1] Mr. S. L. Bethell has tried in his essay, 'Two Streams from Helicon' (in *Essays on Literary Criticism and the English Tradition,* London, 1948, pp. 53–87), to 'press the distinction to ideal limits', listing the contrasting characteristics of the two groups. According to his very useful working definition, the poets of group A (the Shakespeare-Donne-Eliot stream) are characterized by the use of a language founded on the colloquial speech of their day, a rhythm counter-pointed by that of common speech, functional intellectual imagery, contemporary subject matter and a more spontaneous general approach to this matter. Those of group B instead use a language specially created for poetic purposes, a rhythm which fully respects the metrical pattern, pictorial, descriptive and subjectively emotional imagery, subject matter not strictly connected with contemporary issues, and finally, conscious artistry in the general approach to their medium. Mr. Bethell rightly insists on the approximate value of his distinction, remarking that 'in reality every poet has some of the characteristics of each group', but the fact remains that, in attempting to give a picture of a whole literature not as a development of styles through the different periods, but as the expression of a national tradition in which certain constant elements can be found in any period, Mr. Bethell's definition is as good as any. This is why I am trying to see also the position of Dylan Thomas in respect of this twofold tradition.

structure, is certainly not conventionally 'poetic', but rather founded on contemporary colloquial speech:

> If my bunched monkey coming is cruel,
> Rage me back to the making house.[1]

As for the imagery, as has already been illustrated, there can be no doubt on its intellectual character, in contrast with the descriptive one of the second group of poets mentioned.

Thomas seems therefore to belong on the whole with the poets of the Shakespeare-Donne-Eliot group. It is noticeable however that, more than any of them, more even than Donne, Thomas is concerned with himself, with his individual world of physical and mental sensations, which he tries to express emotionally rather than to objectify with a minimum of detachment. This attempt to express strictly subjective sensations with absolute immediacy, before they have assumed rational or logical form, is one reason for Thomas' obscurity, as it leads him to create a whole complex structure of personal and contradictory symbols. In order to render this not wholly conscious world, in which even purely intellectual elements are expressed when still at the stage of sensation rather than reason or emotion, the poet must charge his images with manifold and original symbolical suggestions. The new structure of symbols, created in this way, tends, by its very novelty, to constitute new myths or rather new visions. The preoccupation with the author's self being uppermost, the visions cannot but be continually associated with physical sensations, so that they have a marked anthropomorphic character. The world outside is interpreted and represented in physical, corporeal, we could even say anatomical terms, thought is linked with organic processes and expresses itself through them.

This attitude is not completely new in English poetry. The use of emblems in late sixteenth- and seventeenth-century poetry was already a way of intellectualizing concrete experi-

---

[1] '*If my head hurt a hair's foot*', first published in *The Map of Love*; now in *Collected Poems*, p. 97.

ences, extracting symbols from them. Emblems and conceits however were used more frequently as decorations, or as compressed similes. Only at times in Donne and some of the Metaphysicals they became shortcuts from physical images to intellectual conceptions. But this transition from the physical to the intellectual does not acquire in them the hallucinatory character which it has in Thomas. An emblem forced to the point of hallucination is rather to be found in a poem which is earlier than the Metaphysicals': Robert Southwell's *The Burning Babe* (and we may note how Thomas strove after a very similar effect in his poems *A Refusal to Mourn the Death, by Fire, of a Child in London* and *Ceremony after a Fire Raid,* while he echoed the title—*The Burning Baby*—in a prose piece of his which seems a mere exercise in hallucination [1]); in Southwell, on the other hand, the emblematic foundation of the vision is constantly kept to the fore, giving an absolute prominence to the intellectual element, and very nearly abolishing physical participation.

It is significant that that school of contemporary poets who called themselves the Apocalyptics, and who set as the object of their art the creation of new myths, preferred even in Shakespeare the works where he is deliberately emblematic. They wanted their poetry to be in line with the Book of Revelation, Shakespeare's *The Phoenix and the Turtle,* Webster, Donne, Blake, Hopkins and Kafka. They claimed Thomas, who never formally belonged to the movement, as 'a hero and a mascot'.[2] Actually their connection with him is only in some external features and mannerisms. But whatever their artistic achievement may be, they had the merit of realizing that, in English poetry, there is a definite and constant current, a third 'stream from Helicon', formed by those poets for whom images acquire the physical intensity of vision. In other words, the image acquires for them a kind of physical consistency; it is no

[1] The two poems were first collected in *Deaths and Entrances*; the prose in *Contemporary English Prose,* London, 1939.

[2] See the books already mentioned, by H. Treece, C. L. Boltz and F. Scarfe.

longer a vehicle of thought and a means of expression: it lives and breeds of itself. We could call this stream visionary poetry, provided it is understood that vision is not intended in the sense of allegory (as in *Piers Plowman*) or of a fantastic picture (as in *Kubla Khan*). Vision for them is concrete, capable of continuity and development, endowed with the characteristics of physical experiences—and at the same time, being concrete only in the mind of the poet and not in relation to the external world, it has an indefiniteness which, while making it difficult to fix and express, enhances its incantatory power.

Blake's *London* can be taken as an example of visionary poetry in its least complex form:

> How the Chimney-sweeper's cry
> Every black'ning Church appals;
> And the hapless Soldier's sigh
> Runs in blood down Palace walls.
>
> But most thro' midnight streets I hear
> How the youthful Harlot's curse
> Blasts the new born Infant's tear
> And blights with plagues the Marriage hearse.[1]

Here concrete images create, through compressed metaphors, composite mental pictures which cannot be visualized but preserve a character of actuality, are felt as physical presences rather than abstract conceits. And this is strikingly a feature of visions: they appeal directly to the senses as visible material objects, but at the same time cannot be visualized as pictorial compositions. Another characteristic is their directness: through the senses and only through the senses images are conveyed to the mind—no rationalizing process interferes with the immediacy of the communication. In this way visionary poetry has, together with a certain indefiniteness, a strong physical impact. It was not by chance that Blake, as a painter and engraver, set Michael Angelo as his ideal; whose works, emphasizing the human figures at the expense of their surroundings, were a

[1] W. Blake, *Poetry and Prose*, ed. G. Keynes, cit. p. 75.

visual rendering of the corporeal basis of Blake's visions. These are fundamentally anthropomorphic, not so much because the poet creates a new race of giants to act out his esoteric mythology, as because he is conscious of the physical nature of his creatures, he sees them as structures of nerves and bones, subject to organic processes closely connected with those of nature:

Los heard in terror Enitharmon's words: in fibrous strength
His limbs shot forth like roots of trees against the forward path
of Milton's journey . . .[1]

This is comparable to several passages of Thomas' which I have already quoted. And there are themes common to both poets which produce similarities in diction and imagery. Here is Blake in an early *Prophetic Book*:

                                                The virgin
That pines for man shall awaken her womb to enormous joys
In the secret shadows of her chamber: the youth shut up from
The lustful joy shall forget to generate & create an amorous
        image
In the shadows of his curtains and in the folds of his silent
        pillow.[2]

Here there is an obvious analogy with Thomas' *Into her Lying Down Head* (part of which I have quoted before), and *On the Marriage of a Virgin*.[3] The theme of generation and creation has the same obsessive recurrence in Blake as in Thomas. There is a remarkable closeness between Thomas' vocabulary and that of Blake in a passage like the following:

                In harrowing fear rolling round
                His nervous brain shot branches
                Round the branches of his heart
                On high into two little orbs,
                And fixed in two little caves,

---

[1] *Milton, Book the First,* ed. quoted, p. 394.
[2] *Visions of the Daughters of Albion* (1793), ed. quoted, p. 199.
[3] First in *Deaths and Entrances*; now in *Collected Poems*, pp. 113, 127.

Hiding carefully from the wind,
His Eyes beheld the deep.[1]

It is interesting to note that this is a passage which occurs more than once in Blake's works, showing the importance that it had for him. In the same way we can see how words like *ripeness, winds, odors, figs, seed, fire, virgins, spring* are put to the same use by Thomas and by Blake:

Swell'd with ripeness & fat with fatness,
Bursting on winds, my odors,
My ripe figs and rich pomegranates
In infant joy at thy feet,
O Urizen, sported and sang.

Then thou with thy lap full of seed,
With thy hand full of generous fire
Walked forth from clouds of morning,
On the virgins of springing joy . . .[2]

If this reminds us of the poems contained in the two earlier books of Thomas' (*18 Poems* and *25 Poems*), the pregnancy theme of *The Map of Love* (especially of '*If my head hurt a hair's foot*') is expressed with similar vigour by Blake in the *First Book of Urizen*:

Yet helpless it lay like a Worm
In the trembling womb
To be moulded into existence.
. . .
Coil'd within Enitharmon's womb
The serpent grew, casting its scales;
. . .
Many forms of fish, bird & beast
Brought forth an Infant form
Where was a worm before.[3]

---

[1] *The First Book of Urizen* (1794), ed. cit., p. 226 (see the whole of Chapter IVb and compare *The Book of Los* and *The Four Zoas, Night IV*).

[2] *The Book of Ahania* (1795), ed. cit., p. 241.

[3] Ed. cit., p. 229.

Thomas, then, throughout his work echoes themes, images and diction from Blake's *Prophetic Books* (the works where Blake wanted to express directly his intellectual vision), but while the similarities, even in the use of single words, are obvious, the echoes are not due to a direct derivation, but to the visionary world common to both poets. And the same tone and imagery, with a strong insistence on the physical element of vision, can be found also in some of the poems of Francis Thompson:

> I shook the pillaring hours
> And pulled my life upon me; grimed with smears,
> I stand amid the dust o' the mounded years—
> My mangled youth lies dead beneath the heap.
> My days have crackled and gone up in smoke,
> Have puffed and burst as sun-starts on a stream.[1]

Apart from the direct Biblical allusion, this powerful physical and natural imagery in the poets quoted is partly due to the influence of the Bible itself, but it is also produced by their having a personal vision. Thomas indeed belongs with them as much as with Hopkins, who makes nature rather than the human body the centre of his visionary transfiguration. These poets may be said to form a separate and identifiable current in English literature, connected with the stream of intellectual poetry (in Mr. Bethell's classification) but with characteristics of its own.[2]

Thomas then is not an isolated phenomenon; neither is his poetry the accidental result of haphazard influences. Though remaining extremely individual, he is part of an established poetical tradition, and uses forms which follow the logical development of English poetic expression. Though belonging

---

[1] *The Hound of Heaven.*

[2] It is significant that Bethell hesitates to include Hopkins in his group A; his perplexity may be due to the consciousness of the existence in him of a visionary capacity which tends to isolate him among the other poets of the group. See Bethell, *op. cit.,* p. 54.

to an unusual poetic current—the poetry of vision—he too is a link in the chain of stylistic evolution from Funambulism (something comparable to seventeenth-century Mannerism) to a style akin to Baroque.

The Baroque Theatre

SINCE I wrote the previous essays, Dylan Thomas has died, but left that odd and successful piece of work, *Under Milk Wood,* while Eliot and Fry have produced a new verse play each. As the character of those essays was, at least in part, exploratory, and attempted to assess the present trend in taste and style, it is very tempting to look at the latest works with the deliberate purpose of finding in them a confirmation or a denial of what has already been said. Eliot's *Confidential Clerk* and Fry's *The Dark is Light Enough* seem to offer such an opportunity; while Thomas' 'play for voices' suggests a comparison and a contrast.

Actually *Under Milk Wood* is not a verse play, but seems to be the one fully successful attempt to bring back to the wider public the taste and feeling for the sound of the English language (if with a Welsh accent), for the importance of speech-rhythm, and for the incantatory power of words for their own sake, apart from their meaning. It was just this effect that the early Elizabethan dramatists had produced on their audiences. They too, like the radio script-writer, could not count on much visual aid, and had to create illusion through the power of words and rhythm. They, of course, found a most flexible and apt instrument in blank verse. Now this metric form is worn threadbare, and most verse-playwrights, though feeling that it is still the only serviceable one, try to disguise it as prose with a hidden iambic pattern. Their compromise, their concession to the contemporary audience, is in fact this: to render their verse prosaic—which admittedly is far from easy, and requires a considerable technical skill. Now, Thomas too attempted a compromise. But he started from the other end: he did not try to render verse rhythms prosaic—he wanted to render prose rhythms poetical.

In a letter of October 1951, which accompanied the first part of *Under Milk Wood* (called, at that stage, *Llareggub*) he seemed to imply that he had attempted both approaches:

... I was working on a play, mostly in verse. This, I have reluctantly, and, I hope, only temporarily, abandoned: the language was altogether swamping the subject: the comedy, for that was what it was originally intended to be, was lost in the complicated violence of the words: I found I was labouring at each line as though I were making some savage, and devious, metaphysical lyric and not a play at all. . . . But out of my working, however vainly, on it, came the idea of 'Llareggub' (Please ignore it as a final title). Out of it came the idea that I write a piece, a play, an impression for voices, an entertainment out the darkness, of the town I live in, and to write it simply and warmly & comically with lots of movement and varieties of moods, so that, at many levels, through sight and speech, description & dialogue, evocation and parody, you came to know the town as an inhabitant of it. That is an awkward & highfalutin way of speaking: I only wanted to make the town alive through a raw medium . . .[1]

This statement, for all its picturesqueness, amounts to an acknowledgement of the impossibility of writing a verse-play using the complex diction and metre of Thomas' poetry—and that of most of his contemporaries (for the same reason a quarter of a century earlier Eliot had left *Sweeney* unfinished). At the same time it shows what a limited aim Thomas had set himself: to write an entertainment, which developed those shorter pieces he had been broadcasting since 1945, like *Quite Early One Morning* (1945), *The Crumbs of One Man's Year*

[1] D. Thomas, 'Three Letters', in *Botteghe Oscure*, XIII, 1954, pp. 93–4.

(1946) and *Return Journey* (1947).[1] There is no question of ideas or doctrines to be put across to an audience: the only need that Thomas recognizes is their need of being entertained. Shall we draw once again a parallel with Elizabethan drama, and recall Eliot's words, already quoted more than once in the present book: 'The Elizabethan drama was aimed at a public which wanted *entertainment* of a crude sort, but would *stand* a good deal of poetry'? Thomas thought the same of our contemporary public. But he did not use this notion of what the public wanted to foist off onto them a 'message' through the medium of entertainment. What message there is in *Under Milk Wood,* is not premeditated, but comes directly from his intuitive and poetical recognition of the joy of living and the presence of death. His play for voices is as much a job of work as his film-script *The Doctor and the Devils*—a model in its kind. The alterations he made in the first draft of the play are never meant to enrich the significance of sentences: they are workmanlike improvements in respect to the medium used. Here is, for instance, a speech as it appeared in *Llareggub,* the first part of the play published in 1952:

Me, Mrs. Dai Bread Two, gaudied to kill in a scarlet jumper, yellow petticoat, flashing sash, high heel shoes with one heel missing, tortoiseshell comb in my bright black tousle, nothing else, lolling at the doorway, scowling at the sunshine, lighting up my pipe.[2]

It became in the final version:

Me, Mrs Dai Bread Two, gypsied to kill in a silky scarlet petticoat above my knees, dirty pretty knees, see my body through my petticoat brown as a berry, high-heel shoes with one heel missing, tortoiseshell comb in my bright black slinky hair, nothing else at all but a daub of scent, lolling gaudy at the doorway, tell your fortune in the tea-leaves, scowling at the sunshine, lighting up my pipe.[3]

---

[1] Now collected in *Quite Early One Morning,* London, 1954.
[2] 'Llareggub', in *Botteghe Oscure,* IX, 1952, p. 149.
[3] D. Thomas, *Under Milk Wood,* London, 1954, p. 30.

This, on the printed page, may well look like overdoing things. But the reasons for the additions are obvious: since his medium was the radio, words and sounds had to do service also for colour and sight. Hence the insistence on the descriptive elements, which would never do on an ordinary stage. As a matter of fact Thomas did not fully avoid the danger of decoration for its own sake. It is also true that the second part of *Under Milk Wood* reveals a falling off in the author's powers, especially in the constant intrusions of the narrators' voices.

But in spite of its shortcomings, Thomas' play is significant for more than one reason. First of all as another instance of the tendency among contemporary artists to cater for ever wider audiences. A tendency partly produced by economic pressure on the authors and by the development of the so-called mass-media. But even if these are the main motives that have forced so many authors to try the stage or the radio, the important fact is that a need to communicate with the people at large has asserted itself, in full contrast with the ivory tower conception of half a century (or a quarter of a century) ago. It is difficult in such cases to establish the order of cause and effect: it may well be that the need for mass-communication in the writers developed first and the mass-media offered themselves as a natural fulfilment. What matters, rather, is the new attitude this process has created in the writer towards his own work. The consciousness of the presence of an audience at one and the same time exhilarates and inhibits him. It makes for the grand gesture, the striking posture; but it also suggests the need for some form, for some pattern universally understood—for order.

This, of course, is reflected in the style. The unruliness, the casualness, the utterly individualistic freedom of expression which characterized the art of the first half of this century, will not serve for these public utterances. The manneristic features— lack of symmetry and of constructive balance, fondness for irregularity and linear development—cannot fit the rigid technical rules imposed by the mass-media. Or at least they can fit those media only when the media themselves are still very new, and are still being explored: such was the case with the Elizabethan theatre, a new means of communication which could flourish therefore in a fully manneristic age. But after twenty years, when the medium was thoroughly established, the style of the plays was no longer Manneristic, but Baroque: the rules had been fixed and were respected. In the same way when John Donne, essentially a mannerist in his early poems, became a public preacher and a Dean, he couched his sermons in the most elaborate Baroque style. The same is happening now. The requirements of mass-communication which I have described before, the grand gesture and the need for order and pattern, are the main features of Baroque.

All this applies only in part to *Under Milk Wood*. The radio-play is still a comparatively new medium, which allows an adventurous treatment. A discipline is necessary, a technique of presentation must be devised: but it is not yet a conventional discipline, an established technique. This greater formal freedom still allowed by the radio-play is perhaps the reason why Thomas succeeded in writing it rather than a verse-comedy, which would have meant the adoption of a much more rigid form. The relative looseness of the form he used seems to me very significant, for, while expressing a need for order, at the same time it preserved that scope for improvisation which is characteristic of the romantic attitude. In the general trend towards a more balanced style—so obvious for instance in the tendency of the younger poets to abandon free verse and adopt closed metrical and stanzaic patterns—we can distinguish the permanence of two separate attitudes: the romantic, which seeks an inner imaginative freedom within the closed pattern, and the classicistic, which aims at an ideal correctness, to be verified by comparison with the models of the classical past. The presence of these two basic attitudes in all stylistic periods was recognized by Middleton Murry when he said that 'Romanticism and Classicism are perennial modes of the human spirit'.[1]

[1] J. M. Murry. *To the Unknown God,* London, 1924, p. 136; and compare in

Thomas, then, by the very fact of writing a play showed he was following the general stylistic trend away from the unruliness of manneristic expression towards that movement contained in restful forms, which is Baroque. But his statement quoted a few pages earlier shows once again his romantic attitude towards his imposed formal limits. If from *Under Milk Wood* we turn now to Eliot's last play, *The Confidential Clerk*, we shall see how the elder poet insists instead on the classicistic conceptions of his duties as a playwright. The basic characters and the basic situations are the same as in Eliot's previous plays. Colby Simpkins, the hero of *The Confidential Clerk*, who is tormented by doubts as to his paternity (the religious point of the question 'Who is our Father?' is obvious), and who ends by accepting a call to a mystic mission, is none other than Harry of *The Family Reunion*—a play which also raises the question of earthly, and heavenly, paternity. The guardian angel appears again, this time in the guise of the ex-confidential clerk, Eggerson, who comes forward at the end of the play offering Colby a job as church organist, starting him off on the path of militant faith. There is a girl too, Lucasta, who like Edward and Lavinia in *The Cocktail Party*, settles down in the material, contemporary world, but is at one time on the threshold of the 'vision', of Colby's 'secret garden'. This garden, as we have already seen, represented for Eliot the moment of revelation. But the image loses its magic here, becoming merely obvious, and the moment of illumination is never fully realized, as it had been in his earlier plays.

The themes here are the same: the only difference is, in this case, a more rigid application of the rules of composition which he had formulated. The first of these, which we have already discussed at length [1] was 'the levels of consciousness'. This theory of the 'levels', as systematized by Eliot, is not far from Dante's classification of the 'meanings of writings' in the *Con-*

the present book 'Introduction to Funambulism', and the note at the end of the present essay.

[1] See the essay 'Eliot and the Theatre', especially pp. 139-44.

vivio, a book which Eliot considered important. According to Dante 'writings can be understood and must be expressed mainly in four senses': the literal, the allegorical, the moral (didactic) and the anagogic. An Italian critic, Francesco Flora, has remarked that this formula has seriously hindered the genuine appreciation of *The Divine Comedy.* No less unfortunate has been the result of the formula which Eliot has tried to apply to a drawing-room comedy intended for a West-End audience.

It may be interesting to examine the working of this formula in *The Confidential Clerk.* On the first, the literary level, Eliot presents a comedy of manners. In order to do this he returns to Wilde. Eliot had set down as a basic condition for the new verse drama that it should present characters who 'must on your stage be able to perform the same actions and lead the same lives as in the real world', since they 'cannot be translated to a fairy-land where they may talk appropriately in verse'.[1] Yet this mythical world of millionaires, where none of the real problems of life intrude, *is* in fact a fairy-land. Is it to present such characters that he has put his audience 'on a thin diet of imperceptible verse'?[2] There is a basic misunderstanding in Eliot's conception of theatrical conventions. He has confused the necessity of stage conventions (the soliloquy, the absence of the fourth wall, the stage sets, etc.) with the use of conventions of another nature, such as traditional plot schemes, and stock characters and situations.[3] This second group could be more properly called literary mannerisms rather than theatre conventions, and it is just these which Eliot has chosen to adopt. But this stylization creates the sort of fairy-land he was anxious to

[1] In the already quoted preface to S. L. Bethell, *Shakespeare and the Popular Dramatic Tradition.*

[2] The phrase is used by Sir Herbert Read with reference to *The Cocktail Party* (see H. Read, *The True Voice of Feeling,* London, 1953, p. 148).

[3] For a convincing criticism of Eliot's ideas on theatrical conventions, see N. G. Orsini, 'T. S. Eliot e la teoria delle convenzioni drammatiche', in *Letterature Moderne,* IV, n. 6, Nov.-Dec. 1953.

avoid, and his Wildean treatment, particularly in his last play, has meant the loss of that contemporaneity of character, situation and language which he was so determined to achieve.

The second, allegorical, level of *The Confidential Clerk* rests, as is the case with the previous plays, on a Greek drama, which is meant to provide a close pattern of references to ancient myth. This time the Greek play chosen by Eliot has been identified as Euripides' *Ion*: [1] a story with a happy ending and the sensational intervention of a *dea ex machina,* which Eliot has faithfully preserved. The situation, and especially the final appearance of Mrs. Guzzard, who in Eliot takes the place of Euripides' Athene, is handled however rather superficially and for comic effect; in fact the 'formidable' *dea ex machina* is treated in terms of Miss Prism. It may be interesting to notice how Eliot, in his borrowings from Greek drama, went from Aeschylus' *Oresteia,* so rich in allegorical meanings, to Euripides' *Alcestis,* and finally *Ion*—a play closely linked with the rise of Menander's New Comedy. [2] He moved from great tragedy and myth to a highly refined, tolerant, and artificial representation of life. These three steps are significant pointers to his growing pre-occupation with the technique of stage craft, rather than with genuine poetic values.

The third, the didactic or moral level, is all-pervasive in *The Confidential Clerk.* Eliot sets out to make his audience think, to awaken it to a sense of man's predestination (as exemplified in a few of the 'chosen'), showing with what absolute obedience man must follow his 'call' to a vocation. Noticing the frequency with which certain words occur in the text, it is impossible to resist the temptation to count them. These are the results of a very rough check: the verb *to think* recurs about 130 times in the play (once every 20–25 lines),

[1] B. Dobrée, 'The Confidential Clerk', in *Sewanee Review,* LXII, n. 1, Winter 1954.

[2] See W. Arrowsmith, 'Menander and Milk Wood', in *Hudson Review,* VII, n. 2, Summer 1954, pp. 291–6, where Eliot's elaborations are contrasted with Thomas' directness.

to believe 70 times (once every 37–40 lines) and *to understand* 60 times (once every 43–45 lines). To think, to believe and to understand seem to be the imperatives of the new phase of Eliot's mysticism. These have replaced the more human injunctions of the 'Upanishad'—give, sympathize, control, which in the last lines threw a ray of light over the desolate landscape of *The Waste Land*. The new commandments seem to indicate how far towards intellectual dogmatism Eliot has travelled in his last work.

But over and above the didactic level there is the fourth meaning, the one defined by Dante as anagogical: 'that is, an over-meaning (*sopra-senso*) and this is when you interpret a writing spiritually which is also true in the literal sense, but which through what it expresses, signifies supreme things concerning eternal glory'. Eliot is aiming, in his work for the theatre, at precisely this level of meaning. We have already seen what he has written of this 'over-meaning', the 'meaning which reveals itself gradually'.[1]

It is at this point that we find a more serious equivocation. In authentic dramatic poetry feeling and emotion on the one hand and language and theatrical technique on the other, combine inseparably so as to become indistinguishable from each other. This unity of thought and expression Eliot achieves at times, as we have already said, in *The Family Reunion*; even in *The Cocktail Party* there are moments when he comes near it, but in *The Confidential Clerk* the theoretical conceptions have prevailed. The emotion to be expressed seems in a certain sense to be prefabricated: it is the expression of a religious orthodoxy which has lost its freshness even for the author himself. The scene between Colby and Lucasta in the second act, which is generally considered to be the high point of the play, uses the 'rose-garden' image more as a tired quotation from Eliot's previous works than as a re-invented and living symbol:

> And so you applied for Eggerson's position,
> And made up your mind to go into business

---

[1] T. S. Eliot, *The Use of Poetry and the Use of Criticism*, cit., p. 153.

And be someone like Claude . . . or B. I was sorry,
Very sorry for you. I admired your courage
In facing facts—or the facts as you saw them.
And yet, all the time, I found I *envied* you
And I didn't know why! And now I think I know.
It's awful for a man to have to give up,
A career that he's set his heart on, I'm sure:
But it's only the outer world that you've lost:
You've still got your inner world—a world that's more real.
That's why you're different from the rest of us:
You have your secret garden; to which you can retire
And lock the gate behind you.[1]

This passage is an example of Eliot's new versification, the versification he had so laboriously developed for so many years. Bonamy Dobrée maintains that in *The Confidential Clerk* Eliot had mastered this form completely for the first time, and he remarks also that the metre is an important variation of Shakespearian blank verse, adopting the stresses of common speech. Dobrée illustrates how Shakespeare himself has actually used this metre in some of the later plays.[2] Eliot has attempted, however, to render not only the diction, but also the rhythm more prosaic. Let us compare the passage quoted above with the following, which is not from the same play:

You know everyone. But you don't know them, Gregory.
When an old friend—a friend of forty years—
Asks your assistance—
Instead of giving him a helping hand,
You say, 'Oh, yes, I dare say! Tell me something new.'
A starving wretch accosts you in the street,
You say, 'I know you—if you don't move on,
I give you into custody.' Your son—
Your only son—
The living image of your poor dead wife—
Whom you have turned out like a dog, to prowl

---

[1] T. S. Eliot, *The Confidential Clerk*, London, 1954, p. 51.
[2] B. Dobrée, 'The Confidential Clerk', cit.

The streets—faint, hungry, desolate—
Turns to his father in his sore distress—
You write to him, 'Be off! I've heard that tale before!'
Ay, and you will hear it again on the Judgement Day.
You say you are worth two hundred thousand pounds,
But you are wrong. You are worth nothing!

The metre is similar, with the same basis of blank verse, and the same dramatic artifices of added syllables, rhythmic variations, emphasized caesuras and colloquial fluency. But this second passage is quoted from *A Pair of Spectacles,* a farce which was given in London in September 1890.[1] The text of this play is printed, quite rightly, in prose (I have put it into lines here for the sake of comparison). Its author, Sydney Grundy, made no claim to be writing poetry, or even verse. He was not, in fact, the original author, for his play is a free translation from the French farce *Les Petits Oiseaux* by Labiche and Delacour. The metre Eliot has now discovered is simply the natural rhythm of speech which has so often been reproduced by those with a natural ear for the voices around them, even if only working as translators. Eliot, in conclusion, has re-discovered prose.[2] Those who have read Grundy's play, which has been recently re-printed, may notice several further similarities between it and *The Confidential Clerk.* The most striking is in the treatment of symbols. The titles, including the original French title, are

[1] See *Nineteenth Century Plays,* ed. G. Rowell, London, 1953; the quotation is from p. 527.

[2] These remarks, which I had already published in an article ('La Commedia degli equivoci II' in *Lo Spettatore Italiano,* VII, n. 5, May 1954) can be compared with the following, by Mr. Kenneth Tynan ('Prose and the Playwright', in *Atlantic Monthly,* 194, n. 6, Dec. 1954, p. 76): ' "O God, O God, if I could return to yesterday, before I thought that I had made a decision. What devil left the door on the latch for these doubts to enter? And then you came back, you, the angel of destruction—just as I felt sure. In a moment, at your touch, there is nothing but ruin." Exit, you may expect, into snowstorm; but you would be wrong. The lines come not from Victorian melodrama but from *The Cocktail Party* printed as prose.' Mr. Tynan seems to share my feelings as to the prosaic tone of Eliot's later verse-plays, and as to their nineteenth-century flavour.

symbolical in the same way, and the aim of sound moral propaganda is the moving force. The stock characters are to be found in both, and both have the theatrical mechanism of a comedy of the 'nineties.

These criticisms would be meaningless if Eliot had written his last plays simply as media for the expression and propagation of his beliefs, and without artistic ambition. We know, however, that he had set out to write them as poetry. A recent lecture of his bears witness to this. Published under the title of *The Three Voices of Poetry*, it could be used as a preface to *The Confidential Clerk*. In it he asserts that there are three forms of poetical expression:

The first is the voice of the poet talking to himself—or to nobody. The second is the voice of the poet addressing an audience, whether large or small. The third is the voice of the poet when he attempts to create a dramatic character speaking in verse; when he is saying, not what he would say in his own person, but only what he can say within the limits of one imaginary character addressing another imaginary character.[1]

Eliot seems to retrace his own evolution: from his early lyrics to the meditative monologues, to a more and more prosaic conception of the theatre.

We could say otherwise that the poet, at first closed in his ivory tower—or separated from the rest of mankind by his negative beliefs—felt at some stage the need to communicate with a few, and that later on, when this stimulus became so great as to induce him to devise and adopt propaganda methods, the theatre seemed the one ready to hand. This evolution is not only Eliot's but could be observed in many other contemporary authors. The poets and artists who fully developed the seeds sown by the aesthetic or decadent movement of the 'nineties, succeeded in representing that crisis of beliefs that beset their times in truly poetical though irregular forms. In what I have called a funambulist style, precarious and

[1] T. S. Eliot, *The Three Voices of Poetry*, Cambridge, 1953, p. 4.

daring, they reached poetry, even if it was a poetry of negation rather than affirmation. But when that negative position began to be felt as a limitation to their powers, a threat of sterility, and they started to look for some positive attitude, they were attracted in reaction by the most extreme dogmatic doctrines. Hence Pound's Fascism, hence the Marxism of the young writers of the 'thirties. We may read the same motivation in Eliot's allegiance to the Church of England. Their former isolation had been an evasion from the everyday world. Their new faiths were new forms of evasion from the real world, which seemed still dominated by despair—an evasion from despair into orthodoxy.

This does not mean that, at least in some cases, the new faiths were completely sterile from the point of view of poetry. They did provide new stimuli, as the *Four Quartets* can testify. The comments of Edmund Wilson or E. M. Forster after the publication of Eliot's *For Lancelot Andrewes* were perceptive enough—Mr. Wilson spoke of 'The incapacity [for many literary people] to come to terms with the worlds they live in',[1] and Mr. Forster said: 'what [Eliot] seeks is not revelation, but stability'.[2] Of course, one now must notice the footnote Forster added to this sentence: 'In view of Mr. Eliot's later work I would modify these remarks.' But they were essentially true at the time (1928-9) when they were written. The search for stability is instinctive to those who have not come to terms with the objective world around them. The process which I have been trying to describe has been neatly summarized (though with a different terminology) by Stephen Spender:

The past seventy or eighty years have witnessed three phases of development in literature. First, there is the phase of highly

---

[1] E. Wilson, *Eliot and the Church of England*, dated 24 April 1929; now in *The Shores of Light*, New York, 1952, p. 439.

[2] E. M. Forster, 'T. S. Eliot', dated 1928, in *Abinger Harvest*, new ed., London, 1953, p. 112.

developed individual vision, secondly that of anti-vision and despair; thirdly, that of a return towards the orthodoxy which had been rejected by the writers of the first phase.[1]

This brings us to the much debated question of orthodoxy or conformity in present day literature. Spender himself has attempted a classification of the various forms that dogmatic orthodoxy has assumed: religious, Marxist, and a third sort, characteristic of democratic countries and consisting in the 'conformity with the pervading presence of authority which demands the "responsibility" of the artist'.[2] This tendency is undeniable, and there is no doubt that if it is accepted through external pressures and not, so to speak, invented by the artist in the act of creation, it suppresses that immediacy of expression which is essential to all art. Even a sincere religious impulse, when systematized into a dogmatic faith, results in a basic insincerity, in what Miss Kathleen Nott has aptly called 'the New Philistinism'.[3] Conformity or orthodoxy as such, and especially when it means uncritical acceptance of a dogmatic doctrine, is the death of art. But we must make a clear distinction between accepted faiths and the genuine need for and attempt to reach new points of stability: between escape or a rush for shelter on the one side, and on the other the struggle to define and establish a new (or old) set of values to believe in and live for.

The evolution in style that I have pointed out seems to indicate a trend in this direction—towards what I have called the New Baroque, a trend towards order. Trends in style generally mirror in the aesthetic field the needs of the time that produces them. The fact is that the only alternative that seems to present itself to the establishment of firm values (we can say, if we prefer, ideals or faiths) is destruction. Forty years ago a few writers began to speak of a new apocalypse. In the last decade

[1] S. Spender, *The Creative Element*, London, 1953, pp. 13–14.
[2] *Ibid.*, p. 181.
[3] See K. Nott, *The Emperor's Clothes*, London, 1953.

this notion has become a commonplace of journalese.[1] It has become part of the *Zeitgeist* in its most popular form. In a very sensitive article on *This Age of Conformity* the American critic Irving Howe, deploring the spread of orthodoxy, wrote:

What one conforms to most of all—despite and against one's intentions—is the *Zeitgeist,* that vast insidious sum of pressures and fashions: one drifts along, anxious and compliant, upon the favoured assumption of the moment.[2]

This is true only in respect of the majority who *follow* the spirit of the times, but not in respect of the forces and the individuals who determine it. The artists of the first half of this century (the funambulists), by giving poetic expression to their sense of danger and instability determined a certain *Zeitgeist* which could be called apocalyptic. Both historical events and recent scientific developments went to confirm their intimations. Now there comes the reaction, and at first it may well assume the form of some ready-made panacea, whether mystic or marxist. But it need not remain at that, especially since the remedies we are offered are more than one, and in ruthless competition with each other. Some people are not ready to accept them, are not ready to conform, though still determined to reach a firmer ground, a position of stable balance. It is perhaps significant that a position of this kind is being approached in his latest play by Christopher Fry, a playwright I had chosen in a previous essay to represent the 'popular' phase of a stylistic movement, when that movement becomes acceptable to a very general and unprepared audience.

Once again I must say that, in considering Fry's play *The Dark Is Light Enough* we should distinguish clearly between its absolute artistic value on the one side, and its formal characteristics on the other. As a work of art, the play is far too uneven, laboriously constructed and poetically thin: it does not

[1] See F. L. Baumer, 'Twentieth Century Version of the Apocalypse', in *Cahiers d'Histoire Mondiale,* vol. I, n. 3, Jan. 1954, pp. 623–40.
[2] I. Howe, 'This Age of Conformity', in *Partisan Review,* XXI, n. 1, Jan.–Feb. 1954, p. 20.

even achieve that continued formal brilliancy that made a
delightful and self-sufficient arabesque of *The Lady's Not for
Burning.* But the significance of its intention and the import of
the stylistic changes it shows are worth examining. Fry has
presented it as a 'Winter Comedy', completing his cycle of
comedies on the moods of the seasons. This definition of his
plays is rather misleading, suggesting at first a comparison with
other plays of 'moods': Maeterlinck's atmospheric fantasies, like
Pelléas et Mélisande, on the one side, and Chekhov's far subtler
and more shaded representation of moods in *The Three Sisters*
or *The Cherry Orchard* on the other. Fry's moods are different
from these. In his earlier plays they can be considered as set
themes, on which he composed a series of virtuoso variations.
But in *The Dark Is Light Enough,* for all its talk of snow, old
age, and wintry thoughts, the variations lack sparkle. What
rather stands out is the fact that the play has another meaning,
which it is trying to convey through the apparent casualness
of its action. It is not meant to be essentially entertainment,
though it aims at being that, *too* (if with much less zest than the
earlier comedies). One could even say that the author was so
anxious to let his audience see the existence of a deeper meaning, that he renounced most of the decorations and even the
incantation of his verbal fireworks, his earlier enjoyment of
words for their own sake and for their own sound. The
rhythm of his lines is extremely subdued, often barely audible,
the deliberate exhilaration of verse as such has been succeeded
by an attempt to make the verse sound like prose. We are told
that this less spirited and more prosaic tone best fits the winter
atmosphere that the play is trying to convey. Derek Stanford,
for instance, lists the following three reasons for connecting
the comedy with a winter mood:

One is, perhaps, the new bareness of diction; another, the
general grimness of the plot, with its background of the
miseries of war; and a third, maybe, the notion that this is a
play fitted to the present time, the present apocalyptic age

258

which, for all we know, might see the end of history, as the history of man so far has been enacted.[1]

The allusion to 'the present apocalyptic age' may not be inappropriate; but it goes to prove once more Fry's tendency to seize and represent those conceptions or, to use his own word, 'moods' which have already gained wide currency. As we saw, the idea of a new Apocalypse is among those which have penetrated at present into the awareness not only of the intellectual, but of the common man. As for the 'new bareness of diction', is not that the object of Eliot's dramatic verse as well? More than once in this play we may feel that Fry is modulating into Eliot:

> One must have talent to go from a place to a place,
> But divination to go so deviously
> That north, south, east and west
> Are lost in admiration, and yet to arrive,
> After a short experience of eternity
> At the place and people one set out to reach.[2]

Fry's stylistic evolution seems to be coming full circle. His first model was Eliot's *Murder in the Cathedral,* though at one remove, through the influence of Charles Williams.[3] He developed after that in what seemed the opposite direction to Eliot's, emphasizing the most showy and fantastic qualities of words, rhythm, imagery and rhetorical devices, while Eliot was sobering his diction more and more. But now Fry in his turn is veiling the glitter of his previous verse to reach a discursive language quite near to that of *The Cocktail Party* or *The Confidential Clerk.* His metaphors have lost most of their sparkle and tend to show their serious implications much more

[1] D. Stanford, *Christopher Fry* ('Writers and Their Work', n. 54), London, 1954, p. 32.

[2] C. Fry, *The Dark Is Light Enough,* London, 1954, p. 16.

[3] By a curious coincidence, Mr. Stanford, in order to demonstrate Fry's connection with Williams, has chosen the same quotation from Williams' *Seed of Adam,* which I had used in my essay on Fry in the present book (see before, p. 153, and see Stanford, *op. cit.,* pp. 17–18).

deliberately. I concluded one of these essays by saying that there were indications that 'Fry is proceeding from a Manneristic form towards the quieter Baroque'. Indeed, the last term fits the language of *The Dark Is Light Enough,* even better than that of Eliot's plays. Fry's winter comedy shows the intention to control and hedge in the abundance of fanciful metaphors. In this way Fry's very use of wit assumes the high seriousness which was characteristic of Baroque conceits, a seriousness united to a certain solemnity of tone and orotundity of expression. It is no longer flamboyant, like a euphuist's, but ornate.

The adoption of a more severely disciplined style implies a search for stability also on the 'philosophical' level; or perhaps not a search but a statement, the statement of a faith. This is, of course, the real meaning of the play. A meaning so important for the author that he has stripped his diction of many a decoration in order to make us aware of its presence. We saw that Eliot did something very similar—and we saw what his meaning was: his escape from despair took place through the adoption of Christian beliefs.

It is clear that Fry's attitude too is, and has been from the first, Christian. But his last play is particularly apt to mislead, especially because of its formal resemblance to Eliot's plays. It would be easy to see in Countess Rosmarin Ostenberg an all important Guardian Angel, providing supreme guidance like Eggerson, or like Sir Henry Harcourt-Reilly in *The Cocktail Party*; and in the anarchist Richard Gettner a character like Harry (*The Family Reunion*) or Celia (*The Cocktail Party*) or Colby, finding at last his vocation and ready to sacrifice himself to some sort of transcendental mission. But we should look more closely at the heroine of the play. Countess Rosmarin does provide the centre of stability in the turmoil of the surrounding world; Gettner comments on her, after describing the precarious condition of mankind in the universe:

> In this insecure
> Situation, I found from the first,

Your mother managed to find a stability
Beside which any despair was compelled to hesitate.[1]

The stability offered by Rosmarin is, however, of a very different kind from that offered by Eggerson to Colby in Eliot's play:

I don't see you spending a life as an organist.
I think you'll come to find you've another vocation . . .
Mr. Simpkins! You'll be thinking of reading for orders.
And you'll still have your music.[2]

Colby's vocation is a withdrawal from the rest of mankind into a world of absolute belief, of spiritual perfection, which is symbolized by music. Colby's position is stated even more clearly in Lucasta's words at an earlier stage of *The Confidential Clerk*:

. . . You're terribly cold, or else you have some fire
To warm you, that isn't the same kind of fire
That warms other people. You're either an egotist
Or something so different from the rest of us
That we can't judge you. That's you, Colby.[3]

The heroine of Fry's play has none of this 'apartness'. She believes in man:

Let us say
We are all confused, incomprehensible,
Dangerous, contemptible, corrupt,
And in that condition pass the evening
Thankfully and well. In our plain defects
We already know the brotherhood of man.[4]

The chaos of life does not induce her to seek the shelter of an established doctrine, or of a metaphysical peace, but to confirm

---

[1] *The Dark Is Light Enough*, cit., p. 44.
[2] *The Confidential Clerk*, cit., p. 132.
[3] *Ibid.*, p. 102.
[4] *The Dark Is Light Enough*, p. 20.

her belief in the sanctity of man and of human peace. She does not set out either to show the right road to faith, but acts only through her respect for other people's beliefs:

> Because I have respect for Richard Gettner's
> Wandering and uncertain will, *therefore*
> I have respect for your sheer purpose . . .
> Is is not a quaint freedom, that lets us
> Make up our minds and not be free to change them? [1]

This is her 'divine non-interference', and another character of the play finds another name for it:

> For your sake, madam, I would love
> Anarchy, if I could.

In fact Countess Rosmarin is not a conformist but an anarchist. And Gettner is a convert only in the sense that, from her, he learns that his form of anarchism is simply egotistical, and in the end he rejects it to adopt her selfless, non-interfering attitude. It is clear then that Fry's characters are looking for stability, but they do not look for it in the 'orthodoxies' listed by Spender. The first instinctive reaction of those who felt surrounded by a spiritual chaos and wanted to escape from it was perhaps to turn to these orthodoxies. Fry's play seems to indicate that the search for stabler values need not lead into conformity: personal variations are possible, even if, as in the case of *The Dark Is Light Enough,* they are introduced in a rather timid and deceptive form,[2] so deceptive that we are made uneasy by the evasive meaning of the play, and its impact is thereby much diminished.

But there may be also another reason for the uneasiness we

---

[1] *The Dark Is Light Enough*, p. 30.

[2] Kenneth Tynan, for instance, in his article already mentioned (see note 16) dealing with the three plays I am discussing here, writes of *The Dark Is Light Enough*: 'The play's main action is the regeneration of Gettner, nihilist and traitor, by the Countess, who stands for divine charity, the justification of God's circuitous ways to man.'

experience in looking at the plays of Eliot and Fry. In adopting the dramatic form the poets felt that it dealt with immediate actuality, with the Now. The actual presence of living actors on a stage may well suggest this illusion of immediacy. We saw how most contemporary writers felt the importance of communicating the awareness of the present fleeting moment. This preoccupation spreading not only among poets but also among prose-writers, brought about that closeness between the techniques of verse and prose writing on which we had already occasion to remark. (A very recent and even too obvious example is William Sansom's *Lord Love Us,* a collection of short stories which are only thinly disguised narrative verse, with even the metre and rhymes of popular ballads.) Eliot invested the intuition of the fulness of the moment with a transcendental meaning. Fry had a more impressionistic feeling for it, very akin to Virginia Woolf's, as can be seen from this speech from *The Firstborn*:

> Listen—look—
> What is it, this that has captured me? This 'now',
> This exact truth of time—certainly truth—
> The moment we're now crossing. Can this truth
> Vanish? Look, your shadow thrown over the chair,
> That dog's jerking bark, the distance of whistling,
> A gate clanging-to, the water thrown into the yard,
> Your fingers travelling your bracelet, my voice—listen,
> My voice—your breathing—
>   And Teusret running through the empty rooms.
> It is true for us now, but not till now, and never
> To be again. I want it for myself.
> This is my life.   *Enter Teusret*
>   It has gone.[1]

Fry is conscious of the fleeting character of such moments, as well as of their importance. The implication of all his plays,

---

[1] I am quoting from the first edition (Cambridge, 1946) of *The Firstborn*, p. 35. In the second edition (London, 1952) some lines are abridged.

is that what matters is the present, or rather, 'the awareness of the present as timeless'. These words have been used by Susanne Langer to describe the basic condition of lyric poetry, and *only* of lyric poetry.[1] About drama she writes:

> It has been said repeatedly that the theatre creates a perpetual present moment; but it is only a present filled with its own future that is really dramatic. A sheer immediacy, an imperishable direct experience without the ominous forward movement of consequential action, would not be so. As literature creates a virtual past, drama creates a virtual future. The literary mode is the mode of Memory; the dramatic is the mode of Destiny.[2]

This distinction is useful, since it illustrates the problem of the modern artist, bent on expressing that very momentary impression or feeling, that timeless present which is neither virtual past nor virtual future. The prose-writer at least has faced this problem as a problem from the beginning, fully aware of its difficulties—and has approached it from the right angle. As can be seen in Proust, he started from the mode of Memory, and intensified it to the point when memory became the actual felt reality of the present moment. For the dramatist instead it was difficult to realize that any problem existed: the theatre seemed the natural representation of the present. (It is significant that Miss Langer herself should have said a few years ago: 'instead of creating a virtual Past [drama] creates a virtual Present.')[3] The presence of Destiny was implicit in the plays, and of itself a projection of the action into the future. It is to be found in Eliot (where Destiny is called vocation), and even in Fry, especially in his religious plays. But Eliot missed the fact that this presence was natural to the dramatic mode: he assumed the necessity of underlining it, of creating those moments when the implication of futurity should be made

[1] S. Langer, *Feeling and Form*, London, 1953, pp. 267-70.

[2] *Ibid.*, p. 307.

[3] From an article, quoted in H. Read, *The True Voice of Feeling*, cit., p. 147.

apparent. He treated that presence of Fate which is a natural condition of drama, as a sudden personal revelation to be elaborately conveyed to the listener. The result is over-emphasis. In Fry's case the capacity of drama to imply a sense of Fate is more quietly assumed. He stresses the present in order to imply the future, instead of (like Eliot) implying the future by stressing it.

With Dylan Thomas' radio-play the case is again different. Destiny is present in the constant consciousness of death. But in choosing as his 'story' the life of a whole village in an ordinary day, Thomas did for the drama something very similar to what Joyce or Virginia Woolf had done for the novel: he succeeded in conveying the sense of the timelessness of the present. Each passing moment of the day Thomas describes is so full of its own vitality that the future ceases to matter. One does not expect the development of a plot, but wants all the same the performance to go on. That dramatic quality described by Miss Langer as 'the ominous forward movement of consequential action' is lacking. On the other hand, what Thomas presents is more than 'sheer immediacy, an imperishable direct experience'. It is the realization of the richness of life included in such immediacy, of a movement which is not forward but self-sufficient, of an action which is inconsequential but operating within an instantaneous intuition: the movement and the action of the lyric poem, in which the dramatic element is provided by the ever new discovery of a world in a grain of sand. Dramatic because of the conflict and conciliation of opposites which takes place within one and the same moment, in a timeless present ('all the eccentrics' in *Under Milk Wood,* Thomas noted, 'by their own rights, are ordinary and good').[1]

Perhaps, in view of the traditionally accepted conception of the nature of the dramatic form, *Under Milk Wood* should not be considered a play; as in view of the accepted conception of the narrative form, *Ulysses* or *To the Lighthouse* should not be

[1] D. Thomas, *Three Letters,* cit., p. 96.

considered as novels. Virginia Woolf herself had some mis-
givings on this subject, when she annotated in her *Diary* for
June 27th, 1925:

(But while I try to write, I am making up *To the Lighthouse*
—the sea is to be heard all through it. I have an idea that I
will invent a new name for my books to supplant 'novel'. A
new——by Virginia Woolf. But what? Elegy?) [1]

Yet who questions now the name of 'novel' for Virginia
Woolf's works? In the same way *Under Milk Wood* has been
accepted from the beginning as a play. It is a play which
departs from the norm in so much as it adopts the absolute
present, the moment, as its only temporal dimension; it introduces into drama the same time-unit that Proust, Joyce and
Virginia Woolf had acclimatized in prose-narrative. It is remarkable that in doing this Thomas does not give the impression of wanting to break with the past dramatic tradition (an
impression which is instead produced by Samuel Beckett's *En
attendant Godot,* a deliberate attempt at establishing a timeless
present as the temporal dimension of drama). The unobtrusive-
ness with which Thomas succeeded in introducing what
amounts to a revolutionary change is largely due to the structural balance he imposed on his play. Through the regular
reappearance at different intervals of the same voices, through
the symmetrical contrasts of characters and situation, Thomas
made of his play a unified whole. The Baroque stylization
atones for the revolutionary treatment of the dramatic form.

If we move now onto the stylistic plane, it is possible to
reach one conclusion from the consideration of three plays so
different from each other as *Under Milk Wood, The Dark Is
Light Enough* and *The Confidential Clerk*. Their authors have
been trying to express through a new style the sense of a more
permanent balance, in contrast with the funambulism, the
sense of precariousness and instability, conveyed by the works
produced in the preceding decades.

[1] V. Woolf, *A Writer's Diary*, ed. L. Woolf, London, 1953, p. 80.

NOTE.—In the field of critical terminology, an interesting new suggestion has been put forward by Prof. E. R. Curtius in his masterly work, *European Literature and the Latin Middle Ages* (trans. W. R. Trask, London, 1953); he adopts the term 'Mannerism' as 'the common denominator for all tendencies which are opposed to Classicism, whether they be pre-classical, post-classical, or contemporary with any classicism'. Prof. Curtius adds: 'Understood in this sense, Mannerism is a constant in European literature. It is the complementary phenomenon of the Classicism of all periods. We had found that the twin concept Classicism—Romanticism was not good for much. The polarity of Classicism and Mannerism is far more useful as a conceptual instrument and can illuminate connections which it is easy to overlook' (p. 273). Trying to relate Prof. Curtius' conceptions to the terminology I have used in the present book, I find that by Mannerism he means both the style of periods of unbalance (the style of those whom Pater called 'the Euphuists of successive ages') *and* what I have called the Romantic attitude present in every stylistic period. By Classicism, or, as he says, by 'Standard Classicism', Prof. Curtius designates 'all authors and periods which write correctly, clearly, and in accordance to the rules', that is to say, the style of periods of balance *and* the classicistic attitude in single authors of all periods. My interpretation is absolutely arbitrary, especially since Prof. Curtius, with his vision of the whole of European literature as an 'intelligible unit', disapproves of all attempts at 'cutting it into pieces' (p. 14)—and stylistic periodization is one such attempt. In adopting the polarity Classicism-Mannerism he admits only one vertical division of European literature, a division into two 'constants', while he rules out all periodization, that is to say, all horizontal divisions of literature into stylistic phases in the successive ages.

Prof. Curtius does convince us of the fact that 'European literature can only be seen as a whole'. But I would like to make a few remarks on his choice of the term 'Mannerism' as a 'conceptual instrument'. He writes: 'This is not the place to discuss whether the word "Mannerism" is a good choice as the designation of a period in art history, and to what extent it is justified. We may borrow it because it is well adapted to fill a gap in the terminology of literary science. For that purpose, to be sure, we must free the word from all art-historical connotations and broaden its meaning. . . .' The fact however remains, that he has borrowed a word from art-historical periodization. Had not the same thing happened with another term of the same kind, 'Baroque'? Soon after Woelfflin established the word 'Baroque' to designate a definite stylistic period, a number of other scholars tried to broaden its meaning, so that by 1935 Eugenio D'Ors could list over twenty 'species' of the Baroque 'genus', ranging from pre-historic to contemporary art and literature (see E. D'Ors, *Du Baroque*, Paris, 1935). Baroque had substituted Romanticism in the well-known antithesis with Classicism. For D'Ors and his followers Baroque was no longer a stylistic period but, in his own words, a 'constant in art history'. As a matter of fact this broad meaning of the word did not receive a very wide acceptance, producing only a certain confusion in terminology. Prof. Curtius himself is so aware of this that he writes: 'Much of what we shall call Mannerism is today set down as "Baroque". But this word has caused such confusion that it is better to eliminate it. The word Mannerism further deserves the preference because, compared with "Baroque", it has a minimum of historical associations.' This last sentence can be questioned. In the last thirty years Mannerism has acquired a precise historical meaning, as Baroque had done at the turn of this century. The only difference is that its establishment is more recent. What Prof. Curtius suggests is to take this term and subject it to the same process which 'Baroque' has undergone. It is only reasonable to expect that, when left in less expert hands than his, the same conceptual misunderstanding will arise. The fate of the horizontal stylistic divisions devised by art historians, seems to be that they are seized upon, as soon as they are current, by scholars with a more comprehensive vision, and transformed into 'constant' vertical categories bisecting the whole history of the arts.

What should be kept in mind, is that these words are not so much philosophical concepts as useful empirical definitions of general characteristics in works of art and literature. They are meant to provide a frame of references for the reader, rather than place such works in a rigid abstract system. The two different uses to which terms like 'Baroque' and 'Mannerism' have been put show the need both for stylistic 'period' distinctions and for a definition of the two basic attitudes to artistic expression present at all times. For this reason I have tried to adopt a frame of reference which should take into consideration both stylistic periodization (the alternation of ages of balance and unbalance) and constant attitudes (which I have very broadly called romantic and classicistic).

Index

Index

Index

Index

Index

Index

277

Date Due